*More advance praise for*

# SPEAKING IN COD TONGUES

"*Humourous and intellectual, poignant and celebratory, theoretical and poetic, all in the same space. I am not aware of any
other scholarly or popular book that covers such a wide ground
on Canadian food culture with so much detail and skill.*"
—Irena Knezevic, Food Security Scholar, Carleton University

"*Provocative and accessible, Newman offers a perspective at
once informed and appreciative of Canada's culinary wealth,
as well as vigilant about the need for its protection.*"
—Nathalie Cooke, founding editor of *CuiZine* and
*What's to Eat? Entrées into Canadian Food History*

"*A fascinating culinary tour of Canada. It brought
back memories of the Voyageur Restaurants my family used to stop at on the TransCanada [where] they
served a kid's meal in a paper canoe. Good times.*"
—Janis Thiessen, Food Historian, University
of Winnipeg, and author of the forthcoming
book, *Snacks: A Canadian Food History*

# DIGESTIONS

Publishing established and emerging scholars and writers, **Digestions** is a book series that considers the history of food, the culture of food, and the politics of what we eat from both a Canadian and a global perspective.

**SERIES EDITOR**
Sarah Elton

**For more information about publishing in the series, please contact:**
Karen May Clark, Acquisitions Editor
University of Regina Press
3737 Wascana Parkway
Regina, Saskatchewan s4s 0A2 Canada
karen.clark@uregina.ca
www.uofrpress.ca

# SPEAKING IN COD TONGUES

## A Canadian Culinary Journey

## LENORE NEWMAN

*foreword by Sarah Elton*

**University of Regina Press**

Printed and bound in Canada at Marquis.

Cover design: Duncan Campbell, University of Regina Press
Text design: John van der Woude, JVDW Designs
Copy editor: Dallas Harrison
Proofreader: Kristine Douaud
Indexer: Patricia Furdek
Cover art: FRONT COVER (top row, l to r): "Fruit and Leaves of Amelanchier Ovalis (Saskatoon)" by multik79/Fotolia; "Red Lobster" by Paul Binet/AdobeStock; "Single Fiddlehead" by Bert Folsom/Fotolia; (middle row, l to r): "Rhubarb Stalks" by Valentyn Volkov/Fotolia; "Montreal Style Bagel" by nettestock/Fotolia; (bottom row, l to r): "Cod" by HelleM/Fotolia; "Raw Salmon" by Diana Taliun/Fotolia. SPINE: "Leaf Shape Maple Syrup Bottle" by Casper1774/AdobeStock. BACK COVER: "Poutine, Canadian Cuisine" by uckyo/Fotolia.
Additional Interior art: "A Savory Meat Pie" by David Pimborough/iStock; "Roll Seafood" by Givaga/iStock; "Fillet steak beef" by karandaev/iStock; "Red apple" by anna1311/Stock; "Glazed Doughnut Holes" by Lauri Patterson/iStock; "Fresh bunch of grapes with leaves" by Hyrma/iStock.
All interior photographs by the author.

**Library and Archives Canada Cataloguing in Publication**

Newman, Lenore, 1973-, author

Speaking in cod tongues : a Canadian culinary journey / Lenore Newman ; foreword by Sarah Elton.

(Digestions) Includes bibliographical references and index. Issued in print and electronic formats.
ISBN 978-0-88977-459-9 (paperback).—ISBN 978-0-88977-466-7 (pdf).—
ISBN 978-0-88977-467-4 (html)

1. Food—Canada. 2. Food habits—Canada. 3. Cooking, Canadian. 4. Canada—Social life and customs. I. Title. II. Series: Digestions (Regina, Sask.)

GT2853.C3N49 2016     394.1'20971     C2016-906124-8     C2016-906125-6

10 9 8 7 6 5 4 3 2 1

University of Regina Press, University of Regina
Regina, Saskatchewan, Canada, S4S 0A2
tel: (306) 585-4758 fax: (306) 585-4699
U OF R PRESS   web: www.uofrpress.ca

We acknowledge the support of the Canada Council for the Arts for our publishing program. We acknowledge the financial support of the Government of Canada. / Nous reconnaissons l'appui financier du gouvernement du Canada. This publication was made possible through Creative Saskatchewan's Creative Industries Production Grant Program.

*For Katherine. Your love and support made this book possible.
I'm sorry about all of the potatoes.*

# CONTENTS

# FOREWORD

What is Canadian cuisine? When we ask ourselves this question, we come up with answers such as maple syrup and pancakes, poutine, or butter tarts and Nanaimo bars—possibly perogies in Alberta and Jigg's Dinner in Newfoundland. But there has been no consensus on Canadian cuisine. No meal or recipe or ingredient has offered a satisfactory answer to the question of what is Canadian cuisine today because, as Lenore Newman asserts in this book, ours is a creole cuisine, assembled through the simmering of history, culture, migration, regionalism, colonialism and capitalism.

What Newman experienced and discovered as she travelled (and ate) her way across Canada in search of answers to this question was that the vast differences in climate, geography and, therefore, ingredients of this wide country's regions stand in the way of defining a singular national cuisine in the conventional sense. Canadian cuisine is the food of regions. This is not a surprising conclusion because, as many have remarked, including celebrated food anthropologist Sidney Mintz, national cuisines are in fact regional—such as Italy's supposed national dish *ragù alla bolognese*, which, loosely translated, means "sauce made like they do in Bologna." (This tomato and meat sauce served over noodles is now divorced from region and so globally ubiquitous that I have found it on menus in cities as disparate as Rome, Guatemala City, and Mumbai.) The idea of French cuisine, as Amy B. Trubek documents in her scholarly work, has been constructed in part with the help of the Michelin Tire company in the 1950s. In an effort to grow a market for their tires, they published guide books to entice the French to drive their cars out into the country and seek out what the regions had to offer. What better a reason to travel than to discover some tasty regional specialties. What's different here in Canada is that no advertising campaign or government policy, so far, has successfully elevated any one particular food, ingredient, or dish to national champion.

As Mintz writes in *Tasting Food, Tasting Freedom*, "'Cuisine,' more exactly defined, has to do with the ongoing foodways of a region." A cuisine is defined by a geographic area, a history, a sense of coherence, as well as by a self-consciousness. Part of having a cuisine, he holds, is recognizing our shared experience of preparing and eating as just that—a shared experience.

We keep asking ourselves the question—what is Canadian cuisine?— perhaps because we lack that self-consciousness. Our food rituals are so habitual, engaged in unreflectively, that we don't in fact see them for what they are. And Newman, in this book, recognizes our habits and peculiarities for what they are: cuisine. Like berry-picking, which she describes as a national pastime.

Humans have been nourishing themselves with berries for millennia here on this land we call Canada today. Even though you can buy fresh southern berries at the supermarket all year round, many of us still go out to pick our own summer berries in the backyard, at the U-pick, in the clear-cut, at the side of the road, in the community garden. Which type of berry we pile into our old yogourt containers, dangling from strings around our necks, depends on our region. Newman picks wild blackberries in the west, whereas I grew up collecting raspberries in the thin strip of low brush between the gravel road and crown land behind my grandmother's cottage in Ontario. This shared berry-picking experience is creolized in the way we then prepare the berries. What recipes we turn to depends on who raised our grandmothers, who married our moms, or who passed along recipes for what to do with those berries from the kitchen next door or across the ocean. Blueberry-filled perogies. Bakeapple jam. Gooseberry jelly. Strawberry lassi.

Why does all this matter in the age of the season-less supermarket, where fresh, frozen and processed foods of all kind fly across borders with more ease than a tourist with a piece of unpasteurized cheese in her purse? The power of cuisine in the vastness of Canada is that it roots us to place. It connects us all to the land. In 2005, the United Nations cultural body UNESCO offered their own definition of terroir. While this expression more typically is used to describe the flavours of a wine, UNESCO broadened this notion to include the relationship humans have with the geographical area that feeds them, including all the interactions that take place between the human world and the biophysical world as a result of cuisine. When we eat, we take nature inside of us. Nature—the berry, the animal, the vegetable—becomes us, quite literally as our body builds its cells from what we take in. Through food, and therefore this question of what is Canadian cuisine, we might realize that we are the land. And it is us. No matter where we come from or where we choose to live, Canadian cuisine can be defined as eating the land on which we live. And this is a powerful notion.

Sarah Elton
September 12, 2016

# ACKNOWLEDGEMENTS

I would like to acknowledge the support of the Social Sciences and Humanities Research Council of Canada and the Canada Research Chair program. I would like to thank Bruce Walsh, director, and the entire team at University of Regina Press for believing in this book, and in particular I want to thank editors Karen Clark and Donna Grant for their tireless effort to improve the manuscript. In addition, Dallas Harrison's patience made the copy editing process much easier. I would also like to thank the University of the Fraser Valley, and particularly Adrienne Chan and the folks in the Office of Research for their unwavering support. Thanks also go to Mark Evered for taking a risk on a young scholar. In addition, thanks to Ann Dale, Katherine Newman, and Shannon Blatt for their very careful reading and advice, and thanks to the anonymous reviewers and readers who offered suggestions to improve the book during its final stages. Thanks to postdoctoral scholars Denver Nixon and Lisa Powell, my friend and colleague Priya Vadi, and student researchers Shea Wind and Jen Nickel. I would also like to acknowledge that this book was written on unceded Coast Salish territory.

## PART I

# FROM CONFEDERATION TO CUISINE

I

# INTRODUCTION: SIDEBOARD DIPLOMACY

Canada was born at lunch.

Tension was high in the summer of 1864 in Britain's North American colonies. The American Civil War was drawing to a close, and the colonies faced the prospect of a unified United States that might return to a policy of Manifest Destiny. This threat to the thinly populated and weakly defended settlements came at the same time that Britain, feeling the strain of the expense of its North American holdings, was urging settlers to work together to be more self-sufficient. The colonies of Prince Edward Island, Nova Scotia, and New Brunswick responded, calling a meeting in Charlottetown to discuss unification into a larger and more defendable whole. That the colony of Canada, which consisted of what is now Ontario and Quebec, wasn't invited to the meeting didn't stop eight delegates from Upper and Lower Canada from inviting themselves. These central Canadians were particularly worried about the Americans and were suffering through internal struggles. They were bogged down with the expense of constructing a grand set of Parliament buildings in the remote lumber town of Ottawa, a defensive position that rivalled the great citadel at Quebec City. Why shouldn't these new buildings, resplendent in the Gothic style, not rule over all of the eastern colonies rather than just Ontario and Quebec? Led by George Brown and John A. Macdonald, the Upper Canadians planned one of the greatest adventures in sideboard diplomacy of all time. The two men were not natural allies; in fact, they were thought to dislike each other. They were leading voices from different parties in the Legislative Assembly of the Province of Canada, and they surprised everyone when they joined together in what is known as the "great coalition." It was framed as being necessary to stabilize the government, but Macdonald's larger goal was much grander: Confederation. They stuffed the government steamer *Queen Victoria* with champagne and enough food for a small army and headed from Quebec to Charlottetown, where they would make the case for a broader union. A few good meals, they reasoned, might do the trick.

At 170 feet in length, the *Queen Victoria* was more sturdy than luxurious. However, with just the eight men, their secretaries, and a few other members of government, the steamer served as a fairly roomy base camp with a formidable galley and crew. Aboard this vessel, Brown and his colleagues intended to wine and dine their way to the creation of a country. We are lucky that Brown greatly missed his young wife, Anne, for his letters to her comprise one of the few accounts of the events of that summer. From his lovingly detailed descriptions and reports in the Charlottetown newspapers, we can sketch a general picture of what happened at the conference, and thanks to his enjoyment of fine dining we have an idea of what the meals of Confederation looked like. Even before the conference the men lived well; they steamed along in fine weather, according to Brown, and the general pace of their trip seemed to be more like a culinary cruise than a serious round of nation building. He noted that the breeze was warm while they lounged under an awning on the deck of the *Queen Victoria*, playing chess and backgammon. They had with them an "unexceptionable cook," in his words.

4

The galley chef and his team would play a key role in the talks ahead.[1] The men stopped at Gaspé and took on more seafood, enjoyed saltwater baths, and fished for the odd lobster, anticipating the political cut and thrust to come. Although the politicians of the age often spoke for hours at a time, Brown's letters suggest that the fathers enjoyed themselves, proving that "man does not found nations on bread alone."[2]

It is hard not to be haunted by the surviving descriptions of grand Victorian meals. As the eight founders of Confederation steamed along the St. Lawrence River, they passed a Canada emerging out of the hard-scrabble years of colonization, during which food was more a worry than a recreation. But the rough life described so well in Catharine Parr Traill's *The Backwoods of Canada*—with its bush pudding, bartered meat, and maple beer—was giving way to a period that Dorothy Duncan describes as a time of "prosperity, opulence, and gracious living."[3] The Victorians enjoyed showing off and seldom laid a formal meal that could possibly be finished by the assembled guests. Bonnie Huskins describes the period as heavy eating and hard drinking; she outlines a feast in Halifax in 1863 that included an astonishing array of dishes, including mock turtle soup, salmon and haddock, chicken curry, macaroni, beef, turkey, ham, veal, goose, plum pudding, lobster salad, and Charlotte Russe.[4] The great banquets and balls of the Charlottetown Conference would be no different. As Luella Creighton describes in *The Elegant Canadians*, the 1860s marked the emergence of a sophisticated society in the colonies. The Charlottetown Conference would stand out; she describes it as "the first great convivial occasion in British North America."[5]

The reception that greeted the arrival of the Canadians at Charlottetown did not bode well for the negotiations. The Canadians were slightly ahead of schedule, and thus no one came out to meet them. The *Queen Victoria* anchored offshore, and Brown glossed over the lack of a reception committee, describing the eight men dressing and rowing to shore in a small flotilla since they didn't have one boat large enough to hold them all. Meanwhile, William Pope, a member of the Prince

Edward Island government, the editor of the *Islander*, and a great pro-
ponent of a larger national union, rushed to the docks. He was rowed
out to the *Queen Victoria* while sitting on barrels of oysters and some
jars of molasses. This haphazard beginning was reported smugly in the
rival and anti-Confederation newspaper *Ross's Weekly*,[6] which made
much of Charlottetown being more interested in the arrival of the Slay-
maker and Nichols Olympic circus, the first such event in over twenty
years. The hotels were full, and for the most part the Canadians had to
stay on the *Queen Victoria*; it didn't help that Prince Edward Islanders
were overwhelmingly suspicious of a union with colonists to the west,
for they rightly feared that the larger central colonies might eclipse the
maritime settlements. Brown managed to find a room at Pope's grand
house, Ardgowan, where he and Pope could plan their attack. It was
there at Ardgowan that the first great meal of the conference was held.

6      Precise culinary forensics can be frustrating, but we have a good
account of three key meals at the conference, including that from Brown
of the *déjeuner à la fourchette* held in the afternoon of Friday, September
2, at Ardgowan. After a long morning of speeches, the twenty-three delegates retreated to Pope's lovely house outside town overlooking the sea
to dig into a spread of oysters, lobsters, champagne, and island luxu-
ries.[7] Such parties involved far more than food; Julie Watson describes
Ardgowan as having over seventy acres of grounds, with facilities for
croquet, lawn tennis, and archery.[8] Brown noted that the party "killed
the day" and spent a "beautiful moonlit evening walking, driving, or
boating as the mood was upon us."[9] This lunch and garden party was
the first chance for all of the delegates to mingle informally as a group
and consider the creation of a country. Garden parties were a particular favourite of the Victorians, and public picnics occurred throughout
the colonies. Macdonald was no stranger to using such events for political gain; his favourite campaign tool was to deliver a rousing outdoor
speech accompanied by a grand potluck luncheon catered by the wives of
local supporters. Canadians in eastern Canada still enjoy Tory pudding

with Liberal sauce (similar in recipe to Quebec's *pouding chômeur*), a reminder of the days when voters were plied with food.

The ice broken by the *déjeuner à la fourchette* and the evening's leisure, the Canadians used the next morning's proceedings to forcefully argue for the benefits of a broad confederation. After the day's formal meetings, they invited the delegates onto the *Queen Victoria*, where the galley crew had crafted the lunch that would be the stage for the creation of a nation. Shipboard at three in the afternoon, the delegates sat down to a meal that Brown described as being served in "princely style."[10] Creighton describes this grand meal: "Champagne cooled in tubs of ice; jellies flanked with Charlotte Russe and fragile meringues quivered on the long damask-draped serving tables. Lobsters boiled and chilled and piled on great platters, the gleam of freshly polished glass, flowers, and fruit."[11] The *Vindicator* noted that the steamer had excellent stores and a talented cook;[12] in such a setting, misgivings about union somehow fell away. Brown and the others launched into eloquent, champagne-fuelled speeches, and he noted that, "whether as the result of our eloquence or of the goodness of the champagne, the ice became completely broken."[13] As James Careless, author of *Brown of the Globe*, remarked, "there, in the chief stateroom of the *Queen Victoria*, amid the wineglasses and the cigar smoke, twenty-three men had warmly agreed to found a new nation. Other states might have a more dramatic start— but few surely… a more enjoyable one."[14]

In that convivial setting, a new nation was brought to life as the champagne flowed and the delegates mopped up the last of their Charlotte Russe slathered in the best fruit of the season. The rest of the week dissolved into mornings spent hashing out details of Confederation and afternoons and evenings of fine dining. The conference capstone was a grand ball held on September 8, 1864, in the Colonial Building. Perhaps embarrassed by the conference's rough initial reception of the Canadians, or taken aback by the lavish excess of the luncheon on the *Queen Victoria*, the government of Prince Edward Island spared no expense.

Brown said little about the ball since he had indulged so heavily that he was down with a bilious attack, which he described as "the natural result of such a round of dissipation."[15] Pope's newspaper, the *Islander*, however, reported on the ball in detail. As Creighton notes, never in the island's history was there such a party;[16] from the *Islander*, we are given a vision of a hall resplendent with lamps and mirrors and flowers. The meal, eaten at midnight after a round of dancing, was catered by John Murphy of the North American hotel. The result, the papers claim, did him great credit. He provided "everything that could minister to the taste of the epicure": substantial rounds of beef, splendid hams, salmon, lobsters, oysters, and all kinds of fowl that the season and the market could afford, all vegetable delicacies of the season, pastry in all of its forms, fruits in almost every variety, wines of the choicest vintage— there was "scarcely an inch of vacant table space on the wide tables."[17] The paper describes the quadrilles in the ballroom, the beginning of seven hours of dancing. The legislative library was turned into a room for light refreshment, filled with tea, coffee, cake, and delicacies, along with sherry, claret, champagne, and wine. They planned seven toasts among the speeches after dinner and added a few for good measure; it is interesting to think of the staid Victorians, drunk and stuffed with the finest cuisine, listening to rousing speeches by gaslight far into the early hours of the morning. The evening would live on in many a memory; Creighton notes that a young Robert Harris, there to play in the band, needed no great urging to fill his pockets with snacks for the next day.[18] Nineteen years later he would paint what could well be his best-known work, *The Fathers of Confederation*. The stiff portrait captures a moment that existed in his mind only; his personal experience of the founding fathers at the Colonial Building at three in the morning was without a doubt much more exuberant.

Although many people found a new appreciation for the idea of Confederation during these great meals and balls, not everyone was as enthusiastic; the anti-Confederation *Ross's Weekly* complained bitterly about the upcoming "profitless fandangos" of the ballroom and the fiery intoxication of the midnight banquet.[19] But fandangos aside, the plan came off perfectly. The Canadians invited the Atlantic delegates onto the *Queen Victoria* (perhaps explaining why they had come in such a large ship) and sailed on to Saint John, Halifax, and then Montreal, feasting all the way.

The Victorian era seems far removed from the country that we live in now, but though the food of the time tended to be sweet and heavy, and was washed down with copious amounts of alcohol, the antecedents of Canada's cuisine were already emerging with the presence of local seafood, the best of seasonal produce, and indigenous ingredients prepared in the style of the great chefs of France and Britain (the latter cooking predominantly in a French style). One hundred and fifty years later the country that emerged from the Charlottetown Conference and the meetings that followed has a thriving cuisine that brings together flavours from the land and sea with tastes and traditions of Indigenous peoples; British, French, and Acadian settlers; and the many groups from around the globe who have come to Canada since the nation was founded. Driven together out of a mutual need for company and protection in a vast and formidable wilderness, the Canadian people enjoy a cuisine not based upon recipes and techniques in the classical way; it draws on defining elements mediated locally. Nationally, Canadian cuisine is heavily steeped in the use of wild and seasonal foods. It remains a regionally diverse cuisine, and it is highly multicultural, incorporating recipes from around the world using local ingredients to create an emerging creole that stuns with its ingenuity and devotion to the fresh, the local, and the wild. Canada is a mosaic of evolving culinary traditions held together loosely by the land itself.

When I was given the opportunity to spend several years devoted to the study of our culinary culture, I decided to attempt to position Canada as what Carolyn Steel calls a *sitopia* or "food place." Sitopias, she claims, have strong links to a food-producing hinterland through a

9

lattice-like network, with active markets, local shops, and a strong sense of food identity.[20] But how to do such a thing? Food studies draw on diverse research methods, for often the story of what we have eaten and what we are eating must be teased out of many disparate sources.

I began with a thorough exploration of the existing writing on Canada's cuisine, supplemented with an examination of Canadian cookbooks. However, much more has been written on cuisine in the grey literature, so my research assistants and I collected food blogs and newspaper articles on Canadian cuisine from the past two decades. We analyzed this material in numerous ways, including word cluster analysis, which reveals the terms in most common use at any time.

From this starting point, I plotted a course across the country by boat, plane, train, and automobile. I included several types of culinary sites in my travels, including the big cities with their markets and restaurant scenes, the smaller centres, particularly in agricultural regions, and recreational rural landscapes. Given Canada's vastness, I had to choose my trips to smaller centres. I tried to spread these villages out regionally and was sure to visit places that appeared to be of interest in the earlier literature searches. I had to make one exception out of necessity; in the Far North, I stuck to the main roads, meaning that I didn't get to sample food in the fly-in communities of Nunavut, or visit the port community of Churchill, experiences that I would dearly like to have one day. In the major cities, I revisited key sites such as public markets on several occasions at different times of the year to observe seasonal changes, a technique that Henri Lefebvre called *rhythmanalysis*.[21]

I don't delve deeply into the pre-settlement cuisines of North America save for their influences on post-settlement Canada. However, I do attempt to highlight where Indigenous cuisine has impacted post-settlement foodways.

Blog analysis was particularly useful when I was choosing individual restaurants, and I thank Canada's active complement of food bloggers for their contributions to our culinary culture. On the road,

I interviewed chefs, producers, and other food researchers, and I used photo-documentation to capture both dishes and menus. And, yes, I ate things and recorded my experiences as I did so. The use of smell and taste as a research method is one of food study's more unusual features, and in general I like to position the experience of eating a dish within a context of literature. Where possible I timed my journeys to encounter food festivals and other culinary events, and occasionally I took along companions to share the driving and eating. For those interested, *Food Studies* does an engaging job of exploring the many ways that food researchers approach their subject.[22]

Slowly, a broad picture began to emerge out of the many cuisines thriving in places sometimes thousands of kilometres apart. We are almost without exception a subtle and understated people. When I visited the drowsy and lovely city of Charlottetown and walked the halls of Province House, it felt as if the founding fathers had just popped out to fish for a lobster or two or attend another grand luncheon. There is a lovely lightness to the place; I wandered in with barely a nod from a single security guard and found a series of rooms largely free of grand nationalist statements. Much of the food that I found on my travels had a similar quiet modesty. With few exceptions, there was little over-the-top showmanship to be found at Canada's tables. The ingredients and recipes were left to speak for themselves.

*Speaking in Cod Tongues* is my interpretation of what our cuisine has to say about Canada. One can eat alone, but taking part in a cuisine is a profoundly social act. This book is not entirely about what Canadians eat and certainly not about everything that they eat at home after a long day. This is a story of food as culture, food as celebration, food as performing "cultural artifact capable of rendering the curve of social discourse into an inspectable form."[23] Canada's cuisine emerges largely from what is being served at restaurants, what has been preserved in cookbooks, and what people are saying about food in an age obsessed with all things culinary. I explore Canadian cuisine and its links to place and culture. Food is a language that we use among ourselves and with visitors to strengthen our identity both regionally and nationally. Canadian cuisine sits in a broader international story of trade and globalization, and at some level it is attached to less welcome changes in society. The growing interest in cuisine is closely tied to forces of global capital, gentrification, and the rise of an urban elite. As French cultural theorist Roland Barthes writes, food is not just a collection of products but also a system of communication, a body of images, and a code of use, circumstance, and conduct.[24] Food speaks to us and can tell us who we are or at least who we aspire to be. It remains unclear whether all Canadians will be invited to share in the rise of Canadian cuisine or if increasing inequity will take us back to the class differentials found at the time of Confederation.

This more sinister aspect of food in Canada stretches from the founding of the country to the present day. The same John A. Macdonald who feted the maritime provinces in the dining room of the *Queen Victoria* used food relief as a weapon to crush resistance among Indigenous people of the plains. As explored in great detail by James Daschuk in *Clearing the Plains*, the introduction of new diseases and the collapse of buffalo herds (partly because of overhunting for the pemmican trade) ravaged the people of the plains, and in his role as both prime minister and minister of Indian affairs Macdonald adopted an approach of outright malevolence.[25] Over a century later, videos on YouTube share the outrage that citizens of Canada's northern regions feel about extremely high food prices for poor-quality goods, one of several examples of current inequity and weakness in Canada's food system noted by the United Nations.[26] And though culinary multiculturalism is now widely celebrated in Canada, there is a tendency to gloss over a history of marginalization in which the foods of new immigrant groups were dismissed as bad-smelling, unhealthy, or not suitable for Canadians of western European descent.

To understand these issues of food and culture and shifting internal and external forces, I start with the idea of cuisine as the expression of a people. What, ultimately, does a smattering of dishes drawn from the land, dishes such as cod tongues, poutine, or Saskatoon berry pie, say about us? Cuisine is about more than food. How we practise *commensality*, defined as the "sharing of food at the same table," is a key element of how culinary practice evolves. Brown, Macdonald, and the other Canadian delegates knew that, if they could get the maritime leaders sitting at the same table over a great meal, hopefully with rivers of alcohol in play as well, they would have a chance of selling the idea of a broader union. They were certainly not the first to notice that, if one breaks bread with another person, they will be less likely to come to blows, for commensality can bridge many divides. I also introduce some key concepts that have emerged out of geography's cultural and spatial turn. In the past few decades, a vibrant literature has emerged that allows us to better understand the culinary landscape of a city, region, or even country.

The idea of a national cuisine is not in any way neutral; the creation of national cuisines (and they are created, either unconsciously or consciously) mirrors the larger political projects within states. National cuisines reflect the primacy of certain groups over others. In the case of Canada, our food reflects the dominance of English and French founding settlers (and the tension between these two groups), the marginalization of Indigenous groups, and the tensions between established settler cultures and groups of newcomers. Our national cuisine reflects battles between regions, particularly with respect to the rise of the west as a centre of national power and the shift from a nation of rural people to a highly urban and urbane nation. Issues of gentrification and the rise of the "foodie," along with cuisine as a natural reflection of the conversation between a land and a people and a deliberate exercise in nation building, will reappear throughout the pages of this book.

The idea that the land and the people of Canada are engaged in a discussion mediated by food underpins my description of Canadian cuisine. Setting aside the idea of key recipes and techniques, I frame Canadian cuisine as a series of properties. The first three are that our cuisine draws heavily on wild food, seasonal food, and multicultural aspects of our society. Wild food has always played a large role in the Canadian diet. Although wild foods have faded from many European cuisines,[27] Canadians still head out to the land to forage, much as Brown did when he left the formal ball to fish for lobster (one imagines that the cool evening air did him some good). Our fisheries are still major industries, and many of our best-known foods have wild roots. We also maintain a cultural connection to the winter season unusual in the development of a cuisine. The idea of wilderness, however, has its own complexities. It requires a careful critique since it can downplay the deep conversation between people and the land and erase both nature and culture within the landscape. The role of Indigenous foods and foodways is particularly intertwined with the land, and the status of Indigenous food highlights the lingering injustices imposed on First Nations by an invading settler culture.

14

Closely related to our enjoyment of wild foods is a continuing connection to seasonal foods. This connection is unusual; from a provisioning standpoint, Canada is now deeply embedded in the global food system. After all, we have limited growing seasons across much of the country. However, from the standpoint of cuisine, we are great fans of fresh and seasonal foods. Although this trend must be positioned within a larger global trend that embraces eating in season, Canada's love of what is local and fresh has remarkably wide reach, going beyond the usual fruits and berries to include vegetables and seafood. One of our greatest culinary rituals, the spring visit to a *cabane à sucre*, starts off a seasonal cavalcade that stretches late into the autumn and past the first frosts with the icewine harvest. Across the country, annual festivals celebrate seasonal foods while fostering community, connecting Canadian cuisine to a sense of place.

The third near-universal element of Canadian cuisine is the embrace of multiculturalism. Historically, Canada has incorporated techniques from the far corners of the British Empire and the recipes of newcomers since Confederation. Our status as a formally multicultural society has resulted in a developing Canadian creole. This creole takes recipes from abroad and reinvents them using Canadian ingredients. Our country is known as a mosaic rather than a melting pot, and how we embrace new foods reflects this. As the country that accommodates the highest rate of immigration on the planet, Canada continually responds to new groups arriving on its shores. As ethnic enclaves have given way to thriving ethnoburbs and a much more integrated society overall, we have seen an acceleration of accommodation of new foods and techniques. Indigenous Canadian cuisine has not played as large a role as it deserves in this process, though I highlight elements of Indigenous technique that Canada's settler culture has incorporated. A full account of Canada's varied Indigenous cuisines is beyond the scope of this work. Although the major cities still dominate multicultural culinary trends, small-town variations are emerging, mirroring the success of earlier such incursions, such as the ubiquitous Chinese Canadian restaurants found across the country or the burst of Vietnamese restaurants found in the Prairies. From elk osso buco in Ottawa, to butter chicken lasagna in Toronto, to endlessly innovative sushi in Vancouver, Canadian creole reinvents the world's cuisines with a Canadian twist. This phenomenon is particularly prominent in British Columbia, where it sits within a larger culinary exchange developing around the Pacific Rim. This story of a shift in focus to the peoples of the Pacific is just beginning; in culinary terms, we might look back to see this period as the Pacific Century.

15

The first three properties of Canadian cuisine are mediated by two others. The first is the dominant role of ingredients. This is unusual in a national cuisine and reflects our dedication to the land. Perhaps our short tenure as a nation also contributes to our limited canon of truly Canadian recipes. I explore a few of the ingredients that appear nationally, including our true love of the maple tree. I also look at which recipes and techniques we can call our own, since they tend to be interesting creations. The rise of poutine as a national food over the past few decades gives us glimpses of what the future role of our country might look like in an increasingly globalized system. There is also much to be learned from Canada's cookbooks and the way in which our cuisine is presented.

This focus on our ingredients, recipes, and techniques takes us directly to the idea of Canadian cuisine as regionally based. Our strong regionalism is the final property of Canadian cuisine that I explore, and though there are a few foods that appear nationally the heart of Canadian cuisine is found in the regions. Regional divisions are always open to interpretation, but I divide Canada's culinary profile into eight broad categories: Newfoundland cuisine, Maritimes cuisine, Quebec revival cuisine, Ontario heartland cuisine, Prairies cuisine, Alberta big sky cuisine, British Columbia Pacific cuisine, and Far North cuisine. The assertion that Alberta's cuisine has diverged from that of the Prairies as a whole will likely be contentious, but given the incredible economic and demographic shifts occurring in Alberta it is not surprising that cuisine is shifting as well. In addition, there are several enclave cuisines sprinkled across the country, and I explore them as well, though in many cases these enclaves are fading in importance.

In some ways, all cuisines are regional, and to truly understand the role of food in all but the smallest and most uniform of nations one must break it down to the local level. Canada's cuisine is particularly grounded in the regions, and I give an overview of how culinary trends are evolving in the various parts of our vast land. Ontario and Quebec retain their dominance over many aspects of Canada's affairs, and Montreal and Toronto are two of the culinary flagships of the nation. Canada's cities enjoy an abundance of foods and culinary experiences. As Sharon Zukin notes, food is the new art,[28] and if this is true then Canada's cities are grand museums highlighting the best and most exciting food trends of the nation. Each of the major cities could provide fodder for a book, and each is represented in this book as well as possible, though any attempt to capture a major city's cuisine is at best a snapshot of a moment in time.

In contrast to the central Canadian heartland, British Columbia and Alberta are young and fast-growing provinces that tend to look west across the Pacific rather than east to the traditions of the Old World. Their cuisines are developing quickly and incorporating some of the elements of life on the frontier. Culinary innovation has always thrived in times of economic plenty, and the wealth of the west is contributing to excellence in cuisine both in the cities and in the recreational landscapes of the region. In contrast, the areas of Canada outside the central and western centres of power can seem very quiet and uninteresting, but as explored in Chapter 9 these overlooked regions boast long-standing culinary traditions. These regions are treated together since they have much in common with each other and show a different face of Canadian cuisine than their urban-centred counterparts.

Within our cities and larger towns, market spaces play a large and quickly growing role in our evolving cuisine. Canadians have firmly embraced the market tradition in the past decade, a surprising outcome given that forty years ago the public market and farmers' market seemed to be on the edge of extinction in our country. Markets have thrived and become some of our most popular and influential culinary spaces; in some regions, they vie for and even eclipse the presence of celebrity chefs and region-defining restaurants. Canadians are also increasingly interested in street food, a response to a general North American trend and a new direction given that Canada endured decades of very limited street cuisine. These shifts are influencing our cuisine and, at a larger level, our use of urban space. I separate these trends for closer examination since they are emerging as particularly important generators of Canada's cuisine.

One challenge of any comprehensive study of Canada is the size of the country and the difficulty of covering such long distances. During my travels, I covered 40,000 kilometres of road, passed through airports time and time again, rode the rails, and took ferries in just about every sort of weather possible. Eating on the road was a big part of my experience of

Canadian cuisine; in a country this large, travel is an important part of our experience. We tend to be a little more conservative in our culinary choices when on the road, which might explain why so many of us find ourselves at the Canadian chain Tim Hortons. However, there is ample evidence that food is no longer seen simply as fuel; it is an important element of the experience of travel. The penultimate chapter explores the mobility of Canadian life, and descriptions of my travels slip into the text here and there. From the time of the founding fathers and their journeys by steamship and rail to today's airports and highways and ice roads, Canadian life is at least partly defined by movement through a vast and sometimes hostile land.

I have always been fascinated by food. It is intensely personal, and though I enjoy travelling almost to the point of loving motion for the sake of it my real interest in this project lies with the food of our land and the culture that surrounds it. As Deborah Lupton notes, food is a "liminal substance; it stands as a bridging substance between nature and culture, the human and the natural, the outside and the inside."[29] *Speaking in Cod Tongues* is my understanding of Canadian cuisine, and though it does jibe with what many other people are saying about the foods of Canada it also presents a personal journey to understand myself as a Canadian. My life began in the food industry. I was born into a fishing family with five boats, and we lived and worked the waters of the Salish Sea. After a stint in the pure sciences, I became interested in sustainable food systems and spent thirteen years in central Canada as part of a quest to better understand why we eat what we do. My interest in public market spaces took me around the globe and eventually led me back to the West Coast, where I was granted the great privilege to spend five years addressing the big question of what Canadian cuisine says about our country and the world at this point in history.

In the course of conducting research for this book, I ate many interesting meals, met many dedicated and innovative people, saw places that I might never have seen otherwise, and gained an appreciation for the importance of food and cuisine in our daily lives. People have asked me what my favourite culinary experience during my travels was, and I can't really give a fair answer: so much of what I encountered was profound in its own way. Research changes the researcher, and as a whole the experience of exploring Canadian cuisine has changed how I look at my country, my food, and myself. My hope is that this account of Canada's cuisine can be one small piece of the puzzle of a country that came about almost by accident. I believe that I now have a better understanding of what cod tongues have to say and will return to them in the last chapter. I am sad to report, however, that despite my best efforts I have not yet mastered the preparation of Charlotte Russe, which if served with a local berry of choice would be an excellent national dish for Canada Day.

Cuisines aren't static. They must constantly adapt and change if they are to stay vibrant, relevant, and alive. By the time that these words are printed, Canadian cuisine will have already started to diverge and change. The final chapter of the book looks at possible future influences on our cuisine, from the damaging (climate change, farmland loss, and decline of wild species) to the transformative (population shifts and internal migration, continued multicultural blending, rise of the west, and ongoing explosion of interest in food in general). The cuisine of Canada is extremely rich and varied and will continue to be so.

2

# THE LANGUAGE
# OF CUISINE

On the surface, food is simple. It stands between us and hunger, staving off the third horseman of the apocalypse for another day. Ubiquitous and quotidian, the food system uses roughly 20 per cent of the global energy supply and nearly 40 per cent of the Earth's land area to feed (adequately or inadequately, depending on where one lives) the Earth's billions.[1] Sitopias (food places) have a wide reach, and beneath this practical surface food exhibits a deep cultural complexity. We use food to define ourselves and to mark the milestones of our lives. We use it to bond in groups and to distinguish ourselves from others. And, of course, we use food for enjoyment. The people who prepare our food for us have their own processes and rituals that have developed and evolved over millennia. The challenge for the food researcher is to grapple with the fractal nature of food; there is a universe hiding in every meal.

The concept of sitopia embraces two major loci, one geographical, one cultural. This chapter explores some of the theoretical underpinnings of these two areas of exploration. Geography plays an inevitable role in cuisine, for food comes from the land, and the scope of a cuisine's raw materials is thus bounded by the land. These raw materials also contribute to our opinion of a place, creating a sense of *terroir*. But much of this chapter is necessarily focused on cultural concepts. People come together over food, a property known as commensality, and together they use food to help define their identities. On a larger scale, cuisine is actively shaped as a nationalist project, but it also emerges as a reflection of national projects such as multiculturalism. This chapter highlights how cuisine is both actively shaped and curated, such as through national and regional events and the written word, but cuisine is also shaped and constrained by forces such as the landscape and population. But first a little history is in order: what exactly is cuisine?

The idea of cuisine emerged as thinkers struggled to separate food as necessity from food as cultural artifact. "Cuisine" is a slippery term, complicated by the necessity of daily sustenance. Not all meals are cuisine, by any means, and experiencing cuisine doesn't necessarily meet one's basic requirements for the day. The word *cuisine* literally means "kitchen," descending from the Latin *coquina*, from *coquere*, "to cook." The word entered popular use in late-eighteenth-century France and was brought to life in the writing of Jean Anthelme Brillat-Savarin, a lawyer-turned-epicure who survived a lifetime of complicated politics. After revolution and intrigue, he was happy to settle into the study of a few good meals. The first Western food essayist whose writings have survived, he knew five languages and drew heavily on the classics. Brillat-Savarin would fit in well today and likely be pleased to see the state of gastronomy, a study that he largely invented in his masterwork *The Physiology of Taste*, published in 1825, a few years before his death. I suspect that he would understand the cleverness in the sideboard diplomacy that the Fathers of Confederation brought to Charlottetown; after all, as he once remarked, "let one open any book of history, from Herodotus to our own days, and he will see that, without even excepting conspiracies, not a single great event has occurred which has not been conceived, prepared, and carried out at a feast."[2] Brillat-Savarin believed strongly that food was much more than fuel, arguing that "food is all those substances which, submitted to the action of the stomach, can be assimilated or changed into life by digestion, and can thus repair the losses which the human body suffers through the act of living."[3] Many a fine meal has been prepared to soothe the soul as much as the body. This was an opinion shared by the man who was arguably the co-founder of gastronomy, and perhaps the first culinary critic, Grimod de la Reynière. He opined that "life is so brief that we should not glance either too far backwards or forwards.... Therefore study how to fix our happiness in our glass and in our plate."[4] His guides to food established the idea that a meal, like a work of art, can be judged. A colourful character not known for diplomacy, Grimod was disinherited for a time on account of his lavish dinner parties, and late in life he staged his own funeral to see who would come to it.

A good modern definition of the word *cuisine* that goes beyond the dictionary definition is supplied by Priscilla Parkhurst Ferguson: "Cuisine is the formal and symbolic ordering of culinary practice."[5] This definition suggests that cuisine is about far more than the act of cooking: it includes coming together over a meal and encountering the food served. We partner with food to create a moment in time. The ubiquity of this collaboration makes food an invaluable tool to the scholar of culture and environment. That food and culinary habits escaped study for so long seems odd, for food, in Warren Belasco's words, is "our biggest industry, our greatest export, our most frequently indulged pleasure."[6] Food speaks to us and reflects who we are and who we want to be.

Brillat-Savarin and other early writers who discussed food did so in a cultural context in which an overly sharp interest in such a material aspect of life was seen as rather suspect. The separation of purity of the mind from base needs of the body dominated much of ancient thought; as Proverbs 23:20–21 tells us, "do not be with heavy drinkers of wine, or with gluttonous eaters of meat; for the heavy drinker and the glutton will come to poverty, and drowsiness will clothe one with rags."

The idea that thinking about food was somewhat sinful gradually gave way to a less damning association between gastronomy and the idle rich. To spend too much time dwelling on food was seen as rather trifling, and this attitude influenced Canada's early years, particularly English Canada. Gastronomy was for the very wealthy and not particularly of interest to serious scholars. This attitude waned in the late nineteenth century but didn't entirely fade until modern times.

The second half of the twentieth century saw two trends arise that greatly changed how food is viewed in society. First, the development of the global food system and a rise in disposable incomes made quality food vastly more accessible. Statistics Canada tells us that the expenditure on food as a percentage of total income plunged from 18 per cent in 1969 to 10 per cent in 2009,[7] continuing a general trend that began in earnest after the Second World War. Second, urban cores began to repopulate, giving rise to a large and influential group of people much more interested in trying new and exotic foods, preferably cooked by someone else. The growth of the restaurant scene in major cosmopolitan areas in Canada and elsewhere is somewhat astounding. Each of Canada's major cities boasts several thousand restaurants, a number unimaginable in earlier periods. Even thirty years ago the numbers would have seemed boggling. Zukin captures this shift in her writings on the late-twentieth-century city, documenting the rise of the loft dweller and the class of well-paid knowledge workers who linger in cafés with a laptop rather than toil in an office cubicle. For this demographic, she notes, food is the new art.[8] The resurgence of the urban village drove the emergence of a food elite that demands quality traceable to origin, and for them food consumption helps to frame identity.[9] This trend-setting behaviour in major urban areas has trickled down through the emergence of food as entertainment in the form of Internet blogs, glossy food magazines, and the rise of the Food Network on cable television.

The Canadian cuisine emerging at this point in history is a product of both time and place. It is driven largely by chefs and producers in

23

the food industry, with only a small nod to the role of the cook in the home, a reflection of the shifting dynamics of domestic roles. It is centred on a locality that both stands in opposition to globalizing forces and brands itself as a product for those seeking to buy an experience. It grounds itself in historical tropes of Canadian identity: fresh, wild, seasonal, multicultural, and regionally distinct. Perhaps nothing captures the global era as well as adventurous travellers coming together at the same table to try a new cuisine and through that cuisine become one with a place.

Although writing and talking about and snapping photos of food are currently trendy, they only explain the recent rise in interest in gastronomy. Interest in food itself, and food as a marker of culture, is a latent human trait. Eating together is one of human society's most universal experiences; as Pierre Van den Berghe noted, we are food-sharing animals and use food to establish, express, and consolidate societies.[10] Yet commensality, the sharing of food, is not something that we tend to think about in our individualistic society. The concept has deep roots; the desire to seek out company when eating was observed and written about rather extensively in antiquity by thinkers such as Aristotle: "As to common meals, there is a general agreement that a well ordered city should have them."[11] He believed that commensality was the glue that held cities and societies together, a form of soft infrastructure as critical as roads and bridges, creating a society out of a loose collection of individuals. Aristotle thought that everyone should be included in public feasting, a sentiment unusual today. Plato also studied commensality and argued that public discipline and citizenship could be encouraged through the common meal.[12] In recent times, scholars have begun to understand that commensality is still a major part of modern life; Claude Fischler, for example, calls it "one of the most striking manifestations of human sociality."[13]

This book is largely about what Canadians eat in public, with other people, and outlines a particularly Canadian commensality. The formal restaurant is perhaps the most obvious place where people come together to enjoy cuisine, but one finds people eating at roadside stands, in public markets, on trains and ships, and in public squares and parks. I've watched Canadians line up for food trucks and snack on "beaver-tail" pastries while skating (much harder than it looks). Our country has dockside fish-and-chip stands, *casse-croûtes*, chuckwagon breakfasts, *cabanes à sucre*, and lobster boil-ups. I've eaten in lighthouses, next to the world's biggest apple, and at a café called Eat in a one-building town in Saskatchewan (in my journal, I noted that the pie was excellent). The modern restaurant provides an individual experience in a communal setting, a phenomenon even stronger in the case of street food or market food, a property that Katherine Newman and I once described as eating separately together.[14] Communal tables in restaurants are also becoming popular across the country. I say little about what Canadians eat alone at home since it falls outside the scope of my study, but that private cuisine is likely quite different from the public cuisine explored in these pages. There is a difference between food for sustenance and food as cuisine.

25

One of the most striking changes from the days of the gourmand is how widespread the "food as art" mentality has become. Along with this shift we have seen the rise of a new avatar for people who seek out interesting foods and then write or talk about them (or post pictures of them all over the Internet). This avatar is the foodie, a creature with both positive associations (likes adventure, supports innovation, cares about quality food) and negative associations (obsessive, privileged, self-aggrandizing). The foodie is an expert but has a certain detachment, a shallow engagement that avoids the real dynamics of new neighbourhoods, glosses over the struggles of food workers, and ignores the environmental impacts of highly desirable foods. But for better or for worse, this is the age of foodies, and their cameras and keyboards flood us with information. We have never had such a good grasp of what is being eaten where!

The foodie is a paradoxical creature. The low and incremental cost of entry into the world of food makes the culinary world democratic, but the amount of time and knowledge required to take part fully suggests a sense of privilege.[15] The most accepted definition of the word *foodie* was first articulated in *The Official Foodie Handbook* as "a person who is very interested in food" and "considers food to be an art, on a level with painting or drama,"[16] and is often contrasted with the "food slob" who eats fast food and processed meals. The foodie seeks out the exotic and the authentic, concepts explored further later in the text.

The foodie might seem new, but the idea of food as a distinguishing cultural feature is familiar if considered in the context of Pierre Bourdieu's work on cultural capital and *habitus*.[17] In his discussion of distinction, Bourdieu explores the role of self-identification and niche knowledge as a way of creating group identification. The foodie, however, is much more varied than the gourmand and in many ways has a larger impact on cuisine through breadth and number. Where the gourmand stuck rather steadily to iconic elements such as French cuisine, truffles, and champagne, the foodie is just as likely to blog about the best diner pie in a city or the most "authentic" Vietnamese café. Canada has its share of celebrity chefs, food bloggers, and glossy food magazines.

The idea of a geographer, even one known to be perennially hungry, writing extensively about food and cuisine is a fairly new turn of events grounded in a larger shift in how geographers understand the world. In my own case, I became a geographer who writes about food because I am curious about the untold stories of what we eat. As an environmental geographer, I was heavily influenced by the urban studies of William Whyte, who filmed public spaces in New York to determine how people use such urban spaces. Whyte faced a seemingly intractable problem: why did some public spaces succeed and fill with people while others became dangerous and empty wastelands? By studying hours and hours of film taken from cameras hidden in public squares (his graduate students must have become adept at climbing ladders), Whyte began to establish general

26

categories of human behaviour. The people in his landmark videos act in extraordinarily animalistic ways.[18] They seek protection from the wind. They move from sun to shade as needed. They gather where they can sit easily and avoid places where they feel trapped or alone. When water is present, they touch it. Above all, they form clusters where there is something to eat, causing Whyte to remark that "if you want to seed a place with activity put out food."[19] As I watched those shaky videos of people huddling around hotdog vendors, my interest in public food spaces grew, and later I studied urban public markets, restaurant clusters, suburban farm markets, and finally cuisine at the national level. But I wasn't alone; interest in culinary matters has exploded over the past two decades.

In my examination of Canada's food pathways, I have followed in Whyte's footsteps, examining the culinary spaces of the country. The work follows a broadly phenomenological method described as topography or "place-writing,"[20] capturing spaces full of sights, sounds, smells, and flavours. Where people eat is a critical element of cuisine, one that fits well into a growing interest in the study of space. One of the most striking elements of food, in my mind, is that its relationship with space doesn't flow just one way. What we eat is partially dictated by the spaces and climates that we inhabit; certain crops grow in certain places, for example. But what we eat also shapes our spaces. We rework our environments to favour preferred crops, and we reshape our culinary spaces to best suit our cultures. This two-way conversation between space and culture mediated by food is a good example of what geographer Edward Soja calls a "socio-spatial dialectic." He argues that "people are constantly modifying and reshaping places, and places are constantly coping with change and influencing their inhabitants."[21] A cuisine, in this respect, is a language that mediates the evolution of culture and space. Canada as a landscape influences its cuisine, and the cultural forces shaping that cuisine shape Canada itself.

The landscapes and spaces created by cuisine tend, on the whole, to have positive associations. People tend to have their favourite farm stands, truck stops, diners, or restaurants. They associate some of these spaces with special occasions. During my research, I was told on count-less occasions that I had to drive out and try a little hole in the wall or check out a special nook. All of us are food experts in some ways, if only in a local geography. Ian Cook and Philip Crang describe this personal understanding of culinary geography as the creation of "geographical knowledges,"[22] in which the global flows of the food system are medi-ated locally. In effect, the challenge of truly understanding a national cuisine is to gather all of this local knowledge and distill the common-alities. Something odd happens in this process, though. Because food is so emotional, so primal, it is almost impossible not to develop deep attachments to the spaces of culinary knowledge that we inhabit. This lasting fondness is called *topophilia*, "the love of place," and is inextricably linked to the existence of cuisine.

The term "topophilia" comes from the writings of philosopher Yi-Fu Tuan, who has spent the bulk of his career pondering the bond between people and place. Tuan captures many of the elements that bind us to a place, such as intimacy and associations with happy times in our lives. A good restaurant or café makes an emotional connection with its cus-tomers, creating within them a sense of contentment and security or in some cases excitement and belonging. National cuisines have to foster the same sense on a larger scale. A national cuisine distills elements of what it means to live in a place and perhaps more critically to be of a place. A good café becomes a sitopia not just because of the food that it serves but also because of the orbits of human lives that cycle through the space in a day or season. The coffee house in Figure 2.1 is a place to work on a laptop, a place to meet friends, a place to watch people, and, yes, a place to drink coffee.

Many descriptions of national cuisines tend to focus on the food itself to the exclusion of place, but the microgeography that surrounds cui-sine is critical to understanding how individual dishes and ingredients imprint themselves on a culture. Commensality is inherently spatial,

28

and when we avoid the question of where cuisine is unfolding within a landscape we can lose our perspective and see cuisine as a rather neutral and intrinsic property of a culture. This isn't all positive. The inclusion of space in the discussion makes it obvious that culinary communities are as much about exclusion as inclusion. Food is one way that boundaries get drawn and insiders and outsiders become distinguished, and these boundaries might be drawn economically but are enforced spatially; commensal spaces often meld the public and the private and can become areas where spatial injustice occurs: not all Canadians are represented within Canadian cuisine. As David Bell notes, "we are who we eat with."[23] This is explored in depth in later chapters, but it is worth noting from the beginning that the idea of national cuisine in Canada embraces only certain Canadians.

Commensality is one of the fundamental pieces that make up a cuisine, and class structure, economic distribution, and privilege within a culture have impacts on how cuisine is formed and presented. In the

Figure 2.1. Granville Island coffee house

Canadian context, the years from 1970 to the present have seen a sharp increase in inequity in income distribution and significant shifts in the urban landscape and whom it serves. These shifts are mirrored in our restaurant culture and the very idea of who gets to craft the national cuisine. This book celebrates Canadian cuisine, but I have been cognizant that the emergence of a coherent national cuisine composed of strong regional culinary elements might never have occurred without the global rise of a large group of educated, cosmopolitan, and relatively wealthy people who value cuisine as a cultural product.

It is hard to write the words *Canadian nationalism* without feeling a bit lost; we are known for many things (cold, hockey, doughnuts, maple syrup, canoes, apologies), but national sentiment is not one of them. I've always believed displays of Canadian nationalism to be rather uncommon and was thus rather surprised one Canada Day to turn a corner in Covent Garden in London, England, to find a great number of people wrapped in Canadian flags, wearing red and white face paint. They were spilling out of the Maple Leaf pub, which serves a variety of Canadian beers, sells ketchup-flavoured crisps, and offers an attempt at poutine. Such obvious nationalism is rare in Canada, save for at Olympic hockey games and in Ottawa on Canada Day, where the entire city eats red and white sheet cake and drinks great amounts of beer in the street. Usually, Canada just isn't a very nationalistic place.

I believe that this lack of overt nationalism leads to the assumption that there really isn't a national Canadian cuisine. It would be easy to answer that, no, there isn't and then go on to argue that there is no national cuisine anywhere on the planet; at its roots, all cuisine is regional. As Igor Cusack notes, national cuisines are built by appropriating and assembling a variety of regional or ethnic cuisines,[24] and ours is no different. They are the products of dominant ideologies and power structures and created by governments, writers, members of diasporas, and other actors such as bloggers and web designers. Even great mother cuisines such as French and Chinese break into regional components upon moderate inspection. But to dismiss the rise of national cuisines is to ignore another construct that isn't always grounded in inevitability: the rise of the nation itself. Benedict Anderson writes extensively about the rise of nations, and he claims that "nation-ness is the most universally legitimate value in the political life of our time,"[25] but this wasn't inevitable and certainly hasn't been universal. As Anderson makes clear, the very idea of nations as organizing concepts is new, and nationalism invents nations where they did not originally exist. It's not easy to accept at first that something that seems as "real" and lasting as a nation could be what Anderson describes as a cultural artifact, but certainly the historical path that united French and English colonies to form Canada had its twists and turns. For example, when the Charlottetown Conference was struck, there was no time to notify the remote colony of Newfoundland, and it remained outside Confederation until 1949. Its identity, as we shall see in Chapter 9, has thus had three-quarters of a century less to acquire common elements of what it is to be "Canadian." Quebec contains a minority who believe that their province should stand as a nation-state of its own, and in British Columbia a much smaller minority think that the entire Pacific coast would be better served if organized into a new country called Cascadia. To date, Canada has been held together as a conglomeration of regions, but these ongoing tensions and questions might explain why we have very few strong national symbols.

31

Anderson explores the role of print media and language in creating a national bond, but cuisine is certainly another tool in the nation builder's workshop. Nations exist in a comparative field among other nations, and from the outside some cuisines certainly seem monolithic and well defined compared with our rather nebulous cuisine. But Anderson argues that even the leading national cuisines, such as French or Italian, are the cuisines of vernacular regions combined into national projects by capitalist administrative organizations. In a world dominated by globalization, this might seem odd. Why wouldn't cuisine converge on one great global mélange?

The interesting reality of life in a global era is that diversity emerges as both a reaction to and a marketing technique of globalizing forces. Cuisine acts as a glue that can hold groups together and help to define a nation's boundaries, and it acts as a central product for the growing tourist and export trade. As Rebecca Spang describes in her seminal book on the development of the restaurant,[26] travellers and tourists spurred the development of places where they could grab a meal away from home. Although the French developed the term "restaurant," the Chinese, with their tea houses and inns, could also claim to be the first restaurateurs. Little stages upon which local specialties could be presented and highlighted, restaurants (along with cookbooks and place branding) help to explain why localities are emerging strongly within a globalized system.

Returning to the idea of the nation-state as a social construct, lately there has been a small flurry of research into how cuisines have been used to bring people together under one umbrella identity. These works include a discussion of how Japanese cuisine is part of an imagined national identity built upon the myths of samurai[27] and Cusack's commanding work in Equatorial Guinea, where a very weak state with little historical justification for its chosen boundaries borrowed regional dishes to present a national cuisine largely created through cookbooks. The clear role of cuisine in a nationalist project spurred Cusack to remark that "cuisines are not just innocent concoctions but reflect the dominant ideologies of the societies in which they emerge."[28] Even the Charlotte Russe from the first chapter is steeped in political intrigue. Invented by Marie-Antoine Carême, the dish is named after Princess Charlotte of Wales, the daughter of Carême's former employer, George IV. The Russe refers to where Carême was working when he developed the dish, the court of Czar Alexander I. Ours is not the first age in which food has served as diplomat.

Canadian national identity has emerged in stages, each corresponding to different iterations of nationalism. Early colonial expansion exported imperial identities to the New World, giving rise to Nouvelle-France and British North America. Even after Confederation, linguistic differences and the persistence of colonial identities separated settler Canadians into the "two solitudes." There might not have been a coherent Canadian national identity, but at least two different forms of nationalism were dominant in Canada. The current emergence of Canadian nationalism can be traced to efforts to militate against both Quebec separatism and claims for Indigenous sovereignty. In 1971, with the legitimacy of the Canadian state being actively contested, Prime Minister Pierre Elliott Trudeau declared Canada to be an officially multicultural country and adopted a policy that affirmed respect for the diversity of languages, customs, religions, and ethnicities in Canada even as it upheld English and French as the official languages. The Canadian Multiculturalism Act was passed in 1988, enshrining respect for cultural differences in law and declaring the preservation of cultural heritage a fundamental right of Canadian citizens, with corresponding impacts on cuisine (discussed in detail in later chapters).

Although official multiculturalism has been viewed as an alternative to Canadian nationalism, it should be understood as a form of nationalism itself. As the national ideology, multiculturalism has become a distinct national identity. The inculcation of a "multicultural self" is a central goal of civic education in Canada. However, Katharyne Mitchell argues that this ideal form of citizen has largely been replaced by what she terms the "strategic cosmopolitan," a person "motivated not by ideals of national unity in diversity, but by understandings of global competitiveness, and the necessity to strategically adapt as an individual to rapidly shifting personal and national contexts."[29] Discourses of Canadian nationalism nevertheless still promote the value of multiculturalism and diversity, yet as much as possible multiculturalism is leveraged into competitive advantage. It has become part of the Canadian brand, and the current iteration of Canadian nationalism can perhaps be best understood as an exercise in branding.

Yet cuisine as national brand is just one facet of the role of food in our lives. Cuisine is also deeply personal. We all have relationships with food shaped by fleeting encounters that resonate through the years. I have my own food moments, but throughout this project one in particular has returned again and again to my mind. On my sixteenth birthday, the only birthday from my teen years that I remember well, a friend and I rowed out to a small island in British Columbia's Howe Sound for a picnic. I can't recall exactly what we ate, but the last course was chocolate cake, chocolate ice cream, and tea. To this day, whenever I eat chocolate ice cream, I think about that little trip: the smell of the ocean, the cry of the gulls, the sun on my shoulders as I rowed. This is a pleasant memory, but it can be deconstructed to reveal the elements that come together to form cuisine: the place itself, an active part of the experience, the cultural elements of the food, which in this case reflected the rhythms of an individual life. There is a day in April when I eat cake, a rhythm separate from the agricultural seasons of the year. Every dish, every group, every place has its own microgeography, creating a landscape so complex that it can never be totally captured in words. Food writing is at best the description of a few strong themes, trends, and historical contexts.

34

And there is much more to the food system beyond microgeography. Beyond the food itself, largely hidden but ever-present, are the producers, the chefs, and the production and transportation chain that underpins every meal. Canada's love of local food and embrace of chef culture have brought some of these people into the limelight, but for the most part the people who grow, process, prepare, and serve our food are behind the scenes. In the case of my birthday picnic, we made the cake ourselves, but the recipe was one popular in our community and thus part of our local culture (if I recall, it was a moist, dense chocolate cake made with a little brewed coffee to give it added flavour. The fellow who invented the recipe opened a successful chain of bakeries). The ingredients had to be produced in various parts of the world and then shipped by ferry to my hometown of Roberts Creek, British Columbia. For the chocolate and coffee, the trip was long indeed! Commensality also played a critical role in the experience of the meal. Our rather pleasant picnic would not have been the same had I been alone on that rock, but since that day I've enjoyed picnics alone on beaches and in market squares where many other people were eating at the same time; commensality can be found among strangers as long as the circumstances are right. Finally, our little meal had a grounding in the biological, for the food consumed represented a cornucopia of plants and animals harnessed for the pleasure and maintenance of the diner, just another animal in need of food. At the edge of our picnic, gulls circled hopefully, a reminder that at some level all of nature is engaged in one ongoing communal meal.

## 3

# FROM A COLD COUNTRY: THE CUISINE OF AN IMAGINED WILDERNESS

There is something very soothing about a day spent berry picking. The mind quiets in the search for bursts of colour among the leaves. The quarry might hide in a bog, on a beach, or on a mountainside, and a berry hunt can be a short jaunt to harvest a bit of flavour for breakfast or a hard day's work to gather needed food for the winter. Many Canadians have a beloved berry patch, whether bakeapple, partridge berry, blueberry, Saskatoon berry, raspberry, strawberry, haskap, or blackberry. Berries show up again and again in the dishes that we serve to the world. My berry of choice is the blackberry, and my personal berry patch occupies a scrubby zone where my family's orchard ends and the forest begins. It is unproductive land by most measures, but the season's bounty keeps me in berry crisps and pies year round. In my little town, it was common to glean food from the edges of places; we found cuisine on riverbanks, wild beaches, and forest verges. This story plays out across Canada. In my travels, I have heard many rural Canadians refer to nature as a grocery store. Having lived such a life as a child, I sometimes look at the mountains or the ocean and see the potential for a good meal.

Canada is an excellent country for people who love wilderness and a paradise for fans of wild foods. Our population density is the second lowest of the 100 most populated countries on the Earth, bested only by Australia. If we were to spread out evenly, there would be just four Canadians per square kilometre, and one is never far from wilderness, not even in our biggest cities. Canadians can canoe pristine lakes in the Canadian Shield, climb glaciers in the Rockies, hike and ski in British Columbia's temperate rainforest, and lose themselves on endless prairie, even when within easy driving distance of a nice cappuccino. And, yes, they can pick berries on crown land. It is no wonder that the idea of wilderness is deeply engrained within our national identity, even if the wildest thing that many of us do in a year is scrape the frost off the car's windshield on a morning when it is thirty degrees below zero. The idea of wilderness runs deep within our psyche.

Although 150 years have passed since George Brown amused himself by fishing for lobsters from his vantage point on the deck of the *Queen Victoria*, our cuisine reflects a tradition of wilderness provisioning at all levels. At our homes and in our restaurants, wild foods still play a role—more so than in almost any other cuisine on the Earth. Home use of wild foods is strongest in rural areas of the country, of course, but many city dwellers tell me of wild foods sent by rural relatives or of days spent foraging or fishing to help fill a freezer. Restaurants are embracing wild foods, and foraged cuisine appears right across the country. To be fair, places such as Scandinavia, England, and France are also enjoying a resurgent interest in wild foods, but Canadian chefs have such an abundance at hand that they can easily embrace the flavour of the wild. Foraged food is still a large industry in Canada, if one includes the fisheries, and wild food buttresses a somewhat fragile food security in many regions of the country.

37

My interest in food systems really began with wild foods. I come from a large fishing family, and my earliest memory is catching herring one morning with my uncle so that he could troll for salmon in the afternoon. When we weren't gathering food for commercial sale, we engaged in an astounding array of foraging. We dug clams, we trapped crabs and prawns, we filled the freezer with venison each year, and every summer we spent a seemingly endless amount of time picking various berries for the winter. My father still puts out crab pots regularly near my hometown of Roberts Creek. The opportunity to harvest food from the wild abounds in Canada; in Haida Gwaii, it is possible to catch crabs by hand, simply by wading in the surf. It's hard for food to be more local or fresh than that!

As a child, I also helped out when we sold fresh fish at the dock, and I experienced a different side of wild provisioning through that work. Every day there were sociologically interesting encounters between wild fish and urbanite, mediated by a "real" fishing family. Many people were disappointed to find out that we didn't live on the boat, that we had a house, a car, and other trappings of civilization. My father, though, usually let people believe that we lived on the boat; as anyone who has ever sold food knows, one also sells a story. Both fish and fisherman are the "other," in the ideal "wild" encounter, and this "wild imaginary" associated with much Canadian food has been noted several times in the literature. Atsuko Hashimoto and David Telfer discuss the link between Canadian identity and the natural environment at length, noting our love for wild foods and exploring some of the regional specialties still gathered from the land.[1] Patricia Hluchly describes "wildness" as one of the three defining features of Canadian cuisine.[2] In *Northern Bounty*, Jo Marie Powers and Anita Stewart describe an official diplomatic menu of salmon, fiddleheads, wild rice, and maple mousse, which sounds like a rather nice meal and offers a good cross-section of Canadian foods, all wild.[3]

A full account of Canada's wild foods could fill a book. In my travels, I sampled fiddleheads and nettle pesto, wild blueberries and Arctic char;

went to a very odd mushroom festival; ate wild leeks in Ontario; tasted crowberries, partridge berries, and bakeapples; and drank a madrona wine that made the room spin. Faced with such a rich banquet, I have chosen to highlight a few foods of particular importance or interest. It is important to understand that such foods are not inevitable in Canada's cuisine, even though its geography makes their presence more likely. Wild foods were a particular and rather surprising focus of the cuisine of Expo '67, discussed in more detail in Chapter 6. But for the most part, the early to mid-twentieth century was a period when interest in wild foods declined, and the appearance of wild foods at Expo '67 might have drawn in part from the back-to-the-land movement of the 1960s and the popular book by Euell Gibbons, *Stalking the Wild Asparagus*.[4]

In earlier times, reliance on wild foods was a necessity; as late as the 1930s, local cookbooks offered a comprehensive array of methods for dealing with deer, moose, duck, grouse, and other wild foods. Cookbooks such as that of the Victoria *Daily Colonist* featured several venison, duck, grouse, quail, and pheasant recipes, with an extra section on how to cook rabbit. However, the narrative arc of cookbooks in Canada over the twentieth century shows a shifting opinion of wild foods from a central part of life to a second choice compared with processed, farmed foods. This shift reflects in part the enclosure of wild lands that saw huge portions of the country converted from a culinary commons to private farmlands. This shift was particularly striking on the Prairies, where many wild hunting and foraging grounds were lost. Enclosure in other areas of the country remains incomplete, allowing for substantial wild harvesting to occur.

By mid-century, most of us could no longer feel much kinship with Catharine Parr Traill, and by the early 1960s our cuisine drew heavily on what Warren Belasco calls the "populuxe,"[5] and food was taking a modernist turn. Browsing the cookbooks of the time reveals some interesting experiments in chemistry, including apple pie with no apples and more casseroles built around condensed soups than can be imagined (I won't speak of the things done with Jell-O). In hindsight, Joshua Gitelson said it best when he commented that "to describe suburban cuisine in the 1950s is to invoke images of hellish concoctions,"[6] and these bland, processed, and overly sweet dishes that dominated restaurants and kitchens were displacing the more challenging flavours of wild game and produce.

This followed earlier trends in Europe; when the 2004 Oxford Symposium on Food and Cookery addressed the topic of wild foods, the main argument was that they began to vanish in the eighteenth century and were largely gone from day-to-day life. The participants noted that only a few elite wild foods remain in Europe; Ken Albala highlighted the sometimes-wild truffles, as well as capers from the Cycladic Islands of Greece (and fish, of course, which we sometimes forget is wild).[7] In the same volume, Susan Campbell described much wild food as "nasty."[8] Most presenters were quite negative, though one writer, Steven Kramer, perhaps sums up the difference between North America and Europe nicely with the claim that "in wildness there is freedom."[9] The idea of wilderness, and the glorification of free access to wilderness, have reasserted themselves in the Canadian identity. For many people, the move away from a connection to food drawn from the land lasted little more than a generation, if it reached them at all.

The strong role of wild foods in Canadian cuisine suggests that wild foods never became marginal in the same way that they did elsewhere. "Marginality" is another interesting and slippery term. Just as authenticity is a relational concept, so too marginality is always in relation to the flavour of the moment.[10] What is completely accepted in some situations can be met with disdain in others, and the fortunes of wild foods rise and fall with the fortunes of the people with whom they are associated. Elizabeth Finnis describes this well in the study of foods associated with Indigenous peoples, migrants, and disadvantaged locals.[11] In my own research, I was struck by the rising interest in the sea urchin and geoduck, two rather unlikely popular foods of the BC coast. At one time, urchins were left largely to sea otters, yet an experimental dive fishery now gathers them from the muddy bottoms of BC ocean channels. And I will admit that geoducks seem more the stuff of nightmare than the dinner table. They resemble a giant prehistoric clam with a phallic neck and dwell a metre or more below the surface of the beach at lowest tide. Both foods have gone from marginal bordering on inedible to delicacies for one reason: sushi. People risk quicksand and freezing water for geoducks and line up for the freshest urchins. However, when only Indigenous peoples ate them, settlers were not so quick to add them to their tables. Many of the foods eaten in precontact North America are lost to modern cuisine.

Wild foods in Canada range from the mundane to the obscure, the invasive to the extinct (if one wants to roast a great auk, it's too late). These foods can be foraged, as with fiddleheads and berries; they can be controversial, as with seals; they can be expensive, as with Canadian caviar; and they can be delightfully obscure, as in the case of pickled spruce tips and bottled cattail hearts. Some, unfortunately, have been endangered by overharvesting, and many interesting wild foods have fallen out of favour and been lost to our cuisine. The best example of this latter sort of food is pemmican, which helped to build Canada as we know it yet is now largely a meal left to history.

Little undisturbed prairie ecosystem remains in Canada, and few of these patches are large enough to support bison. It is sobering to think that these giant animals once roamed the plains in the millions and that large bands of nomadic peoples once followed them. As numbers of captive bison rise, bison burgers have reappeared on Canadian menus, particularly in Alberta. I recall that they were for sale at Head-Smashed-In Buffalo Jump, Alberta, an Indigenous site where bison were run off cliffs and processed into food. In those times, much of the bison ended up in the form of pemmican.

*Pemmican* is a Cree word, and the food is a mixture of powdered meat, grease, and occasionally dried berries. Compressed into blocks, it carries an impressive 3,500 calories per pound and stays edible for

41

up to five years.[12] Pemmican was also made on the West Coast out of salmon and traded widely around western Canada by Indigenous groups. However, it was its role in the settlement of the western regions that made "pemmican" a household term, even long after it was regularly eaten. Pemmican proved to be the magic bullet for the most pressing problem faced by the fur-trading voyageurs from the east. Although they filled their boats with corn and Ontario wild rice, they arrived at Lake Winnipeg half starved. To access the rich fur-trading grounds of the North, the voyageurs needed a way to carry a lot of calories, and pemmican, basically an early protein bar, fit the bill. A rich trade in pemmican began. Cree and Assiniboine hunters traded pemmican for European goods, and Métis communities began producing pemmican in bulk for the fur trade. At first, this was mutually beneficial; however, when the Hudson's Bay Company established a monopoly over the fur trade in 1821, it could press down the price paid for pemmican, which by the 1830s had fallen by 75 per cent.[13] This was a contributing factor in elimination of the plains bison: Indigenous peoples had to overhunt bison to maintain their income stream (though many other factors, including habitat disruption, deliberate extermination, and diseases from cattle, were factors). Collapse of the bison herds placed the surviving people of the plains in a situation of dependence on the government for famine relief. As explored in *Clearing the Plains*, the government's use of food as a tool to move starving survivors onto reservations led to the destruction of many bands. Weakened by hunger, Indigenous groups vanished as diseases brought from the Old World ravaged populations. The grim aftermath of the pemmican trade on the plains saw the Indigenous peoples of the region nearly eliminated.[14] Pemmican as a concept, however, was taken up by settler culture, and pemmican was used by many polar explorers years after it had fallen out of favour in the general population.

What is interesting about pemmican is its almost total absence from Canadian cuisine, even as a curiosity. In my interviews with chefs specializing in Canadian dishes, I was told several times that tourists ask for the dish, but for the most part it remains on the pages of the history books; it's difficult to make and doesn't suit modern tastes. As for the bison, they are making a comeback; on my way to Yellowknife, I had the pleasure of driving through one of the last unfenced herds, and I marvelled at their size. Perhaps pemmican belongs in the history books, and perhaps it is simply an example of overkill; few people these days need to slam back 3,500 calories of rancid grease and powdered meat to survive the day. Still, it would make a bold appetizer for some adventurous chef, and I encountered a few attempts to present it to the modern diner. A recipe is provided in the excellent *From Pemmican to Poutine* for the bold.[15]

Although pemmican has largely vanished, the other voyageur staple, wild rice, continues to gain in popularity. I have seen wild rice waving in the sun at the far edge of Manitoba where the prairie meets the Canadian Shield, and I've been entranced with the gentle wash of noise that the ripe seed heads make in the wind. Wild rice isn't actually rice at

43

Figure 3.1. Free-roaming bison near Yellowknife

all: it's a different grain, *Zinzania aquatica*, one of the few edible grains native to Canada.[16] It is an annual, sleeping through the winter and then shooting two to three metres into the air in the shallow waters at the margins of lakes in Ontario, Manitoba, and northern Saskatchewan. Its lush seed heads wave in the wind and shatter easily to cast a future crop on the water. It was a staple for the Indigenous peoples of the region, who used its easily stored calories as a valuable trading item and took advantage of the power of the rice beds to attract birds. The grains puff up into a delicious nutty dish, a wonderful reward for a rather difficult harvest. Historically, the grains were gathered by canoeing through the stands of rice and knocking ripe grains into the canoe with a paddle. The rice must then be cured by drying. Although this method sounds relaxing, the modern approach using airboats is probably much faster and more economically rewarding. The harvest is still a mainstay of Indigenous peoples in the area, many of whom have capitalized on the durability of the crop to sell it over the Internet. Even today wild rice is an expensive treat, and costs are likely to rise as popularity of this dish grows across the country; it pairs extremely well with many Canadian favourites, such as salmon and Arctic char. Wild rice country runs south of the border as well, where it captivated Thomas Vennum to write the only thorough book on the subject, *Wild Rice and the Ojibway People*.[17]

Wild rice is often paired with fiddleheads, a combination that brings out the wild, nutty flavour in both foods. The popularity of fiddleheads is an excellent example of the process described by Wilk, in which a regional food is elevated as an element of national cuisine. The tightly furled fronds of young ferns, fiddleheads are enjoyed across central and eastern parts of the country but are an uncommon wild harvest in the west. They are usually harvested from ostrich ferns and always gathered from the wild. Their popularity might stem in part from their early appearance, for in many cases they are the first green things in the eastern forest. They grow in damp areas and on riverbanks, are a shade-loving plant, and have a taste somewhere between fresh peas and asparagus.

They were popular with the Mi'kmaq, and their use as a food was incorporated by the Acadians. Their popularity is increasing along with the general interest in Canada's cuisine, and along with culinary efforts in general, and fiddleheads appeared in a number of the menu analyses I conducted during the spring season. They can be toxic if undercooked, though I've encountered them in quinoa salads and survived; to be honest, the flavour is better after a light blanching. They are a pretty food and carry a little bitterness that can be tempered with butter or another fat.

Fiddleheads are an interesting example of the rural to urban food chain that exists in Canada. Although they seem to appear in markets and restaurants as if by magic, they are gathered by hand in rural forests and sold to buyers who bring them to market. Harvesting fiddleheads in bulk is hard, cold work that involves hours of stooping, but the income comes at a critical point in the year and can be important in regions with little employment outside the summer months.

Not all greens come from the land. When I read about the dulse of Grand Manan, New Brunswick, in Margaret Webb's excellent *Apples to Oysters*,[18] I couldn't stop thinking about the men and women who wander out onto the slippery floor of the ocean at low tide to gather the red seaweed for which the island is famous. They then dry it, in a manner that has changed little over the centuries, by spreading it onto dark rocks. They ship the bulk of it to Japan, a new twist in an old economic chain. I couldn't really justify going so far out of the way to see something that another writer already captured, but when I stood in front of a small pile of the seaweed at the public market in Saint John I just had to learn more. I was going to Grand Manan.

The island didn't disappoint. It was a beautiful and ghostly place, with gnarled trees on grey rocks and lobster pens built out of sticks on the shallow flats. The dulse is high in protein, iron, and trace minerals, and it grows best at the aptly named Dark Harbour, where the island's formidable shadow shades the sea bottom. Dulsers, who inherit their grounds in complex family arrangements, gather the weed by hand in

45

what seems to be some of the hardest and coldest work that I've seen in
a country infamous for hard and cold work. At Roland's Sea Vegetables,
customers are free to buy dulse on the honour system from the mountains of bagged samples. Almost purple, it tasted strongly of the sea.

Later at the ferry terminal, I found some islanders passing the time,
and they told me a little more about this odd food. Most of it is exported,
but they eat it locally crumbled onto dishes as a spice or added as a
thickener in stews, where it functions rather like the *filé* of the Cajuns. A
group of helpful teens showed me how to toast it using a lighter, which
gave the dulse a nice crunch, much like popcorn. Although the work of
gathering seaweed on a bed of slippery rocks is difficult, it pays well, and
dulsing supplements other seasonal fisheries around the island. In all of
my travels around Canada, I can honestly say that Grand Manan was
the most hauntingly beautiful place that I have been. However, there is
a sad lesson in Grand Manan, for part of that haunting beauty comes
from the ruins of another great wild harvest, the herring fishery. The
island was once a hub of the smoked herring trade, and in Seal Cove
buildings now abandoned were once filled with the noise of workers
unloading the fish, filleting them, stringing them up, and smoking them.
The fishery collapsed in the 1990s, leaving barely a ripple in the international market but greatly damaging the local economy. The ruins of the
once bustling town lie largely abandoned, save for the odd lobster fisherman and tourists looking for nice photos at sunset. If we wish to enjoy
wild foods, then we must act as better stewards of our national culinary
resources. And, though the loss of the local herring fishery is a serious
blow, it pales next to one of the greatest collapses of a food system in
recorded history, the loss of the Atlantic cod.

It is hard for me to write about cod. As a fisherman's daughter, I grew
up fearing shipwreck and fishery collapse, and it is difficult to fathom
that a 500-year harvest could come to an end through gross mismanagement and the inability of the global economic system to adequately
signal local environmental depletion. If the same fate were to befall the

Pacific salmon (discussed in Chapters 6 and 12), the foodways of my home region would be ruined. Cod played a similar role; they were both a major driver of settlement of the eastern rim of the country and an underpinning of cuisine everywhere along the East Coast of Canada. Durable, nutritious, and multipurpose, cod supported hundreds of communities and made daily appearances on thousands of tables. The grand history of the Atlantic cod is documented in a book by Mark Kurlansky,[19] who describes cod's prized white and flaky flesh as supporting the greatest fishery in world history. He notes that it was likely the Vikings who discovered how easily cod could be salted or dried, creating a convenient and lasting source of protein. The Basques brought the fishery to the attention of Europe, secretly travelling to the Labrador coast, where they processed great quantities of cod on shore in spaces that came to be called "rooms" or "flakes." The dried or salted flesh then graced the tables of Europe, usually draped in a heavy sauce to disguise the damage of long-distance travel. When John Cabot stumbled across this fishery in 1487, he sparked a frenzy for cod. It is from him that we get the stories of a fish so docile and plentiful that one could dip it out of the ocean in baskets.[20] By 1550, half of the fish eaten in Europe was Atlantic cod.[21]

47

To better understand the social importance of cod in Newfoundland, I sat down with "Dr. Cod," Dean Bavington, at Memorial University in St. John's. In his book *Managed Annihilation*,[22] he argues that the very idea of management of such a resource is fundamentally flawed. He pointed out that between 1960 and 1975 as many fish were caught as between 1500 and 1750; technology simply overwhelmed the fish stocks. All of the management in the world couldn't compensate for the technological advances that allowed for the fishing equivalent of strip mining, particularly given the political dangers of limiting the cod catch. This combination of the ability to fish cod heavily right from the shore to the deep ocean and the need for politicians to respond on a five-year electoral cycle, at most, is in effect fishing the cod into oblivion. On July 2, 1992, fishing was halted, putting 30,000 people out of work and ending 500 years of fishing. As we sipped rum in St. John's (not the iconic screech, since Newfoundlanders are trying to encourage consumption of some of their finer distillery products), I asked Dean to go beyond the numbers; what did the loss of such a keystone food do to society? He sighed and tried to explain just how badly Newfoundlanders missed fresh cod. As a staple eaten several times a week by almost everyone, the loss of the fish felt like a betrayal, a body blow to the culture. On rare occasions when fish caught as part of scientific experiments to measure stocks were offered to the citizens, long lineups stretched back from the dock.

It was Dean who interested me in the strange tale of the cod tongue, an unlikely food if ever there was one. A small, fatty piece of flesh under the jaw of the cod, it isn't really a tongue at all. A cod head yields this treasure and two pieces of cheek meat, and in the days of the fish plants locals would pass some time cutting tongues and cheeks from the discarded heads. Often children would do the job, and once enough tongues and cheeks were gathered they would be fried with pork scrunchions and perhaps some carrots and potatoes. The feast, or "scoff" as it is called locally, would be eaten outside on the dock, and no one would have thought either to feed cod tongues and cheeks to tourists or to pay a price for them. But with the moratorium on fishing, the feasts on the docks came to an end, and perversely cod tongues moved into the restaurants as an adventurous food for tourists.

I first ate cod tongues at Cornerbrook's grand old Glynmill Inn, in the Carriage Room. They are a marvellous dish, fatty and rich, and the pork scrunchions add a touch of salt and flavour. Such a dish says something about Canada: fresh food heavy in calories designed for a people who spend a lot of time outdoors in a cold and unforgiving environment. The fact that I was eating cod tongues in a hotel that could have been straight out of a Victorian novel said something else about Canadian cuisine: the link between the people and the food can be broken and forgotten.

Although the meal was excellent, I would rather have eaten it standing around a great iron pan on the dock.

The cod tongues fried up on the dock weren't the only missing cod dishes that I heard about; I found signs of the vanished fish all over Newfoundland. As Kristen Lowitt describes in her excellent work on Newfoundland foodways, cod was the staple of many people's diets,[23] and it created a cuisine based upon seasonal and local additions such as pork, berries, potatoes, and cabbage. Cod simply dominated discussions of this rural cuisine; Holly Everett notes that the iconic cookbook *Fatback and Molasses* has forty-nine seafood recipes but that thirty-four are for cod![24] The outports of Newfoundland evolved a culinary cultural identity linked to the sea and seafaring traditions, reflective of an economic history tied to the fishery that produced fish for subsistence and sale. As Dean reminded me, the right to fish for cod for one's personal consumption was a term of Newfoundland joining Confederation in 1949, when the work of the Charlottetown Conference was finally concluded and Canada took its modern form. The mismanagement of the cod was a profound betrayal of trust.

The cod seem to be returning, slowly, and there is hope that one day they can once again be available to all Newfoundlanders and that cod tongues and cheeks will once again be fried with scrunchions on the dock. And across the country there is a growing understanding that wild foods can and do play important roles in our foodways, and interest in protecting wild foods is growing. Yet the disaster that befell cod has deeper lessons for how we need to interact with our environment. The small inshore fisheries thrived for 500 years before government mismanagement and exponential gains in technology eliminated cod in a matter of decades, yet across Canada local hunters and gatherers have been labelled as marginal and backward, banned from hunting grounds and punished for following their own local knowledge while being sidelined in policy discussions.[25] Reconciling wild foodways with agriculture and the global industrial food system can be very difficult; as Hugh Brody argues, hunters and farmers live in incommensurable worlds that require different ontological perspectives to be understood. Farmers, he argues, see nature as a domesticated object; hunters deal with it as an animate subject.[26] The reality in Canada is perhaps a little more complicated. Many of the rural farmers whom I know also hunt and forage for wild foods, and many Indigenous groups practised forms of agriculture, but on the larger societal level bridging such a gap requires the clashing of worlds. Wild foods available in one province are not legally allowed for sale in others, and often such foods aren't processed in inspected kitchens. Although food safety laws are most often valid and reflect actual risks, at the margins ideals about what is an acceptable food source can damage long-standing cultural traditions. The wild foods most accepted on the table are those that have been successfully commodified and incorporated into the larger food system. Many people need to be reminded that fish, in particular, is a wild food, for it is easily purchased in the supermarket as part of the normal diet. Other wild foods, such as wild rice, are heavily advertised as such and command high prices. These foods have moved from the subaltern to the luxury good.

Wild foods represent a hybrid edge between humanity and nature, and as Richard White notes we spend our lives in hybrid landscapes.[27] To understand the successful incorporation of wild foods into a cuisine is to understand that the very idea of the wild is profoundly strange. As William Cronon remarks, we need to rethink our notion of "wilderness,"[28] for the idea of a pure wilderness free from human presence is historically false and creates a dualism that gives us permission to evade responsibility for the lives that we actually lead. By treating the cod fishery as an "other" to be managed, the 500-year fishery was lost.

In the end, we can't really talk about "wild food" without realizing that the term is not without baggage that needs to be unpacked. The trouble with our hunger for wild food comes back once again to the concept of the authentic. When urban day trippers used to ask my family if we lived on the boat, it was another example of an encounter; as they returned to the city, they could imagine us, sailing through the island channels, living another possible life. The same goes for the romanticism behind some of our attachment to wild food: the idea that we could live off the land in an unspoiled Eden if only the world were slightly different. This idea of pristine and almost sacred wilderness, however, ignores the reality that the boundary between nature and culture is never a sharp line. It is blurred, and it is subtle, and it has implications for how we view the land and certain groups.

A good example is the little-known Indigenous clam garden of the BC coast. Clams were a vital food store for coastal Indigenous peoples; they were easily available, plentiful, and, unlike other seafoods, had the delightful property of staying still. Such an important foodstuff was to be encouraged, and as explored by Judith Williams[29] Indigenous communities improved clam habitat by moving rocks to the absolute low-tide line. The beach behind the rocks would build up, providing an expanded area for the favoured *Saxidomus gigantea* or butter clam (the clam used by BC Ferries in its chowder even though it is not the most common commercial clam). These tasty little clams live in the lower third of the intertidal zone, and their cultivation by Indigenous peoples was a form of mariculture that has left an extensive archeological record on beaches along the coast. That settler culture didn't notice the curious stone walls along the BC coasts could be partly because such changes go against the idea of Indigenous groups living off the wilderness. In addition, of course, settler governments had a stake in viewing the lands of North America as undeveloped, and if Indigenous people were farming clams that conception of an empty wilderness would disappear. As Williams remarks, "if native mariculture was as extensive as it seems, I can no longer completely refer to it as wilderness."[30] Interestingly, tending clams in this way is unique to coastal British Columbia and thus can be seen as a truly Canadian method of producing food.

If a wild food is tended in some way, then at what point does it cease to be wild? There might be no real answer to that question. Returning to the berry, similar patterns are evident; almost every Indigenous group that harvested berries also conducted controlled burns to increase yields, and in rural communities today many Canadians, settler and Indigenous, continue to lightly manage berry patches with a little fire, brushing, and weeding or, in the case of blackberries, a good thrashing with heavy equipment. As Sarah Whatmore notes in *Hybrid Geographies*, the reality of inhabiting a place goes against the idea of wilderness as pristine, undisturbed, and unpeopled.[31] The Himalayan blackberry, *Rubus laciniatus*, an invasive species, is itself a creature of boundaries, appearing at the edges where human and wilderness blurs. As I have written elsewhere, it is a source of up to 20,000 pounds per acre of delicious berries, but it is also an unbelievable pest.[32] These blackberries create dark, tangled thickets guarded by heavily barbed canes, often hide bees' nests, and hinder the growth of native species. Yet I love them. There is something so calming in the smell of their leaves and in the incredible abundance of their fruit. They are a fellow traveller, thriving at the edge of the not quite wild. And this ambiguity, this hybridity, is a defining feature of Canadian cuisine. But berries also highlight another feature of the Canadian table: they are one of many foods that create significant annual anticipation. In an age of global food chains that can provide endless culinary summer, Canadians still value seasonality.

52

4

# SEASONALITY IN AN AGE
# OF ETERNAL SUMMER

The summer of 2012 came late in Vancouver, and customers at the Trout Lake Farmers' Market were restless. As each rainy Saturday market came and went, volunteers were besieged by people wondering when the berries would arrive; as the market host, I had to explain again and again that maybe the next week they would be in luck. Meanwhile, farmers were telling tales of muddy fields, mouldy flowers, and a decided lack of bees. When the strawberries finally arrived, there was a collective sigh of relief.

The Fraser River basin is one of the great berry-growing regions on the Earth; 100 million pounds of blueberries are grown there each year, along with a major portion of North America's cranberries. The people of Vancouver and the Fraser Valley incorporate this bounty into their cuisine at every opportunity. Raspberries and strawberries are equally popular and appear on almost every menu in the late spring and early summer. We are a culture that loves our berries, and even though nature was behind schedule in 2012 consumers felt some inner clock ticking, suggesting that strawberries should be ready and insisting that blueberries and raspberries should not be far behind. When it comes to seasonal tastes, we don't like to be kept waiting.

In an era of global food production and transportation, it is reasonable to assume that eating seasonally would fade into history. Global food producers call the continuous availability of food the "endless summer," and it is true that seasonal rhythms have been muted in many regions. Seasonality, however, is a lasting and growing element of Canada's cuisine. In the study of market spaces, in menu analysis, and in field visits around the country, I encountered a strongly rhythmic progression of fresh foods. This resurgence of seasonality is part of a larger global trend tied to the rising interest in food in general and can be traced back to the late 1990s. This change reversed a half-century-long trend in which the idea that foods are meant to be seasonal was increasingly lost in a flood of imports from other countries. A study in 2001 by Anne Colquhoun and Phil Lyon in the United Kingdom, which historically also had a strong history of eating seasonally, documented the retreat of seasonal eating as the global food system grew.[1] The writers lamented this loss, suggesting that the impatience that I witnessed at Trout Lake is shared elsewhere. Their research showed that in the United Kingdom consumers miss the seasonal parade of foods that lends a cadence to the year. Their study captured a small niche of the population increasingly interested in eating in season, and it discussed a glimmer of interest in seasonal food in high-end restaurants, hinting that perhaps the seasonal cadence wasn't quite gone after all. My experience across Canada suggests that, as a nation, we are ahead of the trend when it comes to our interest in eating what is fresh locally. Canadians love to eat what is in season.

Traditionally, seasonality is a strong feature of cuisine anywhere far enough from the equator to have distinct harvest times, and, despite a long decline in seasonal eating throughout the twentieth century, seasonality has remained a factor in our food choices. Seasonality, best understood today as the consumption of foods during the time of year when they are ready for harvest, is partly a cultural property of food rather than a direct reflection of the reality of farming and harvesting, though that reality can also play a role. Consider kimchi, made and eaten in great quantities in Korea as a central culinary element. Kimchi is made throughout the year, but it is in November when the cabbages are ready for harvest that the *kimjiang,* or "kimchi-making season," occurs. Employers still grant a kimchi bonus at this time so that families can purchase the needed crocks and cabbages. The *kimjiang* might seem to be tightly coupled to the harvest, but cabbage is one of the easiest vegetables to store and transport a long distance. The persistence of the *kimjiang* in an era when global transportation supplies cabbage year round is a cultural phenomenon as well as an agricultural one.

Taste and freshness are huge factors, of course, in the desire for seasonal produce. An extensive study of Canadians who shop at farmers' markets noted that consumers regularly want seasonal food and will pay a premium for it on the ground that it tastes better and on the assumption that there is a health benefit to eating fresh food in season.[2] However, there is more to seasonality than freshness, for many traditional dishes are eaten only at specific times of the year. A 2009 study of northern European consumption of seasonal dishes, such as the foods associated with Christmas and Easter, explored how we continue to eat these foods only at certain times even though in theory they could now be consumed at any time of the year.[3] The study found that, rather than experiencing a weakening of the coupling between these dishes and certain times of the year, these foods remained highly unlikely to be eaten "out of season" even if they diffused to new regions of the world removed from the climates and seasons of the original locations. Physical availability was not enough to override the cultural expectations of when and where certain foods were found. Turkey remains an excellent example: it is mainly eaten at Thanksgiving, Christmas, and Easter in Canada, even though turkey burgers have a small following year round.

Does such an attachment explain the behaviour observed at the Trout Lake Farmers' Market in 2012? Eating a berry out of season

55

is different from having Christmas dinner in July, but it appears that similar factors are in play. This mysterious seasonal internal clock has been examined at length by Jennifer Wilkins of Cornell University. Her interest in our relationship with the seasons began when, in 1996, she noted that people in food co-ops were much more likely to value eating in season.[4] This is an important observation because it suggests that exposure to seasonal food tends to reinforce our relationship with seasonality, which might help to explain why Canada has always had a strong seasonal element to its cuisine and why the increasing interest in seasonal foods can be seen even more strongly here than in many other countries. Wilkins and her team remained intrigued by this link and conducted a landmark study of university undergraduates to measure our understanding of the seasonal cadence of food.[5] The results were shocking: 78 per cent of the students identified fruits and berries that they ate only in season, and 67 per cent identified fresh vegetables that they ate only in season. Outside the season, many of the subjects still ate these foods but only in canned or frozen form. Moreover, they identified the dishes that they made with these ingredients as distinct from those that they made in season, which makes sense given that canned and frozen foods are significantly different from their fresh counterparts in texture and flavour. Almost all of the students could name a wide variety of seasonal foods, and their understanding of what grew locally at what time of year was accurate. Somehow they had an internal clock counting down the growing season; the berry-seeking Vancouverites were likely experiencing a similar effect, and the kimchi makers of the *kimjiang* also likely have an innate understanding of when the local cabbage is ready.

Seasonality has persevered in Canada for a number of reasons. We have clearly defined seasons, and historically Canadians had no choice but to eat within the dictates of climate. Our early foodways involved dealing with luxurious plenty during harvests and storing as much food as possible for our long winters. We retain an enjoyment of seasonal foods that appear either early or late in the year, since they were the first and last fresh foods available on our early tables. This strong attachment to seasonality provides a grounding for seasonal cuisine even in the age of the global food system. Similar elements can be found in other northern cuisines, such as those of the Scandinavian countries. Thus, at least part of our seasonal connection is geographic.

This geographic connection to seasonality does not completely answer the question of why Canadian cuisine is becoming increasingly seasonal. There is a global trend toward fresh local food. Our cuisine in particular is influenced by the importance of California's cuisine in North American foodways. Trends observed in Canada extend well beyond our borders; fine dining in many countries incorporates local food in season. All of these elements—a historical imperative to eat in season that has left an imprint culturally, a continuing relationship with seasonal wild foods, and a larger culinary turn that stresses freshness and locality over complex recipes—come together to make Canadian cuisine observant of the wheel of the year.

Seasonality does have its limits, however. In the age of the global food system, we have the luxury of ignoring seasonality when it suits us. A follow-up study by Wilkins in 2002 found that staple products such as grains were almost never seen as seasonal and that few people identified meat and fish as seasonal, with the occasional exception such as lobster or turkey, or highly regional experiences such as the BC spot prawn season.[6] This matches what I have found in Canada; although people understand that iconic foods such as salmon follow a seasonal cycle, they continue to consume these foods year round when possible. The other interesting exception is exotic foods; people do not learn the seasonal cycles of other places, and with few exceptions they ascribe an aseasonality to their bananas and oranges, though in the big cities I noticed a growing interest in unusual seasonal citrus such as pixie tangerines and tree-ripened mangoes. For the most part, people embrace seasonality where it is culturally encoded and when fresh flavours far

57

exceed those of imports, but usually they will not eat seasonally when doing so greatly limits the diversity of their diet or when a crop is a dietary staple.

I found seasonality in every region of Canada, and higher-end urban restaurants in particular are stressing their use of fresh local ingredients. In Vancouver, the trend made menu analysis difficult; many restaurants have replaced a permanent menu, and even seasonal menus, with a daily fresh sheet. These seasonal foods create a calendar of sorts; one can measure the year in harvests and dishes tuned to the seasons. In Montreal, in fact, the Corporation de Gestion des Marchés Publics de Montréal produces a handy chart outlining what is in season throughout the year.[7] I've selected a few representative seasonal foods to explore, and the earliest foods in the Canadian culinary calendar emerge not from the fields but from the oceans and forests.

One of the first seasonal foods in the Canadian calendar is also one of the most controversial. Seal meat is still eaten in Newfoundland, the Far North, and parts of the Gulf of St. Lawrence, and it was once key to survival in these harsh environments. The seal hunt occurs in March, and historically seal was often the first fresh meat of the season, providing badly needed nutrients. Bottled seal and flipper pie is still available in Newfoundland but rarely found anywhere else in the country aside from the Far North. Seal meat enjoyed a mild resurgence in popularity in 2009 after the European Union banned Canadian seal products. Former Governor General Michaëlle Jean attracted global attention when she ate seal heart at a Nunavut festival shortly after the ban, and several chefs also began to offer the meat in solidarity. This small burst of interest was similar to the rise in domestic beef consumption when the United States closed its borders to Alberta beef during the mad cow scare;[8] Canadians are quietly patriotic for the most part, but we are proud of our food. The Montreal restaurant Au Cinquième Péché continues to serve seal in season and faces occasional protests for doing so. The Newfoundland grocer Bidgood's offers several seal products, including take-away flipper pie (Figure 4.1). Controversy aside, seal is an acquired taste: it is both chewy and fishy, though it is lean.

In most of Canada, the year's culinary calendar begins in April with the sugaring season. As the best-known national food, maple syrup is discussed at length in Chapter 6, but the rituals surrounding its short production season are worth noting for their seasonal elements, which form one of the oldest culinary traditions in Canada. These activities predate the arrival of colonists, and anthropologists have documented sugaring festivals among the Indigenous populations of eastern Canadian regions.[9] The third full moon of the year was known as the sugar moon among the people living near the Great Lakes, a name adopted by the colonists. Today maple syrup time is celebrated in numerous ways, including the Elmira maple syrup festival in mid-April. This event is recognized as the world's largest maple festival, with over 60,000 people visiting in a day. The festival highlights pancakes and sweet treats, as one might imagine, as well as the production of maple toffee (*tire d'érable*), one of a handful of recipes in the world that requires snow as part of the cooking technique (and what other country would cook with snow?).

59

Figure 4.1. Flipper pie

In Quebec, maple syrup season is the time to visit a *cabane à sucre*, a ritual examined further later in the text. Eating at the boiling sheds in the sugar bush was once a family affair; relatives would gather to make sugar and share food. This private space evolved into a rustic restaurant experience centred on simple rural dishes. Popularity of the *cabane à sucre* has grown to the point where hundreds of them can be found near the major cities in Quebec, where most of the syrup is produced. Maple sugar festivals are also found in Ontario and New Brunswick, but I have also attended a lovely sugaring-off in British Columbia in early March made from the sap of the broadleaf maple. The province's small syrup industry produces a product with a strong apple overtone.

The next widely observed moment on the food calendar in eastern Canada is the annual arrival of fiddleheads. I discussed them at length as a wild food, but it is worth noting here that fiddleheads are an unlikely candidate for inclusion in the modern culinary canon. They can be bitter, grow in difficult terrain, and if prepared improperly can be dangerous. Perhaps they have endured because they are the first fresh vegetable of the season. In many places in the east, they are literally the first green things visible in the forest. This might also explain their regional limitation; they are much less well known in the west. In the interior of British Columbia, wild asparagus often fills the role of fiddleheads and can be found in many damp sandy areas in the valleys.

Spring comes late in many parts of Canada, including the ruggedly beautiful coast of Newfoundland. I arrived at Cape Bonavista on a clear but chilling day and was glad to crowd into the kitchen of the lighthouse, likely once the scene of masterful cooking that made do with few ingredients. Built in 1843, the lighthouse sits on a landscape of rocks, grass, and wind. Offshore, the occasional iceberg floated by. I wondered at the meals made in the tiny kitchen high above the ocean and pictured salt cod and pork, flour, and dried beans. As I wandered the grounds, I came across the stone foundation of a long-vanished house. No trace of wood remained or any hint of who had lived there. I can reasonably assume that they enjoyed rhubarb pie, though, for a clump was thriving happily in the shelter of the ruins. No matter how harsh the winters at the Cape Bonavista Lighthouse, they likely started their year with a tart treat enjoyed right across our country. During the spring harvest, rhubarb rivals maple syrup and salmon as a Canadian iconic food. It is the definition of a culturally seasonal food; rhubarb freezes well, and is always cooked, yet we still tend to enjoy it during its growing season when it is fresh. Its lack of versatility largely limits it to a once-a-year treat, though rhubarb tarts are growing in popularity. And, for what it is worth, rhubarb was the only food that I encountered everywhere across the country. It was never the most important food, or the most flashy food, but it was there growing in healthy clumps from Tofino, British Columbia, to St. John's, Newfoundland. There is a clump outside the window of my office, oblivious to the poor quality of my East Vancouver soil. Easy to transport as a rhizome and medicinally useful, rhubarb travelled with settlers to every corner of the country.

In Judith Comfort's description of a seasonal cuisine embracing all twelve months of the year near the maritime shores, rhubarb took pride of place as the first pie of the year.[10] It is greeted with welcome after a harsh winter and has been associated with Canada since colonization began. Duncan claims that rhubarb is one of the oldest Canadian foods,[11] and analysis of period cookbooks suggests that it was often simply called "pie plant," a name that captures its most common preparation. It can also be served as a crisp, pudding, or even relish, but for the most part it is offered as a pie or jam. Rhubarb is a fascinating food plant, one of only a handful of perennial foods that we grow. It is technically a herb, though it is often called a vegetable and has been legally classified as a fruit on occasion. It is an ancient companion plant of humanity and was grown as long ago as 3,000 BCE in China. It spread west along the spice routes and became naturalized in European Russia. It grows easily from a rhizome, so it is very hardy and easy to transport and propagate. It was not actually used as a food until the sugar trade made sweeteners readily available. Historically, it was most often used as a medicinal plant. Today many Canadians have rhubarb in their gardens, and it is available at farmers' markets and groceries early in the season. The rhubarb festival in Shedden, Ontario, falls near the end of the rhubarb season and features a baking contest. The best use of rhubarb that I've encountered lately is as an addition to the iconic Canadian butter tart, examined more closely in Chapter 7.

Late spring and summer bring a parade of fresh products that feature in culinary preparations. There are early peas and greens such as kale and chard, and then succulent green beans appear along with cucumbers and tomatoes. Fruits such as cherries and peaches fill the markets, along with all of the berries: first strawberries, then raspberries, and finally blueberries. Strawberries are a historical favourite and an interesting product of the Columbian exchange, in which North American and Eurasian flora and fauna intermingled for the first time in millennia. Modern strawberries are hybrids of the South American and European varieties.

Summer erupts with fresh vegetables, from spring peas to the first tomatoes of the season to tender young green beans. Fresh corn appears in the market as the season progresses, a food popular in the hot late-summer months, boiled or roasted with butter and salt. Fresh corn is a feature at barbecues and picnics; I enjoy mine roasted in tinfoil over hot coals, and the newer, sweeter varieties such as peaches and cream have only improved the experience. As autumn arrives in Canada and the parade of seasonal foods slows down, a number of festivals mark the harvest bounty, including several foods stored for the winter. One of my favourite events is the University of British Columbia's apple festival, an annual celebration of the wonderful diversity of a favourite fruit. Five dozen varieties of apple are available for tasting, along with sales of trees, apples, cider, and, of course, pies. I am always amazed at how popular this event is; tasting so many apples quickly can lead to grief, but each year thousands of people line up for the pleasure. My family has a small orchard, and the heritage varieties that we grow are coming back into vogue both for culinary use and as a base for traditional ciders. The Northern Spy in particular is a quintessential Canadian apple: cold loving and not ready until late into October. Sea Cider on Vancouver Island uses Spies in one of its popular artisan ciders.

Few fruits benefited as much from the Columbian exchange as the apple. Native to a region centred on Kazakhstan, the apple has been popular since antiquity. The settlement of North America, however, led to an explosion of apple varieties. An apple seed does not yield a tree that is a copy of its parent. Thus, apple trees must be grafted onto rootstock to create true copies of a desirable tree. During the settlement of North America, orchardists didn't have the time for such niceties; they planted acres of apple seeds, generating hundreds of new varieties of apple then sold to settlers in need of a reliable fruit for the frontier. Many of those apples were likely poor quality, but some of them had desirable properties such as good flavour and texture and the ability to be stored (a subset worked well for cider and helped to dull the monotony of a Canadian winter). Particularly in Upper Canada, almost every account of settlement involves simple apple pies and crisps, and early Canadian recipe books contained dozens of variations for this staple crop. Wherever settlers went, apple trees followed.

Apple pie has always been popular in Canada, and apple festivals are common from Saltspring Island to the Annapolis Valley. The diversity of Canada's apple crop, though, is dropping. As the population urbanizes, old orchards are falling into ruin, and varieties of apple that don't suit the industrial food system are being lost. Renewed interest in local and regional food has revitalized apples somewhat. Old trees are being revived, and the public is expanding its interest in the great variety of North America's apples. And apples, of course, remain popular on Canada's fall menus.

As autumn nights lengthen and the final stages of harvest begin, we encounter some of the year's most interesting culinary cultural events. Canada is a deeply multicultural country, and it is impossible to describe its seasonal festivals and observances comprehensively. But the Thanksgiving meal marks an interesting example of cultural seasonality. In "Talking Turkey," Andrew Smith and Shelley Boyd describe the holiday that in Canada is on the second Monday of October as a secular holiday that marks the end of the harvest and the changing of the seasons.[12] Thanksgiving feasts originated in England and became popular during the reign of Queen Elizabeth 1. The first such feast in North America was Martin Frobisher's 1578 Thanksgiving Day on Baffin Island, where the explorer hoped to establish a colony (it did not succeed.) Centuries later biscuits and peas were unearthed in an archeological expedition, perhaps the first Thanksgiving leftovers in North America. That meal was likely a high point of the expedition; Frobisher was a privateer hired by the British to find the Northwest Passage and establish a mining colony, but the ship with the prefabricated buildings foundered, a quarter of his men sailed home without him, and Frobisher, ready to cut his losses, was giving thanks for the most part that he had survived the high Arctic.

64

Smith and Boyd paint Canadian Thanksgiving in stark contrast to the pageantry of the U.S. holiday, with its focus on Pilgrim mythology, shopping, parades, and football. Canadian Thanksgiving is more recent and draws more deeply on the English tradition of Thanksgiving harvest feasts. The meal, however, is both seasonal and unchanging. The traditional dinner of turkey, stuffing, seasonal vegetables, mashed potatoes, gravy, cranberries, and pumpkin pie has been in place roughly since the mid-nineteenth century. The period from Thanksgiving to Christmas is likely the only time that a person will encounter most of these foods. French Canadians, as a rule, do not take part in this holiday. Although *Action de grâce* is a literal translation of Thanksgiving occasionally used, most French Canadians with whom I discussed the issue are glad to have the day off but don't do anything in particular to celebrate it. Given the rather grim associations of Thanksgiving with colonization, one can hope that one day the meal will lean more heavily on its roots as a harvest festival and downplay celebration of the conquest of North America.

My favourite part of the holidays in late fall is pumpkin pie, and the ripening pumpkin patch is a nice endpoint for the Canadian culinary season. Pumpkins are grown in great quantities in Canada, though they are mostly eaten from Thanksgiving to Christmas, as noted above. Almost all pumpkin consumed in Canada is premade; canned pumpkin is much easier to use than fresh pumpkin, so most pies are made from a variety of pumpkin that can be had year round if desired. Although a North American crop, pumpkin has spread around the world and is used in a wide variety of cuisines. Ironically, fresh pumpkin is starting to creep back into Canadian culinary use from abroad; I recently enjoyed a decent pumpkin curry, and pumpkin tempura is appearing in Japanese restaurants.

Few people bother to make pumpkin filling from scratch, but there is at least one time of year that Canadians buy pumpkins in great quantities: Halloween. This odd holiday has strong roots in Canada, thanks largely to the Irish and Scottish influence on our culture. Halloween celebrations are thriving in Canada and spreading to parts of Asia. I was puzzled by the great number of pumpkins in Montreal's Marché Atwater in the autumn,[13] but given the number of jack-o'-lanterns that decorate the neighbourhood of Saint-Henri the orange wonderland at the market made sense. Farmers in rural areas near big cities have had some success with U-pick pumpkin lots, and in some places an outing to choose a jack-o'-lantern is combined with other elements of rural agritourism, such as corn mazes. The use of a pumpkin to represent the light carried by Jack of the Lantern is a North American invention, perhaps rooted in Montreal, though I can't provide definitive proof of this. In the original Irish legend, Jack carries a piece of hellfire in either a carved apple or a turnip as he wanders the fens and moors; North Americans quickly determined that the pumpkin was much better suited to this task. In my old neighbourhood near the University of Toronto, we walked along the streets pulling a wagon on November 1 salvaging jack-o'-lanterns and then make a large batch of pie and soup, proving that graduate students will go to great lengths to find free food. Storing food for the winter is still common across Canada, though gathering activities don't quite come to a stop. In many parts of the country, the depths of winter are the time for ice fishing.

The seasonality of Canadian cuisine deserves a deeper theoretical examination. Our interest in wild foods certainly helped to preserve seasonality in our cuisine, but it doesn't explain why these practices are so persistent. Culture plays a role, as in the case of Thanksgiving dinner, but other factors are at work, including deep links to place. Importantly, experiencing food at the ground level can locate research in place and track how localities are experienced.[14] Our fixation on the regional and local is driving a resurgence of seasonality.

To understand seasonality in Canada, I studied several public markets over three years: Granville Island in Vancouver, St. Lawrence Market in Toronto, and Marché Atwater in Montreal. I visited each market in each season of the year, documenting the foods on offer. In this longitudinal study of Canada's public markets,[15] cuisine didn't emerge as a fixed object; it changed with the year according to the foods fresh at the time and the foods culturally expected at the time. Returning to Ferguson for a moment, cuisine can be described as an ongoing process in which nature is turned into culture,[16] which implies a rhythm to the process. If we consider the conversation between people and their spaces, there is a rhythm regarding food that follows an annual cadence. Hersch Jacobs noted this element of Canadian cuisine as emerging from the inherent seasonality of the landscape,[17] but there is a deeper desire for reoccurring order at play. To fully understand the seasonality of Canadian cuisine, one must look at Canadians and their relationships to the rhythms of place. Seasonal foods map out a calendar deeply linked to landscape, and the trick is to imagine why this cadence remains important in an era when fresh food is available year round. The study of restaurants, markets, and festivals reveals a strong and growing relationship with seasonality, opposite to what one would expect as global transportation perfects the just-in-time delivery of perishables. Why do we crave a rhythm to our food and feel slightly uncomfortable when that rhythm is ignored or violated?

The idea of rhythm is understudied in geography, where timeless interpretations of space have dominated. However, research on the different rhythms of spaces is not a recent invention; Lefebvre was not only a master of the spatial but also introduced a less well-known concept, that of rhythmanalysis. He thought that everywhere there is an interaction among place, time, and energy—in short, a rhythm.[18] Understanding the rhythm of a place is central to understanding how it functions. To do so requires a longitudinal study; in the case of food, there is a clear daily rhythm and a longer yearly cycle revealed only after observation (and other cycles and changing trends superimposed on that cycle; in this respect, food studies start to look a lot like astronomy). A three-year study of Canada's public markets clearly demonstrated the long pulse of the year, and restaurant analysis shows the same trends, as do cookbooks organized by season. But the interesting outcome of this seasonality is that Canadian cuisine doesn't present an unchanging face to the world. This isn't unique; certainly, French cuisine presents different dishes in different seasons, as do California cuisine and several others.

The rhythm of culinary encounter is influenced by both space and time. Our culinary spaces take on a characteristic that we describe as a "polyrhythmic ensemble,"[19] and the rhythms that we find in these spaces reveal the "various and contested ways in which place experience is created, controlled, consumed, or commodified."[20] Going back to the idea of sitopia, a fundamental property of a food space is change that occurs with the rhythms of life: the food that we enjoy in a place depends on the time of day, the day of the week, and the cadence of the year. This temporal element of our food spaces brings diversity to our lives and establishes rituals that persist even when traditional harvest seasons no longer constrain availability. So, even in a world where food is available year round, we still conceive of it as having a harvest season, and we

67

incorporate that rhythm into our cuisine because historically it has been inscribed into our spaces and our histories. Canada is a seasonal country with a deep connection to winter; we pride ourselves in the annual test of the long, cold, dark season. This cycle is self-reinforcing; as fruits and vegetables become plentiful in season, we enjoy an annual indulgence. Tim Ingold argues that "a place owes its character to the experiences it affords to those who spend time there,"[21] and I believe that a cuisine is no different. We don't just eat Canadian cuisine, we spend time with it, and the longer we do so the more sides of it we see.

The wild foods that we forage are largely seasonal, and even if we are removed from foraging directly there is an almost unspoken assumption that seasonal food is more "natural" and more closely linked to our defining property of wilderness and the outdoors. Where the foraging and harvesting of wild foods is a direct link to nature, the purchase of food in season represents a more subtle desire to reunite with the rhythm of the seasons. I love the idea of "soft fascination" with nature,[22] a term coined by Agnes Van den Berg to describe our fascination with landscapes, even at the level of a single tree in a city park or a tiny square of beach. Similar forces could be driving the desire to plant urban gardens and orchards and to eat seasonally at the local market. When we eat in season, we take part in primal natural rhythms.

In 2014, the berries came early to the market, and customers rushed to eat, bake, freeze, and preserve them. In some cases, such as maple syrup and fresh salmon, we continue to enjoy the foods out of season even if we celebrate their harvest at the appropriate times of the year. In other cases, such as fresh berries, fruits, and vegetables, we eat them in the largest amounts at the times of year that they are harvested.

It is important to note, though, that interest in seasonality does wax and wane; in my study of Canadian cookbooks from the 1930s to the 1960s, I found that, though berries were still described in great detail (along with rhubarb), for the most part fruits and vegetables were used canned when they were used at all, and they were cooked a frighteningly long time. For example, the *Edith Adams' Thirteenth Prize Cookbook* from 1950 features only one page of salads, and of six recipes one is pickled beet, one is macaroni, and three are Jell-O based.[23] The cookbook also has only one page for vegetables, and of the six recipes two are for fried preparations and two involve baking vegetables for long periods in heavy sauces. There are several pages of pies and tarts that do feature some seasonal fruits. The moral is that, though geography does create a precedent for local seasonal food, culture can introduce some fairly strong variations in what the cuisine actually looks like. But from the first settlement to the populuxe era of canned and frozen food, and then back to the farmers' market, Whole Foods Market, and 100-mile diet, seasonality gives a cadence to Canadian cuisine that cannot be ignored.

5

# THE CANADIAN CREOLE

When I was growing up, a trip out to eat was a rare treat taken to celebrate some special event. In our family, there was one exception: once a month or so, we would go to the Seaview Gardens restaurant, where we would take our fill of Chinese Canadian cuisine from the smorgasbord. The food was fairly simple and reassuringly unchanging. There was a long table filled with sweet-and-sour pork (in a bright red sweet sauce thickened with cornstarch), chop suey (complete with bean sprouts, baby corn cobs, and water chestnuts), chow mein, beef with broccoli, fried rice, lemon chicken balls in a bright yellow sauce, ginger beef (though that dish was added in later years), and puffy deep-fried eggrolls with plum sauce. When I left home to attend the University of British Columbia, I would pick up similar eggrolls at the Varsity Grill, which offered much the same experience. And on rainy days, I still love to settle into a booth at the local Chinese Canadian café for wonton soup.

This strange cuisine was found throughout North America, and even then we knew that it had little to do with what was eaten in China. Chinese Canadian restaurants prospered in even the smallest towns.

Although today Chinese cuisine in Vancouver is much more nuanced and more closely represents the different regional cuisines of the vast country of China, occasionally I still crave those sweet tangy hybrid dishes of my youth. Across rural Canada, Chinese Canadian restaurants continue to flourish, and almost every BC town has one. In *Eating Chinese*, Lily Cho sums up the cuisine's resilience nicely: Chinese Canadian restaurants are old but not extinct.[1] During their ascendancy, when the mainstream food eaten in Canada was still heavily rooted in British and French traditions, the widespread love of the Chinese Canadian restaurant reflected the beginning of a multicultural element to Canada's cuisine. This nascent willingness to blend the cuisines of incoming groups into regional diets didn't rest only in restaurants. Cookbooks from the mid-twentieth century were filled with "ethnic" sections that taught the home cook the mysteries of the perogy, curry,

Figure 5.1. A traditional Chinese Canadian restaurant

71

and, of course, chop suey. Unfortunately, for many of these groups, of which Chinese Canadians were one, their food was accepted long before their people.

Chinese Canadian cuisine is both a product of a distinctly Canadian experience and a variation of a larger global pattern that emerged wherever the Chinese diaspora established communities. The historical reception of Chinese immigrants in Canada was not a happy one, and the rise of the Chinese Canadian restaurant reflects a long history of discrimination. The first Chinese people to immigrate to the West Coast and Prairies came in the late nineteenth century seeking gold, followed by labourers from Guangdong province, who came to help with construction of the national railway. Toronto's Chinatown arose as this first wave of workers relocated from California, where they faced particularly strong discrimination, and Montreal became a hub for Chinese railway workers. As immigrants, they faced significant barriers and were stigmatized as a threat to Europeans in the job market. This led to the Chinese Immigration Act of 1885, which imposed a steep head tax on immigrants from China. In 1923, immigration was banned entirely and wasn't reopened until 1947, though barriers remained into the late 1960s. This is particularly stark since Canada at that time was experiencing the highest rates of immigration on a percentage basis in its history, even compared with today. As Italians, Germans, Britons, Scots, and Ukrainians poured in, the Chinese were frozen out. The cuisines of these other groups are also critical to the story of Canada's cuisine, and they will appear in the chapters on regional cuisines, but the story of Chinese Canadian cuisine, born of prejudice, followed a different path. During much of this period, Chinese people already in the country were banned from almost all occupations. Restaurants were one of the few businesses that they were allowed to operate, and they were often the only such establishments in towns and served as de facto town halls. In addition to Chinese offerings, they usually served "Canadian" dishes as well, such as hamburger, steak, and simple fish-and-chips. But they are best known for their unusual take on Chinese cuisine, bright red sweet sauce and all. A mix of Chinese techniques and Western flavours, Chinese Canadian dishes foreshadowed the current multicultural state of Canada's cuisine in general.

In the past decade or so, a number of scholars have explored the Chinese restaurant. In *Sweet and Sour*, John Jung notes that Chinese cooks faced two limitations on their cooking: first, the ingredients that they were used to back in China simply weren't available; second, the mainstream food of the time was "creamy, meaty, and sweet."[2] They drew loosely on the dishes of Guangdong province since many of Canada's first wave of Chinese immigrants were relocating from that part of China. The 1850s had not been kind to Guangdong; it went through war, rebellion, and natural disasters. As Jennifer Lee demonstrates in *The Fortune Cookie Chronicles*, immigrants opening new restaurants also began innovating new dishes. The iconic fortune cookie, she found, likely arose in San Francisco.[3] Canada has its own list of non-verified additions to the cuisine; legend suggests that the Chinese smorgasbord was invented in Vancouver's Gastown, where Scandinavian loggers suggested to a Chinese cook that the food be served all at once on a sideboard rather than one dish at a time.

Canada is not the only country where a version of Chinese cuisine has a strong presence. In *Globalization of Chinese Food*, editors David Wu and Sidney Cheung call Chinese food a powerful global force.[4] The key is the willingness of Chinese cooks to amend the cuisine to suit local conditions; Lee describes Chinese cuisine as having a philosophy of mixing local ingredients with Chinese techniques.[5] The historical diaspora included people from Fujian province and Guangdong province, and Hakka people from the mountains. They have given the world Chinese Malaysian food, Chinese Indian Hakka cuisine, Hawaiian plate lunches, the tiki Polynesian food offered by entrepreneurs such as Trader Vic, along with our own Chinese Canadian food.[6] By 1931, a full one-fifth of Canada's restaurants were run by Chinese, even though

73

Chinese Canadians represented less than 1 percent of the total population.[7] Chinatowns flourished in cities and provided points of contact between curious urban diners and Chinese cuisine, including chop suey, fortune cookies, and rumours of second menus offered only to Chinese diners. Until the 1970s, Chinese Canadian cuisine remained relatively static; Jean Duruz calls these styles of food fortress cuisines, predictable havens that don't change.[8] The Chinatowns of Toronto, Vancouver, and Montreal represented a certain vision of East Asia, and though eventually strange ingredients and exotic fare did appear, chop suey was never far away. But in the last decades of the twentieth century, a multicultural revolution would wash over Canada, affecting how we now look at food.

Change has come at long last to Vancouver's Chinatown. Although there are still places there to buy Chinese vegetables and pick up oriental screen prints, there are also pubs, bike shops, condominium developments with vaguely Asian names and styles, a pie shop, and everything else that one might expect to find in a rapidly gentrifying neighbourhood. In the broader city, Chinese vegetables are available at every grocery store, and most Vancouverites know how to cook them. A barrier that stood for far too long has been breached. A similar change has descended on Toronto's Gerrard Street as the traditional customer base has expanded rapidly in the suburbs. The era of urban ethnic enclaves in Canada is over, save as tourist attractions. This is the age of the ethnoburb.

In the case of Chinese Canadians, rapid changes to immigration patterns took place in the 1980s as a first wave of Taiwanese immigrants was followed by heavy immigration from Hong Kong, shifting the demographics of Canada's major cities and, in particular, their suburbs. Vancouver's suburb of Richmond shifted from 95 per cent Caucasian to a 60 per cent visible minority population over a few decades, and Toronto rapidly became one of the most multicultural cities in the world, a phenomenon explored further later in the book. These changes also reshaped our culinary landscape. Chinese Canadian food was displaced by regional Chinese cuisines that more closely represented current regional Chinese cooking. New ingredients became available, and more people became used to culinary techniques such as the use of hot spices. Large populations of South Asians also moved into the suburbs, where strip malls became dotted with excellent restaurants serving cuisines from around the world. Suddenly, Canadians were being exposed to a vast array of cooking styles and cuisines.

This massive shift is directly linked to vanishing urban ethnic enclaves within Canada's cities. Vancouver's Chinatown is a disappearing remnant of a dark period in Canadian history. The Vancouver suburb of Richmond and clusters surrounding Toronto's so-called ethnic malls exemplify how Canada's multiculturalism is playing out in the twenty-first century. These areas are known as "ethnoburbs," a term coined by geographer Wei Li to describe the suburban expression of the classical enclave, a neighbourhood whose key institutions and business enterprises are owned and operated by members of the same ethnic group. Li formulated the ethnoburb while she studied settlement patterns in Los Angeles, and she describes them as a new sort of settlement that is a child of global restructuring.[9] In the classical description of immigration, incoming groups settled in the inner city and moved out to the suburbs only once they had assimilated into the dominant culture. Ethnoburbs, on the other hand, form through chain migration in a world where immigrants have the resources to move into suburban communities. Because these communities never attain the overwhelming demographic homogeneity of classical urban enclaves, much more mixing occurs. This is another driver of the deep multicultural nature of Canadian cuisine. In the suburbs, these cuisines run together, forming new and surprising combinations.

Toronto has the most extensive ethnoburban development in Canada. There are four Chinese ethnoburbs and several Italian ethnoburbs. The two historical Chinatowns are secondary and minor in comparison. Of the 7 per cent of the Greater Toronto Area (GTA) population that is ethnic Chinese, for example, 21 per cent are in the inner city, and 79 per cent are in the suburbs.[10] There are over sixty ethnic malls in the GTA, offering a dizzying array of foods. In the Vancouver area, the suburb of North Vancouver has a strong Persian community, the suburb of Surrey has a vibrant South Asian community, and the suburb of Richmond, as mentioned, remains a preferred destination for new arrivals from China. A visit to an ethnoburb offers incredible variety in dining; Richmond is the site of night markets, which have developed around the Pacific Rim as the Chinese diaspora spreads. Richmond's night market might not be open as late as those in Hong Kong, but it does offer a great selection of street food. On my last visit to it, I enjoyed squid rings and *miso tonkotsu*, pork buns and tofu skewers. The night market is a long way from the Seaview Gardens, but in 2015 Asian flavours just don't seem as strange and exotic. Multicultural cuisine isn't an unusual departure for Canadians: it is part of everyday life. Flavours from around the world are as common now as maple syrup and smoked salmon.

76

It is tempting to roll out a problematic word and say that the current state of Chinese cuisine in Canada, with food on offer from several regions of China, is more *authentic* than the cuisine offered in the glory days of the Chinese Canadian restaurant. However, the idea of authenticity in cuisine masks a deeper understanding of the interplay among national cuisines in a world of globalization. A cult of authenticity arose in the last decade of the twentieth century, a movement critiqued heavily by Lisa Heldke in her excellent work on culinary tourism, *Exotic Appetites*. She reminds us that cuisine is not a static entity, and thus no cuisine is perfectly authentic.[11] Heldke argues that the word *authentic* is really just a problematic synonym for the word *good* and that food should be judged on its individual merits. Arjun Appadurai agrees, arguing that the idea of authenticity seems to imply a timeless perspective on profoundly historical processes. How, Appadurai asks, can one generate stable criteria of authenticity for traditions that are always changing?[12]

The word *authentic* is derived from the ancient Greek word *authentikos*, but the Greeks used it to refer to what were in effect "do it yourself" projects; for example, the food that one grew and cooked at home was authentic.[13] The modern twist stems from the strange relationships that North Americans have with the foods of other countries. In the early to mid-twentieth century, immigrants to North America were expected to assimilate, and often their only links to the Old World were culinary. However, all cuisines evolve, and as immigrants were cooking the foods of their pasts ethnic enclave cuisines tended to change little if at all. Cut off from the land that created it, a cuisine of memory dies little by little. In this case, authenticity is about nothing more than the cook who best invokes memory. In the mid- to late twentieth century, the quest for the exotic came into play. Heldke wonders whether "what we identify as authentic in that culture is often simply what is new to us: which may or may not represent what insiders to that culture would identify as significant, traditional, or genuine elements of it."[14] Richard Handler sees authenticity as part of the same shift in urban life that gave us the foodie; authenticity is little more than a cultural construct, a search for the unspoiled, the pristine, the traditional, an individual quest to find something new.[15]

Attempts to identify certain foods and cuisines as authentic depend largely on an idea of culture as something bounded, externally observable (and thus scientifically measurable), and exclusive. Although the concept of culture originates in the European Enlightenment,[16] the modern understanding of cultures as plural derives in part from anthropologists such as Franz Boas. He argued that inherited customs and traditions helped to shape ethical and aesthetic norms of groups, and thus different cultures cannot be judged against each other. Although he rejected the idea that cultures are static, his argument in favour of cultural relativism held that cultures are largely incommensurable and thus bounded enough to be independently identified and studied.[17] The language of authenticity relies on this view, which might admit change

77

within defined and delimited cultures yet doesn't allow for the blurring of these boundaries. However, emigration and the creation of diasporic communities, as well as immigration and the introduction of other groups into different nation-states or the homelands of ethnic groups, often lead to the use of new ingredients, cooking techniques, and recipes that challenge the distinctions used to categorize ethnic cuisines. This shift goes far beyond Chinese Canadian cuisine, and new examples continue to emerge.

Authenticity was a hot topic of conversation as Priya Vadi and I sat down to lunch at the Vancouver restaurant Rangoli. A doctoral candidate at Royal Holloway University in London, England, Priya is on the cutting edge of understanding how cuisine is changing in a globalized world of diaspora and multiculturalism. She and I were investigating Canadian culinary trends, and authenticity seemed to have gone right out the window. We visited Vij's Railway Express food cart one sunny Saturday at the Vancouver Farmers' Markets, and as we enjoyed halibut curry and blueberry lassi we began to wonder why so many Canadian chefs are willing to do what the inventors of Chinese Canadian cuisine had to do: mix local ingredients with the techniques and recipes of other cultures. The blueberry lassi seemed to be so Canadian, even if it did have the requisite tang of yogourt and the bite of cardamom and star anise.

Vij's, the flagship restaurant of Vikram Vij and Meeru Dhalwala, is one of Vancouver's most popular restaurants. Meeru's strong dedication to quality ingredients and food security issues in general has shaped Vij's into a series of restaurants, a popular home product line, and successful cookbooks. Their food, always excellent, sometimes raises the eyebrows of those who value authenticity above all else. From the start, Vij's deviated from what was expected of Indian restaurants. A recent menu featured a grilled sablefish in a tomato yogourt with an onion masala and a fresh BC trout in coconut and fenugreek. When we sat down with Meeru at Rangoli, she spoke passionately about local food. She explained that she had become interested in the environmental impact of food through fish, which might explain the frequency with which local fish appears on their menus. In that context, the blueberry lassi is obvious; as Meeru noted, if we were in India, "it wouldn't be blueberry. It would be lychee or mango, maybe papaya. The blueberry is pretty much from here."

Food from here. Ironically, this is exactly what the ancient Greeks would call authentic. We asked Meeru, rather timidly, what she thought about the word *authenticity*. She replied forcefully that it is a stupid word. What about *fusion*? She scowled. "That's another word I want to spit on. I hate that word, I will not even entertain a conversation about that word." I should have stuck to talking about fish.

But how did Meeru see their food? In her view, it is her own creation, a deeply personal craft that she shares with others. If food is art, then who am I to argue with an artist? A living cuisine braids together strands like rivers on a delta plain, incorporating the new, the available, and above all the vision of its chefs. Canadian cuisine might be as alive as any cuisine can be, with such a vibrant chef culture, such wondrous raw materials, and such strong flows of people with new practices and ideas. I might not go as far as to hate the term, but in Canada "authenticity" makes no sense because we don't have enclaves within a dominant culture in the same manner as in other places and times. We have a multicultural mosaic, and Priya and I realized that it was creating exactly what has appeared in other periods of history and other places where mixing and innovation come together. We were witnessing a culinary creole, beginning in Vancouver but with shades appearing across the country. A truly Canadian creole.

Understanding the growth of creole in Canada requires first considering the rise of multiculturalism itself. As late as the 1970s, Canada was still a country locked into French and British culinary traditions, Chinese Canadian restaurants and the odd Italian place notwithstanding. Will Kymlicka has written extensively on multiculturalism in the twenty-first century, a period during which, he claims, we have seen a

79

shift from espousing assimilation to enshrining the right to practise culture as a matter of fundamental justice. Kymlicka reminds us that cultural diversity remains the norm, with 5,000 ethnic groups and 600 active languages worldwide.[18] One can extrapolate from this that there are many culinary traditions out there and great potential for any number of new mixes. Kymlicka distinguishes between diversity in founding population and diversity in immigrant composition, and he notes that Canada is both multinational, since it was founded by a French population and an English population, and was influenced by the Indigenous groups already present. Canada is now decidedly polyethnic since it has accepted so many waves of immigration over its history. The Fathers of Confederation had to design a much less rigid federal system than was the norm of the day, with power sitting in the two founding groups. The uneasy tension between French and English meant that Canada never established a monolithic identity. That said, before 1960, immigrants were required to assimilate to either a French or an English identity in what was an officially bicultural country, and until recently Indigenous cultural expression was systematically and institutionally discouraged. The food of the time reflects this; a look at cookbooks from the early twentieth century reveals British and French dishes, with dominant immigrant groups represented at most with separate "ethnic" sections. Kymlicka notes the exception of the Chinese and suggests that, because they couldn't be assimilated, they were relegated to their restaurants and ethnic enclaves. Chinese Canadian is a compromise cuisine.

Change came rapidly in the 1970s. Today Canada is one of the three top destinations for immigrants: Canada, the United States, and Australia take half of all immigration worldwide. In *Canadian Multiculturalism*, Michael Dewing and Marc Leman interpret the concept of Canada as a multicultural society in three ways: as a sociological fact, as a state ideology, and as a policy with political implications.[19] Their statistics remind us how much things have changed: at the time of Confederation, 60 per cent of Canada's population was British, and 30 per cent was French, yet the demographic makeup of the country now is remarkably different. By 1913, immigration would peak at an annual rate of 5 per cent of the population. People from all parts of Europe flooded into Canada, often pushed by traumatic events at home or lured by the promise of cheap farmland and the chance to start a new life. More recently, immigration has shifted to Asia, the Caribbean, and South and Central America, and with recent upheavals in the Middle East we can expect a significant influx from this region. A full account of Canada's immigration history is beyond the scope of this work, but from a culinary point of view the fact that one in five people in Canada was born elsewhere can't be ignored when considering the national cuisine. Even if they arrive with little else, newcomers carry their cuisines with them.

According to Dewing and Leman, the period before 1971 saw gradual acceptance of ethnic diversity as legitimate and integral to Canadian society.[20] Partly in response to the rise of Quebec nationalism, the 1971 policy of multiculturalism officially encouraged cultural groups to retain and foster their identities and to promote creative exchanges among all Canadian cultural groups. Adoption of the Charter of Rights and Freedoms in 1982 officially recognized the multicultural heritage of Canadians in the Constitution. The Charter acknowledged multiculturalism as a fundamental characteristic of Canadian society. By 2010, 56 per cent of Canadians saw multiculturalism as a symbol of Canadian identity. Although some parts of the country are much more deeply multicultural than others, this profound shift in viewpoint had a correspondingly profound shift in cuisine.

Understanding creoles begins with what they are not: fusion foods. A fusion dish occurs, as noted by Joyce Goldstein and Dore Brown in their excellent book on California cuisine, when a chef borrows flavour combinations, signature ingredients, or cooking techniques from one culture's cuisine and applies them to another culture's dish.[21] Los Angeles is a hotbed of fusion cuisine, where Wolfgang Puck, perhaps the best-known practitioner of fusion, noted that fusion is the embodiment of American cooking.[22] On the surface, the same type of effect is visible in Toronto in particular, with strange mixes such as the Jamaican jerk and Italian fusion in Kensington market or the Hungarian Thai restaurant. But ultimately fusion is the mixing of two things from two different places or traditions. When groups with distinct identities live together for a long time, something else emerges, something more lasting. The term that we use for this mixing is "creole," from the Latin word meaning "to create." A cuisine becomes a creole once mixing is so established that a generation of people is born into it. As an example, when two groups who speak two different languages occupy the same region, they first develop what is called a pidgin language to communicate with each other that draws on both of their first languages. Once they have children who speak the pidgin language as a first language, it is known as a creole; the cultural and culinary traits are known as a creole as well. This hasn't happened in Canada in terms of language, but it has happened in terms of cuisine. In Vancouver, in particular, a generation is growing up with combinations such as butter chicken poutine and Vancouver-style sushi. These are seen as local foods, Canadian foods, not as representatives of other ethnic cultures.

82

The most famous creole cuisine is that of New Orleans, where Acadian, Spanish, American, French, West Indian, and Indigenous groups came together to create a lasting pocket of cultural difference. New Orleans creole is so long-standing that it has developed into an entire suite of recipes that bridge culinary divides from po'boy sandwiches to gumbo *filé*. But there are other long-standing creoles as well, including Hawaiian creole, studied in detail by LeeRay Costa and Kathryn Besio.[23] They chart over a century of culinary history currently re-emerging as a local movement based upon *ā ina* or "the land," which mixes all of the peoples to come to the islands, from the Polynesians to the Japanese and Chinese through to the Americans. Hawaiian cuisine combines sugar plantation and native dishes, canned meats, and preparations such as plate lunches and *poke*. Hawaiian spam sushi, or spam musabi, would be quite at home in Vancouver.

Farther south on the Pacific Rim, Brisbane cuisine charted a course similar to that of Canada. At first, fusion and creole did not occur, but Asian Australian cuisine adapted to the lack of ingredients in a similar way to Chinese Canadian cuisine. In the 1950s, these adapted recipes were popular with white Australian housewives, and true mixing didn't occur until multiculturalism became more widely established.[24] Today Brisbane, a very multicultural city, is home to many fusion dishes, including a mixing of Thai and Western dishes. An older creole occurs in Malaysia, where Malay and Fujian Chinese cuisine come together. In his study of this cuisine, Eugene Anderson describes such a cuisine not as a hybrid, like a mule, but as a braided river in which channels come and go and thousands of traits mix.[25] Why Pacific Rim cuisines are so rich in creole requires further study, but such a creole is readily observed on the West Coast and across Canada. Jacobs noted this phenomenon as the interpretation of recipes originating elsewhere,[26] and in "Delicious Diversity" Joanne Hlina argues that we adapt, blend, and recreate food from around the world.[27]

Canadian creole expresses itself in a few ways, though most often as either a recipe from elsewhere reimagined with Canadian ingredients or as a Canadian recipe reimagined with ingredients from elsewhere. Priya argues that Vancouver is the heart of Canadian creole, with the three foci on Lebanese Canadian, Asian Canadian, and South Asian Canadian combinations, but I did find evidence of similar culinary innovations across the country. In Newfoundland, I encountered ginger moose in Port Aux Basques (a twist on the Albertan recipe ginger beef). In Ottawa's Byward Market, I sampled elk osso bucco. In Halifax, I enjoyed donair spring rolls with a local craft beer. Blueberry lassi fits the category of a recipe reimagined with local ingredients, and the butter chicken poutine popular in both Toronto and Vancouver represents the inverse. Butter chicken in particular suits the Canadian palate, and butter chicken lasagna is available frozen in major Ontario supermarkets. In Vancouver and its surrounding areas, restaurants serving both

83

Italian and Indian food are common. Calgary's Laurier Lounge serves a very interesting and filling poutine bourguignon, and in Montreal I enjoyed a twist on what Canadians have come to know as a "typical" dolma in which grape leaves were replaced with local chard. Even in homogeneous regions such as New Brunswick, I encountered a curried lobster roll. However, Priya is likely right that the case for a fully developed Canadian creole is most strongly made in Vancouver.

Let's begin with a hotdog. Japadog broke ground by mixing Japanese flavours with traditional street hotdogs and has since become one of Vancouver's most famous street foods (and a featured favourite of Anthony Bourdain.) However, it nearly didn't come to be; when Noriki Tamura and his wife, Misa, moved to Canada, they wanted to open a food cart to sell East Asian street crêpes. Strict vending laws made such a venture impossible, though, so the couple settled for a hotdog cart that they immediately began to customize. Japadog brought wasabi mayo, nori, and grated daikon to Vancouver's street food scene. Opening in 2005, they featured items such as the terimayo dog, with teriyaki sauce, mayonnaise, and seaweed. They have since expanded and opened a storefront café, and now they offer fries in flavours such as butter and shoyu, curry, and *shichimi* and garlic. The *okonomi* dog is topped with bonito flakes, and the *negimiso*, my favourite, sports shredded cabbage and miso sauce. A survey of customers, however, revealed something interesting; there is a generation of Vancouverites who would never see such cuisine as Japanese or ethnic or fusion. They see it as Vancouver cuisine, as local as a sablefish fillet or blackberry pie. Vancouver has its own creole, and it likely began with Canadian sushi.

Sushi burst onto the Canadian landscape sometime in the 1980s. In her fascinating thesis "'Processing' Sushi/Cooked Japan," Rumiko Tachibana charted the increase in mentions of the word *sushi* in Canadian newspapers, from a low of eight mentions in 1980 to nearly 1,500 mentions in 2007. In British Columbia, sushi is widely available, from grocery stores to gas station convenience stores to chain restaurants. Even my university cafeteria has a sushi bar. Tachibana calls sushi a "deterritorialized cultural object."[28] Canadian sushi, she notes, uses less fish, more vegetables, and often has the rice rolled on the outside to mask the flavour of the nori. Of the ninety rolls that she documented in Victoria, British Columbia, only seven were common in Japan. This variety, blending local flavours with traditional preparations, seems almost endless and can reach somewhat extreme levels. The Eatery, a thirty-year-old Vancouver restaurant that embodies the spirit of Vancouver sushi, offers rolls with names such as Electric Banana and Green Eggs and Ham. Shizen-Ya capitalizes on Vancouver's health-conscious population with quinoa sushi and whole-wheat tempura with maple mayo. In the Izakaya scene in Vancouver, restaurants such as Guu and Hapa pair excellent fresh local ingredients with traditional preparations; I ate a lovely simple kale *gomae* at Hapa, for example. But if there is a beginning to Canadian sushi, it lies at the top of Vancouver's Japanese restaurant culture: Tojo's.

85

Priya and I interviewed Hidekazu Tojo on a quiet afternoon in his palatial restaurant on Broadway. I was, I admit, somewhat nervous; Tojo's is arguably one of only a tiny handful of Canadian restaurants that is truly world famous. Known for his excellent use of texture and the finest of local seafood, Tojo prides himself in a cuisine rooted firmly in place. His innovations began out of necessity; in 1971, almost no one in Vancouver would try sushi, save for a small community of local Japanese. Tojo claims to be the inventor of the inside-out roll, a technique designed to hide the seaweed. In Japan, sushi is prepared according to strict rules, and when we asked Tojo what traditionalists think of the inside-out roll he smiled.

> I kept hiding the seaweed, and some customers said, "Oh, Tojo, this is a great idea," but many Japanese people, they would punish me and say, "Oh, Tojo, this is a wrong idea, you are breaking tradition," so I stayed quiet.... A lot of international people said,

*"Oh, this is a very good idea," you know especially the American people, and they go back to California, where it becomes the California roll.*

Tojo also faced a shortage of ingredients; unable to find *unagi*, or "eel," he used salmon skin to develop his signature BC roll. He believes that these adaptations and their popularity helped to brand sushi as local. One Japanese trait for which Tojo is known is his dedication to seasonality. In British Columbia, he found a wealth of seafood and produce tuned to the seasons:

> *In Japan, the seasons are very clear; in Vancouver, we have BC spot prawn starting at the end of May to the end of July, and pine mushrooms are after summer, and daikon, and carrot, and in October chestnuts. In winter, we use root vegetables to make soup as the weather is very bad and cold. And in spring we use tender leaf vegetables. In summer, it is cooler foods, cucumber.... My style is I'm here in Vancouver in the Pacific Northwest, so I use as much local ingredients as possible.*

A meal at Tojo's is a significant investment and rare treat, but his preparations are of such quality that they serve as high notes for meals. His sashimi draws on the best geoduck, salmon, snapper, and tuna. He particularly delights in the delicate local sablefish, which I have enjoyed at his restaurant steamed in a brown paper package served on cedar bows and melted into a delicate buttery soup. To eat at Japadog and to eat at Tojo's are to span a gulf of price and formality, but both places speak to the ingenuity and persistence of newcomers and to the multiculturalism, grounded in place, that defines the West Coast.

If Vancouver is at the heart of a Canadian creole cuisine, Toronto is a raging forge of multicultural culinary mixing, though not all dishes are quite as adventurous as chef Susur Lee's cheeseburger spring rolls and

86

the Hunanese-style lobster ravioli at his latest restaurant. Lee is a pioneer of the mixing of Eastern and Western flavours and is credited with helping to found Toronto's thriving restaurant scene. Elsewhere, Banh Mi Boys serves Vietnamese-style *banh mi* sandwiches stuffed with duck confit and in the past has served bulgogi beef on Indian paratha bread. Indian bread also figures in the great Toronto roti debate.

I was last in Toronto on a cold and windy winter day, shivering among the crowds on Queen Street West, once a down-at-the-heels strip but now home to what Richard Florida would call the creative class and the rest of us would call the hipster invasion. I love the grit of Toronto, and the pounding clang of the streetcars, and the general busy urbanity missing from most of Canada. I crave Queen Street sometimes, but mostly I crave Gandhi Roti, ground zero for the great roti debate. Toronto has West Indian roti, an import from the Caribbean, and East Indian roti, which I have come to believe is actually a Toronto invention. The use of roti as a wrap began in Trinidad in the 1940s as a way to serve spicy curries as a fast food. Hummingbird Roti in San Fernando claims to be the first place to have done this, but the technique spread rapidly, and the dish is also popular in Guyana. The bread and the name came to the Caribbean along with indentured servants from India. However, the curry and bread used to make the West Indian dish are quite different from those used in the East Indian version found in cities such as Toronto. Who started making a Caribbean dish based upon Indian bread with typical Indian roti and curry? Likely someone in Toronto, Montreal, or New York, for the dish is found in all of those cities but not elsewhere. Roti with East Indian filling isn't the same as the West Indian variety, but given that the bread itself is originally from India it is an example of a food that has been modified multiple times. I stood in the tiny Queen Street hole-in-the-wall restaurant, one of the best-smelling places in Canada, and left with a delicious wrap of *muttar paneer* curry and a *malai kofta* curry to smuggle back to Vancouver in my luggage.

87

Fifty years ago, even thirty years ago, the sort of mixing occurring in Canada's major cities wouldn't have appealed to the tastes of the time (this is true elsewhere in the world as well; Priya's primary case study is London, another hotbed of multicultural cuisines that is a far cry from traditional fish and chips or shepherd's pie). Is a multicultural *mélange* the future of food? In fields as varied as urban planning, culinary study, tourism, and interior design, researchers have noticed the strengthening of what Sheldon Pollock names "the cosmopolitan vernacular,"[29] a style of life, culture, and design found in the cities of the globalized world in which the richest and most powerful create trends that really know no country. Bell agrees, describing a new global culinary geography that results as cuisines collide and hybridize; he argues that "nothing sums up the post-modern metropolis better than the frantic co-mingling of cultures and cuisines."[30] This doesn't mean, however, that global cuisine will converge; as should be clear from the Canadian examples cited here, the use of fresh local ingredients has arisen as a counterpoint to the widespread mixing of recipes and techniques drawn from all cultures. In the future, these twin forces of mixing and localization will likely continue to shape Canadian cuisine and indeed all cuisines in the world.

It is hard not to notice that among all of the mixing of culinary cultures across Canada, to the point of creolization in places, one group is largely missing. The culinary voices of Indigenous Canadians have been tragically silenced for most of Canada's history. As Kymlicka reminds us, until recently they were treated as wards of the state.[31] Indigenous Canadians make up nearly 4 per cent of the population, and that percentage is increasing rapidly. Their cuisine is a founding element of Canada's culinary identity, but it is usually unacknowledged, save for a smattering of restaurants that have come and gone over the years. This absence is parallel to that of another culinary group on the other side of the world; in her 2010 study of Māori cuisine in New Zealand, Carolyn Morris found a total absence of formal Māori restaurants and a general distaste among the public for Māori food, viewed as "bad," "strange," and not worth advertising.[32] Māori food, of course, is no stranger than many other cuisines, but as a rule oppressed groups do not get the chance to market their culinary traditions to others. Canada's Indigenous cultures are only now recovering to the point where their cuisines can be revived, and much of the cultural knowledge associated with those cuisines exists only in anthropological reports. Change, however, might be on the horizon. On a winter day last year, I sat down for a meal at Tea-n-Bannock in Toronto, the first restaurant that I can think of that tries to reconcile the reality of settlement and colonization with Indigenous culinary tradition. It serves a wonderful array of precontact dishes, such as northern pike and elk stew, but it also has postcontact dishes such as the trapper's snack, which features Klik luncheon meat on bannock, and blanket dogs, which feature a wiener wrapped in fry bread. Bannock itself is a rather mysterious food; it is thought to be Scottish in origin, though no one knows whether the flour version replaced an earlier Indigenous baked bread, perhaps prepared using a starchy tuber. Hybrid though it is, bannock is the best-known Indigenous food, and bannock burgers can be purchased at a high-end food cart in Calgary or at non-descript stands across the Prairies. One of the nicest bannocks that I ate in my travels was on Lennox Island in Prince Edward Island, where I was warmly welcomed at a bannock stand with sizzling bread fresh from the pan. On the western shore of the country, Vancouver's Salmon n' Bannock serves, well, salmon and bannock, game, and a lovely cedar jelly. Indigenous foods aren't as well known or widely available as they should be in Canada, but they will likely grow in importance and popularity.

89

Canadian creole, in which a recipe is reimagined with local ingredients highlighted, or inversely in which a local recipe is recreated with ingredients from other cultures, is occurring against the backdrop of a profound shift. Where once the Atlantic coasts were the centres of global trade, now the Pacific Rim is increasingly emerging as a place of trade, mixing, and power. I believe that the appearance of creole in Canada's cuisine reflects a growing acceptance of the multicultural nature of our country. The major diasporic groups in Canada bring new flavours to our tables, and the combinations that emerge from those flavours are increasingly framed as Canadian rather than hyphenated dishes. However, this emerging creole often carries a fixation on ingredients; the recipes often provide the stages, but the ingredients are the stars. It is to Canada's ingredients that I now turn.

# 6

# INGREDIENTS: AS CANADIAN AS MAPLE SYRUP

One of the most striking features of Canada's cuisine is the strong tendency to highlight fresh local ingredients over complex preparations: we put ingredients forward. In contrast to many other cuisines, there are few truly Canadian recipes. As the previous chapter suggests, one hallmark of Canada's culinary style is to recreate a recipe or technique from elsewhere in a way that substitutes in local products. We are a country of simply prepared dishes whose ingredients are often identified by name; menu analysis revealed a wealth of discussion on the individual farm or location that supplied the product for the dish. This movement is fed by global trends but has roots that reach back into the grand meals once served on the transcontinental trains. Duncan describes early railway cuisine as a "regional rolling buffet" that presented trout, prairie hens, antelope steaks, and then salmon as the trains moved west,[1] with ingredients often identified by town of origin. This focus on named and celebrated Canadian dishes was also noted by the Bertons in their *Canadian Food Guide*, which highlights the use of ingredients such as Winnipeg goldeye, Oka cheese, and Quebec maple syrup.[2] With ingredients as the stars, chefs in Canada have become experts in taking a light hand in their cooking techniques, and they shy away from overprocessing or hiding food in sauces. As James Murphy and Stephen Smith note in their study of Canadian chefs, their minimalist approach lets ingredients speak for themselves.[3]

Cuisines that function without a strong base of recipes are unusual but do exist elsewhere. In her study of California's cuisine, Amy Trubek noted that, while most regional cuisines have shared recipes, California's cuisine doesn't have a strong canon of established dishes.[4] Scandinavian cuisines have a similar structure as well, drawing instead on the flow of the seasons. New Nordic cuisine also highlights the best ingredients, for example. This focus on ingredients prompts the question of whether Canada, in contrast to a national dish, might have a national ingredient. Is there one flavour or set of flavours that defines us as a nation? Many ingredients highlighted in Canadian cuisine are regional, but a few have achieved a national presence as well. Those deserving special mention include salmon, wild berries, and cheese. Some ingredients, such as fiddleheads, beef, and lobster, are treated in the regional discussions in following chapters but do have a presence nationally. However, one Canadian ingredient was so common in menu analysis that it lives up to its reputation as a national stereotype: maple syrup.[5]

I can think of no other country so deeply associated with a single species of tree. The maple leaf appears on our flag and on our currency. The various maple species line our streets and drop their leaves on our yards. From where I sit, I can see three such trees just coming into their fall colours. Each spring Canadians produce the bulk of the planet's maple syrup, incorporating it in diverse and innovative ways into almost every imaginable dish. Maple syrup occupies a strong place in our folklore and generates an important stream of income in rural areas of Quebec and Ontario. Quebec produces 80 per cent of the world's supply, and demand

92

continues to rise. Canada produces about 35,000 tonnes of maple syrup a year, returning $150 million to Quebec farmers at the beginning of the growing season when cash on hand is in short supply. Our syrup is particularly popular in Japan, and it is carried home by tourists from all over the world. Within Canada, we often use maple as a flavour, sauce, or food in its own right; outside Canada, it is often used as a sweetener for beverages such as tea.

Made from the sap of the *Acer saccharum*, or sugar maple, maple syrup and sugar are native to North America and were important food and trading items for Indigenous peoples. Sap was concentrated in hollowed logs either by heating it to boiling with hot stones or by letting it freeze and discarding the ice on top. The production of maple sugar was a large commercial operation among some Indigenous groups, including the Chippewa and Algonquin peoples.[6] Indigenous groups traded in sugar rather than syrup since it was so much easier to store and carry,

93

Figure 6.1. Canadian maple products

though they also boiled meat in sap to give it flavour, a cooking technique that seems to have been lost to the modern world (similarly, the use of sugar in savoury dishes recorded in medieval texts passed out of vogue in European cooking). With few other sources of sugar easily available, maple sugar became a critical supply for settlers as well, who traded with Indigenous groups for the precious sweet blocks. Jacques Cartier apparently developed a taste for drinking maple sap during his voyages in Canada,[7] though many other settlers apparently didn't take so readily to this local sweetener. In the *Canadian Settler's Guide* of 1860, newcomers were urged to buy large quantities of so-called Indian sugar despite what the author described as a peculiar taste.[8]

Maple established itself early as a key element of settler culture, even though other such innovations taken from Indigenous peoples did not last over time. Maple syrup production is both difficult and fuel intensive, and it might well have disappeared into history if not for the growing political discord in the United States between North and South that spurred Confederation in the first place. Abolitionists described maple as "more pleasant and more patriotic than sugar ground by the hand of slavery."[9] Settlers learned how to make maple sugar from Indigenous groups and took advantage of a growing market to supplement their incomes. Sugar became an important cultural product in these communities, and the taste for this sweet food slowly spread across the nation. Clearly, that "peculiar" flavour grew on us.

Today maple is used both for its flavour and as a sweetening agent, and the iconic product appears across the spectrum of Canada's food scene, from fine dining to the stereotypical order of a maple-glazed doughnut and double-double coffee (two cream, two sugar) at Tim Hortons. Analysis of menus collected over two years of research in both English and French, drawn from across the country, confirmed what was obvious in my fieldwork: maple syrup is used in all regions, and maple sugar makes appearances. Maple is made into pies, fried, made into toffee on snow, and turned into whiskey. It is a complex flavour both sweet

94

and *umami*, and this complexity makes it difficult to craft a chemical alternative. Real maple syrup is the product of cold, clear nights and warm, sunny days that stimulate sap production as the tree readies for spring. Canada's syrup is classed as light, amber, and dark, a nod to the mineral content in the syrup, which increases as the season progresses. Production is regulated in Quebec, though strangely Canada does not have laws protecting use of the word *maple*. In nearby Vermont, a product cannot be described as maple unless the sweetener used is 100 per cent maple. Canada could follow this path, for maple products adulterated by corn syrup lack the quality and flavour of the pure products.

If maple syrup is the best-known Canadian ingredient, choosing an iconic national maple dish is more difficult. Maple is highlighted in numerous regional specialties explored in the next set of chapters, but truly national maple dishes include candied salmon and the traditional breakfast of pancakes and maple syrup. I've enjoyed pancakes at countless diners across the country, including the massive, fluffy pile served up at the Tomahawk Restaurant in North Vancouver, where I have never managed to make my way through the towering stack. I ordered pancakes to my room at the Chateau Laurier the morning after giving a talk for *Walrus* magazine on the threat posed to maple syrup by climate change, and I've made a lot of pancakes myself on mornings when I just needed a little lift. And once, as rain lashed the side of the train as we slid past countless unnamed lakes north of Thunder Bay, I enjoyed pancakes drenched in maple on the transcontinental railway, perhaps the most quintessentially Canadian experience of all my travels.

Pancakes, however, are not Canadian. As explored in Ken Albala's seminal work,[10] pancakes date back at least to biblical times and appear in diverse cultures around the world, from Japan to the Netherlands to Ethiopia, where the injera for all intents and purposes is a pancake. Even pancakes with maple syrup can't be credited to Canada exclusively; it's just as likely that the dish was first served up on the East Coast of the United States. Canadian pancakes tend to be large and fluffy, often served with berries as a topping or with berries added to the batter, and can be found at roadside diners and in the best Canadian hotel dining rooms. They fit the model of North American breakfasts: sweet and carbohydrate heavy, and they often come with typical side dishes such as bacon or sausage. Pancakes are also oddly timeless: the stacks served in the logging camps of Canadian legend sound similar to the pancakes dished out today at the Calgary Stampede or modern brunch spots of our urban centres. However, Victoria's Jam Café certainly tries to give them a modern spin, serving maple sausage dipped in pancake batter then deep-fried and red velvet pancakes with cream cheese drizzle. These more exotic formulations aside, pancakes are most likely to be paired with another national food: berries.

Berries appear right across Canada and play a much larger role in our cuisine than they do in the cuisines of many other countries. The wild element of berries was touched on earlier, and the act of berry picking and the presentation of berries to tourists as an element of cuisine reflect the conflicted idea of the liminal space between the human and the wild. Holly Everett describes berries as icons of a resourceful people and a welcoming and bountiful wilderness. She notes that in Newfoundland nearly a million kilograms of partridge berries are gathered each year[11] and that the bakeapple has its own festival in Labrador, making the berry a central feature of Newfoundland's cuisine. In comparison to more challenging dishes such as cod tongues and seal pie, berries are a "low risk culinary departure."[12] For visitors and foodies alike, berries offer a chance to enjoy a cuisine without having to chance bush meat or unpleasant techniques of preparation.

U-pick berry patches in Canada also abound, giving urbanites the opportunity to interact directly with a slightly sanitized version of farm culture (there is a big difference, of course, between a few hours of pleasant berry picking and a full season of poorly paid labour while being exposed to the weather). Berries have always played a strong role in our cooking, and most recently they were highlighted in Roy and Ali's *From*

*Pemmican to Poutine*, which features a swath of berries, including a simple dish of berries marinated in maple syrup and blackberry merlot. I encountered as many berry desserts as chocolate desserts as I crossed the country during my research, often in reworked versions of classic boiled puddings and slow-cooked deep pies. And it is in the form of pie that Canadian berries present a delicious and historical cross-country dessert experience.

In my opinion, fruit and berry pies are simply culinary perfection, which might reflect my identity as a Canadian. I am not alone in my assessment; in 1853, Charles Smith wrote in his *Curiosities of London Life* that pie is a great human discovery that has universal estimation among all civilized eaters.[13] Ironically, pies started out primarily as containers; Janet Clarkson positions the pie as an early element of culinary technology.[14] The first pies used the crust to hold and preserve the contents, though she doubts that the crust was discarded, since it was made of valuable flour; more likely, it was fed to animals or broken up and incorporated into other dishes. The pie took its modern form by the fourteenth century in the United Kingdom, where there was plentiful wood for firing ovens and lard for making pastry. Sweet pies of the kind popular in Canada had to wait until sugar was widely available, likely by the sixteenth century. England's love of pie was mirrored in many of its colonies. In Australia and New Zealand, this took the form of savoury pies, and Clarkson notes that the "American preoccupation with sweet dessert pies is absolute."[15] Canada, however, fully embraced the pie as both a sweet and a savoury element since both fillings and flour for crust were abundant. This hasn't gone unnoticed; Clarkson thought that, "perhaps more than any other culture, Canada's heritage and history [are] clearly revealed through its pies."[16] However, we don't really have a national pie that stands above all others; we fill our pies with local delights, using recipes handed down over generations. We like our pie varied and in abundance; at Chilliwack's Airport Coffee Shop, customers struggle to choose from among dozens of flavours of pie,

97

representing tastes and preferences from across the west. I am partial to the cranberry-apple-peach pie, which brings together several tastes of the region. Pie recipes don't lend themselves well to innovation (if the recipe varies far from its usual form, then it ceases to be a pie), which gives them a timeless quality. However, I did enjoy a tasty mango-blueberry pie from the Mayne Island farmers' market; the exotic fruit fit well into its Anglo-Saxon container. Rhubarb pie is a perennial favourite and is often topped with meringue.

Although berries and maple syrup might make for an interesting dessert, it is worth wondering whether Canada has a defining protein. What we eat as a main course varies strongly across the country, yet salmon has a strong claim as national main course.

Anita Stewart called salmon "*the* Canadian fish—a fish of legends and so delicious that it is served with pride in the kitchens of dozens of cultures."[17] Although salmon is most strongly associated with the West Coast, there was once industrial salmon fishing on the Atlantic coast and in the Great Lakes. Cod might have been the fish that founded Canada, but salmon is the fish that defined it.

Salmon can act as a component of a larger dish but can also stand alone. Menu analysis turned up salmon prepared in almost every way possible, from gravlax, Montreal-style lox and bagel, to barbecued and baked salmon, to salmon sushi and sashimi. Sport fishing for Atlantic and Pacific salmon is still a popular tourist activity, and on Cape Breton and the central BC coast salmon excursions can include some of the most exclusive tourist experiences on the Earth. On the West Coast, entire tourist events and festivals are crafted to view salmon returning and enjoy their bounty. Local residents also indulge in the fish: half of all fish eaten in British Columbia is salmon.

Salmon is a keystone food on the West Coast and the source of the historical richness of the Indigenous coastal peoples. Prior to colonization, salmon was the primary food source for many of the coastal and river peoples of British Columbia, who ate the fish fresh, smoked, dried, and pounded into pemmican. Salmon was an invaluable food that returned on an annual basis, allowing the establishment of large perma-nent settlements near river mouths and streams. Salmon grounded the coastal peoples of British Columbia deeply to place. The fish were har-vested in nets and traps and harpooned and speared as they passed by on their way to spawning grounds. This steady source of food that could be processed and stored for later use allowed the development of compli-cated agricultural and maricultural practices and long-term habitation of sites. Salmon was so important a food that it figured strongly in many ceremonial rituals as well. It was central to potlatch culture, in which a tribal chief would host representatives of other tribes and fete them with

> *a lavish feast during which they bore witness as he asserted var-ious privileges and justified his claims to productive resources such as fine salmon streams. At the conclusion of the ceremony, the chief distributed gifts to his guests, with the value of the gifts increasing according to the recipient's social prestige. Having accepted these gifts without objection, guests were virtually stopped from disputing the chief's claims at a later time.*[18]

99

Arriving settlers also realized the importance of this superabundance of food. Already a popular fish abroad, BC salmon were reoriented to export, and large-scale salmon production exported the fish to remote corners of the empire. Canneries dotted the coast, including the larg-est centre of production, Steveston, one of British Columbia's oldest settlements. The rise and fall of Steveston's fishing industry is well doc-umented because of its importance in the British Empire. Monographs give detailed overviews of this vibrant community's rise and fall as one of the world's great fishing ports.[19] Steveston sits on the mouth of the Fraser River Delta on Lulu Island, about twenty kilometres from downtown Vancouver, and was the site of an Indigenous fishing camp. Steveston sits on unceded Coast Salish territory. The townsite was platted out by the Steves family in long, narrow lots to take advantage of the riverfront. By 1890, fifteen salmon canneries were operating in Steveston, and the population swelled to 10,000 during fishing season. The Fraser River salmon run at this time must have been wondrous to behold; contemporary accounts describe salmon so thick in the river mouth that they formed a solid living mass. Amid this thrashing tangle, Indigenous men fished in their canoes, and Indigenous women worked in the canneries alongside Japanese and Chinese workers. Steveston was a rough, boisterous boomtown on the far frontier, a noisy and fishy place, churning out canned salmon that shipped as ballast to be sold in the far corners of the empire. In 1912, an interurban railway was opened to Vancouver; the "Sockeye Limited" ran every half hour and brought workers from Vancouver's Japantown and Chinatown to Steveston, relieving the chronic housing crunch at the townsite during the fishing season. The train returned to the city filled with Lulu Island milk and vegetables and fish from the canneries. For half a century or so, salmon was king.

100

No fishery can withstand such a booming industry for long. Fraser River salmon suffered an ongoing series of setbacks and declines, including a disastrous disruption when construction of the railway through narrow Hell's Gate Canyon blocked the entire watershed to the spawning fish. As the fishery collapsed, canneries in Steveston closed or amalgamated, and the lifeblood of the community was already in retreat when the Second World War dealt the town its most serious blow. Seen as a threat to national security by the governments of the time, all citizens of Japanese descent were relocated to internment camps and stripped of their boats and properties. Two-thirds of Steveston's population, roughly 2,600 men, women, and children, were taken away in this shameful act.[20] After the war, some Japanese families returned to Steveston, but many found that, with their homes and boats sold, they couldn't reintegrate into the community.

Today the Fraser River salmon fishery is only between 5 and 10 per cent as strong as it once was, but even this diminished level is enough to maintain what is still the largest fishing fleet in Canada. Steveston is also arguably one of the best places to enjoy salmon in Canada, and it is home to dozens of restaurants serving salmon and other seafood. Canned salmon and smoked salmon are still popular souvenirs as well. Traditional Indigenous dishes such as smoked salmon became popular among the settler population, as did fusion dishes that incorporate salmon into immigrant cuisines. Salmon has been branded as a traditional Canadian food, and in turn it has been used to brand British Columbia. Smoked salmon is sold alongside maple syrup at tourist shops, both resulting from and further increasing its reputation as a traditional Canadian food. Perhaps the best example of the ubiquity of salmon in BC food culture comes from the BC roll, a popular maki sushi that features barbecued or grilled salmon (or salmon skin in some preparations) along with cucumber and a sweet sauce. This roll is extremely common in Japanese restaurants on the West Coast, and its origin is discussed in Chapter 8. Candied salmon is also a popular snack.

Why is salmon so popular? It is a sweet-tasting fish with firm flesh that lends itself well to many preparations. It lacks the fishy flavour that can mar whitefish, and it is marketed as a healthy alternative to other proteins. The five species of Pacific salmon are all fished heavily, though sockeye remains the most valuable. Each year several million sockeye are caught, with a value in excess of $20 million. Salmon is also farmed on the West Coast, though farmed salmon remains controversial because some see it as an inferior product that endangers the wild runs, and many British Columbians will not eat it.

Maple, salmon, and berries might seem a rather sparse palette with which to create a national cuisine, but across the country they are supported by dozens of regional foods grounded in the physical and cultural expressions of place. The next three chapters discuss these regional foods at length, but before moving on I want to note two other ingredients that stand as national culinary elements. The first is wheat, which tends to be overlooked as cuisine but of course expresses itself as one of Canada's starches of choice. Canada is one of the world's major wheat producers, and when Canadians sit down to eat they often pair their meals with bread. Our pies, pancakes, perogies, and porridges are based upon grain, and we brew our grain into beer, vodka, gin, and whiskey to wash our meals down. Although wheat itself usually plays a supporting role in cuisine, of late the historic Red Fife wheat is again being grown and used by artisan bread bakers, who like the grain for its colour and the excellent crust that it gives to bread. First grown in Peterborough in 1842, cold-hardy Red Fife dominated the Canadian wheat industry until the turn of the twentieth century and allowed wheat production in marginal regions. Nearly lost to history, a small museum collection of Red Fife grown near Keremeos, British Columbia, sparked new interest in this heritage grain. It is now grown in small amounts across the country.

The other oddity on Canada's national food scene is cheese. Through all seasons over the course of the project, cheese was actually the number one ingredient used in restaurant meals. Canadians use cheese heavily. We make it into sauces and bake it into our favourite dishes. Cheese in Canada is seldom the star of a meal, but it tends to appear almost everywhere. Lasagna is one of the most common meals eaten in the home in Canada, but it would not appear on a list of Canadian foods. Canadians are rather blind to the amounts of cheese that we toss onto our foods, but historically we have strong ties to the dairy industry. Cheese was an early arrival in Canada since its production was a convenient way to store food for the long winters. The Vikings at L'Anse aux Meadows didn't keep cows, but Samuel de Champlain and his settlers certainly did, and cheese has been a part of North American life ever since. At first, Canadian cheese resembled cheese made everywhere; it was made in small batches as a local farm product. During this period, hundreds of now vanished cheeses were made and enjoyed in Canada. However, this variety was lost early; as Heather Menzies noted in her discussion of the Ontario cheddar industry, bad harvests in the early years of the twentieth century led many farmers in central Canada to switch from

102

wheat production to the more reliable dairy industry.[21] This concentration led to a thriving commercial cheddar industry, and this durable cheese became Canada's second largest export, behind only timber. This industrial production largely displaced cottage production of artisan cheese, but the most jarring transformation of the cheese industry was yet to come. In her essay on Kraft Dinner, Sasha Chapman describes the journey of J. L. Kraft, who left Ontario for Chicago to perfect a more durable cheese product. He patented the first processed cheese food in 1916, and his great contribution to Canadian culture, Kraft Dinner, was developed in 1937. Kraft's processed cheese was based in part upon MacLaren's Imperial Cheese, a partially processed, sharp, cold-pressed cheddar sold in pots. Kraft bought the MacLaren company in 1905. Today Kraft Dinner, a mix of macaroni and a neon orange sauce, is one of the most purchased grocery items in Canada.[22]

The downside of the rise of Kraft's empire was crushing uniformity in the Canadian cheese industry; in 1971, Kraft controlled half of Canada's cheese production, and most Canadians ate only Kraft mozzarella and Kraft orange cheddar. Quebec's cheese industry remained more varied, but English Canadians were largely stripped of variety in their cheese. Supply management of the industry began in earnest at this time and favoured existing large producers. Supply management rests on three pillars: production limits, price controls, and import restrictions. Foreign cheese could enter Canada only in limited amounts, and long-term deals with dairies ensured that milk flowed only to large producers. Artisan production began to emerge in spite of this tilted playing field and used non-controlled milks such as goat, sheep, and water buffalo. As interest in quality cheese grew, farmers directed some of their milk production to more interesting products. Canada now produces hundreds of excellent cheeses. In 2013, a Gouda from Lancaster, Ontario, won a global cheese award, the first in Canada's history.

One particular cheese product deserves special mention. Quebec maintained a more vibrant cheese culture even during the darkest days of

Kraft's dominance of the industry. A few of Quebec's signature cheeses are mentioned in the next chapter, but the province is perhaps best known for its cheese curds, the solid parts of the soured milk used in cheese making. During a milk glut in the late 1950s, dairies began making and selling bags of curds as a snack food. This bit of innovation stands as a precursor to Canada's one unquestionable national dish: poutine.

In a world defined by nations, the idea of national dishes has emerged as an almost inevitable construct. The idea of a single national dish is sometimes accepted as a natural part of cuisine; as Fritz Blank describes it, "the kitchens of every nation have one dish which is not a dish, nor even a meal, but rather exists as an event."[23] But how can a nation, in all of its diversity, be represented by a single dish? The phenomenon of the national dish has inspired many budding nations to create such a culinary object. In his study of the role of cookbooks in India, Appadurai explores how national cuisines are often created by presenting regional dishes as national,[24] and Cusack agrees in claiming that national cuisines are often built by appropriating and assembling a variety of regional or ethnic recipes.[25] This is the case with poutine, which has emerged as one of Canada's most recognized national dishes.

From humble beginnings as a Québécois snack food in the 1950s, poutine has spread to all regions of the country and can be found in elevated forms in high-end restaurants serving Canadian cuisine. In its simplest form, poutine is composed of hot french fries topped with cheese curds and a brown sauce, though other ingredients do appear. Additions to poutine vary by region, and several classic styles, such as Michigan (topped with a red sauce and cheese curds), have been present since before the food appeared on the national scale. Poutine was almost unknown outside Quebec as late as the 1990s, but it has enjoyed a rapid adaptation right across Canada.

There are several competing origin stories for poutine, though the most popular account places the creation of poutine in Warwick, Quebec, at a restaurant owned by Fernand Lachance called Le Lutin Qui

Rit. In 1957, he was asked to put cheese curds on an order of fries in a paper bag, and he exclaimed that "*ça va faire une maudite poutine*" ("it will make a bad mess"), giving the food its name. A period menu gives some credence to this origin, and Warwick holds an annual poutine festival. The one written work dedicated to poutine, *Maudite poutine!*, supports the Warwick origin story, adding that local Eddy Lainesse claims to have asked for the first order and thus was the first person to eat poutine. Charles-Alexandre Théorêt notes that poutine might have faded as "*une vulgaire curiosité culinaire québécoise,*"[26] but it was embraced as a symbol of Quebec's emergence on the world stage, evoking pride. Like anyone dedicated to good poutine, Théorêt rails at the use of shredded mozzarella in place of cheese curds, the defining feature of the dish. They don't melt on the hot fries and have a "squeaky" texture. They are the mark of a proper poutine.

Poutine found a home at roadside *casse-croûtes* and spread to Quebec's cities as a snack food, particularly a late-night snack food. Nationally, poutine is often enhanced with a local flavour; butter chicken poutine is popular on the West Coast, poutine in the Prairies often includes Alberta beef, Nova Scotia tops poutine with donair meat and sauce, in Prince Edward Island lobster often appears on upscale versions of the dish, and Newfoundland poutine incorporates the local dressing of dried breadcrumbs and savory.

Poutine also varies regionally in Quebec, with cabbage being the most popular topping in Shawinagan, and in Montreal fine-dining restaurants reimagine the dish with caviar and truffles. The most decadent poutine in the country is likely the one at Au Pied du Cochon, served in a foie gras foam with lobes of foie gras on top, though in British Columbia Crab King serves an over-the-top, crab-laden version. Poutine has its own lexicon; for example, back in Quebec, *galvaude* style includes chicken and peas.

Few other dishes have the national scope of poutine, though a handful of other contenders vie for national status. Nanaimo bars and butter tarts appear on most lists of Canadian national foods, though both are somewhat limited to their geographic regions of origin and are discussed further in the regional section of the book. A similar case is that of the doughnut, which isn't Canadian but has found a home here; in his treatise on the doughnut, Paul Mullins calls Canada the "promised land" for the sweet treat.[27] Elaine Power and Mustafa Koc comment on the unusual way in which an American creation became a Canadian food,[28] and the story of the doughnut is indeed a curious one. On one level, doughnuts and doughnut shops are most closely associated with suburban Ontario, but in Canada the doughnut is also deeply associated with the national Tim Hortons chain, which plays an unusual role on the Canadian landscape. The why of Tim Hortons isn't entirely understood, but the connection between hockey and doughnuts is certainly part of its success. As an ex-NHL player, Tim Horton first established the link between his chain and the national game, but it was really only after his death in a car accident that the chain began reinforcing the link. If Chinese Canadian restaurants played the role of town square in the early to mid-twentieth century, Tim Hortons plays the same role in many a Canadian town in the twenty-first century. Tim's opens early and is a haven for parents taking their children to hockey practice. In smaller towns, lingering is not discouraged. Tim's caters to an imagined "average Canadian." The sort of Canadian who drinks a double-double with a maple-glazed doughnut is the Canadian version of the bellwether to the point where appealing to the political views of such people has been referred to as "doughnut populism." The doughnut is seen as a Canadian standard almost solely because of its association with Tim's and its doughnuts, including the iconic round Timbit, a doughnut hole confection actually made separately using a different mix. The iconic roles of the doughnut, the doughnut shop, and Tim's in particular are dealt with in Steve Penfold's book *The Donut*, and Penfold even calls this snack an unofficial national food.[29] He traces the emergence of the doughnut to the small doughnut shops of Ontario that appeared in the interwar years since doughnuts lent themselves perfectly to small-lot industrialization. In all honesty, the doughnuts of that period were likely better than those of today, often baked at a separate facility and then trucked to their points of sale. Doughnuts are best eaten when fresh, and the twenty-four-hour doughnut shops of Ontario emerged as popular places for grabbing a sweet treat and hanging out. Penfold calls the doughnut shop a "passing by sort of business," linked to the geography of convenience that arose at the beginning of the automobile era.[30] He acknowledges that the doughnut really doesn't capture the same devotion in the far west or Quebec, but to date no challenger has managed to displace Tim Hortons as the most Canadian of chains. I can't quite agree that doughnuts warrant status as a national food, however.

On their own, recipes highlight the dishes that a nation holds dear. As a body, recipes are "inscribed cultural tales"[31] that act as historical maps of regional cuisines. Cookbooks are important for the snapshots in time and space that they capture, but they are also one of the few lasting imprints of food. For the researcher, the ethereal nature of the culinary poses a real problem; one must become a detective of menus, diary entries, artworks and photographs, advertisements, and, of course, cookbooks. Canada might not have one book that stands as the "bible of cuisine" in the manner that Georges Auguste Escoffier's 1903 *Le guide culinaire* defined French cuisine for a generation,[32] but it does have its share of engaging cookbooks that help to map the evolution of our cuisine. A full exploration of Canadian cookbooks is beyond the scope of this work; for readers interested in a thorough treatment, Elizabeth Driver's excellent *Culinary Landmarks* summarizes all Canadian cookbooks before 1950.[33]

The first truly Canadian cookbook was *La cuisinière canadienne*, published in Montreal in 1840. Popular well into the twentieth century, this text began to show the North American influences on classic continental cuisine. Fourteen years later the first book in English on Canadian food was even more rooted in the new colonies. The influences of wild food and seasonality are less mysterious when put into the context of the conditions facing settler culture. One of the best descriptions from the era is Catharine Parr Traill's 1854 *The Female Emigrants Guide, and Hints on Canadian Housekeeping*.[34] A prolific writer and an enthusiastic settler (her sister Susanna gave a more nuanced account of the crushing hardships of the Ontario frontier), Traill left one of the most complete accounts of settler cooking. She described techniques for preparing game and lake fish and included harrowing instructions for ice fishing. She provided descriptions of how to sugar off maple sap and which plants were edible and useful. She made good use of local berries and had frequent interactions with the Indigenous people living nearby, who showed her many useful local plant foods. In what might have been wishful thinking or clever advertising for those contemplating settlement, she included British dishes that likely were impossible to produce in the Canadian wilderness.

108    Aside from local cookbooks, surprisingly little was written about Canadian food in the early decades of the twentieth century. These community books, however, shouldn't be discounted, for they show the importance of regional cuisine. Eventually numbering in the thousands, the community cookbook became popular in the 1870s and thrived into the modern era. Driver's expansive survey of these books gives us a preview of what the regional cuisines hold, and her work is referenced in the discussion of the regions. Books of Canadian scope, however, were unusual. One of the first of the modern era was *Helen Gougeon's Good Food Book*, published in 1958.[35] This text separates out Québécois cuisine and a catch-all "multicultural cuisine" section, and it includes some recognizable Canadian dishes, such as tourtière. However, for the most part, it is similar to many books published at the time in Western countries. *The Laura Secord Cookbook* of 1966 explicitly addresses the question of "what is Canadian cuisine?" by collecting and arranging recipes regionally, a technique still used today.[36] The book, as claimed on the reverse of the front cover, celebrates the regional and multi-ethnic diversity of

Canadian cooking. The dishes highlighted in this book for the first time begin to resemble what still appears nearly half a century later. Recipes include maple buns, maple doughnuts, bannock, prairie beef, tourtière, and game meats, including recipes for seal, antelope, bear, and bison. They include cod tongues, fish and brewis, blueberry grunt, and a maple Charlotte, noted as a Canadian adaptation of Charlotte Russe.

The *Laura Secord Cookbook* stands as a precursor to what would become a national reflection on Canadian cuisine: the Centennial and Expo '67 in Montreal. These events began a lasting preoccupation with the seeming lack of Canadian cuisine, and several cookbooks were commissioned to provide insight into Canada's culinary experience. Publishers McClelland and Stewart secured prolific writer and journalist Pierre Berton and his wife, Janet (her inclusion reminds the modern reader that the kitchen was an overwhelmingly feminine place in the 1960s), to write *The Centennial Food Guide*, published in 1974.[37] Born in the Yukon, Berton wrote in a style that contributed to the invention of a Canadian national narrative. His histories draw deeply on wilderness and open space and on living in a harsh land. *The Centennial Food Guide* is no different. Exploring Canadian meals throughout history, the book moves from lumbermen eating pork and beans among British Columbia's ancient forests to sugar socials at which one could eat as much *tire d'érable* as desired. As they move from history to recipes, the couple describe three sorts of Canadian cuisine: natural products such as Saskatoon berries and apples, place-branded species such as Malpeque oysters, and what they call Canadian concoctions, such as pemmican, tourtière, and pea soup. They conclude the book with an all-Canadian dinner that includes fiddleheads, blueberry whip, and Oka cheese.

The cuisine that the Bertons were helping to create was on display to the world at Montreal's Expo '67. In her exploration of food at the World's Fair, Rhona Richman-Kenneally calls the food on offer the greatest dining extravaganza in Canadian history.[38] The food at the fair was highlighted in a booklet outlining all of the restaurants, including

109

fine dining from around the world. The Canadian offering had to be sufficiently grand. La Toundra, the fine-dining restaurant of the Canadian pavilion, featured a tundra colour scheme, sealskin seats, and murals of everyday Inuit life. Drawing on a Canada that most Canadians had never seen, the restaurant served whale meat and muktuk, named ingredients from across the country, and had a section of multicultural dishes that reflected both an ideology and an aspiration.

Canadian cuisine changed after Expo '67. Although community cookbooks continued to draw on local people for their recipes, new national-scale books presented our cuisine as a unified if somewhat nebulous whole. Anita Stewart, now the food laureate at the University of Guelph, does much to build our culinary identity in her writing. In *The Flavours of Canada*, she looks at the cuisine using a regional sweep while exclaiming that, though Canadian cuisine "doesn't present itself conveniently," it is as "exotic and sexy"[39] as any cuisine on the planet. In *Anita Stewart's Canada*, she shifts from a regional approach to an ingredients-based approach, marking the continued unification of the cuisine into a convenient whole.[40]

Cuisine is a three-legged stool of ingredients, recipes, and techniques. Each culture approaches food in its own way, and specific environmental conditions drive local innovations to develop unique methods of preserving and preparing food. Canada is a young country, and as such most of our distinctive techniques are borrowed from the Indigenous peoples, who had a much longer time to adjust their cooking to suit the landscape and the ingredients that it supplies. In *The Flavours of Canada*, Stewart argues that bent box cooking, in which food is boiled in a wooden box filled with hot stones, is the only Canadian cooking method, but there is good evidence that we are responsible for a few more.[41] The making of pemmican can also be said to be a quintessential Canadian cooking method, as can cooking salmon on a plank. Although the latter has been claimed as originating elsewhere, there is strong evidence provided by George Hunt, sent by Franz Boas to live among the

Kwakiutl in the early days of the twentieth century. Hunt was Tlingit by birth and understood the importance of food and preservation to Indigenous peoples. He clearly describes a form of plank cooking in which thin slats of wood, usually fir, were used to pin salmon fillets near the fire. He also describes a lovely technique for eating herring roe in which cedar bows were dipped into the ocean to gather roe, then shared among the group.[42] Hunt captures a world of refined commensality and a complex cuisine that required an entire community to carry out.

Farther east one other truly Canadian technique deserves mention: the people of the Great Lakes region made maple sugar in great quantities and enjoyed the treat known as *tire d'érable* or "maple taffy." It is made by boiling sap, pouring it onto fresh snow, and then gathering the solidifying taffy on a small, clean stick. This simple technique has likely been entertaining children for centuries. And what could be more Canadian than cooking with snow?

The current state of Canadian food writing is rich indeed. From journals such as *Cuizine* and *Canadian Food Studies* to full-length texts such as Nathalie Cooke's *What's to Eat?*[43] and Dorothy Duncan's *Canadians at Table*, Canada's cuisine is an active area of research for food scholars. Chefs are also adding to the literature on the cuisine; a hybrid monograph and cookbook by Roy and Ali, *Pemmican to Poutine*, crosses the country from east to west exploring dishes such as blueberry grunt, fiddleheads, PEI potato fudge, poutine, and tourtière and for the first time explicitly provides a section on Indigenous foods. And, true to the book's title, it includes a recipe for pemmican. Although the cuisine of Canada has become more of a national cuisine, the regional sweep still reveals a key property of our nation's food. And it is to this regional variation that I now turn, beginning with what could be the heartland of cuisine in Canada: Quebec.

# PART II

# A TOUR OF
# THE REGIONS

7

# QUEBEC AND ONTARIO

There is a conversation between place and food. Both nature and culture construct cuisine, and which aspect dominates is dependent on one's perspective. Wild foods and seasonal foods seem to ground Canadian cuisine deeply in the natural world, yet when multicultural influences are considered Canada's cuisine appears to be a product of eternally evolving cultural flows and lasting imprints of history. Both perspectives are valid: the conversation among place, food, landscape, and culture is constantly reshaping cuisine. The balance of natural and cultural forces varies by location, leading to what Jacobs noted as strong regional differences in Canadian cuisine. He attempted to rough out descriptions by province,[1] and most cookbooks and discussions of Canada's cuisine follow that path. However, regional culinary centres do not entirely map onto provincial boundaries; they more closely fit vernacular cultural regions. In this chapter and the next two, I try to capture some of this regional richness, though I confess to falling back onto blanket descriptions at the provincial level as well. However, a few trends are clear: vernacular regions are becoming more sharply defined, partially through self-promotion in a globalizing world, and cultural enclaves left from previous waves of immigration are dispersing. And major cities, hothouses of culinary innovation, are developing culinary identities separate from their home provinces.

What is a region? I like to think of regions as spaces of conversation where culture and nature interact, but in global terms they also respond to events outside their boundaries. David Bell and Gill Valentine devote a chapter of *Consuming Geographies* to regional food systems and call them human-centred ecological systems, a creation of human and natural processes.[2] Regions are paradoxes of resilience and adaptation; Martin Jones and Gordon MacLeod note that forces external and internal continually transform regions and that they are both socially constructed and politically mediated.[3] Geographers are increasingly turning their attention to what has been called the "new regionalism," an umbrella term for research on the social life, relations, and identity of a place, and culinary geography is no different. Place remains the central organizing principle of food studies. This is certainly true in the case of Canada, and there remains a desire to highlight the geographical inevitability of regionalism. Hashimoto and Telfer tried to explain regional culinary divisions in Canada on the basis of product availability,[4] but this approach discounts local agency in framing a region. Local cuisines are actively encouraged, strengthened, and sold to tourists and the international market. In base terms, they can be used as brands, though this is a shallow description of the social and cultural capital embedded in a culinary tradition. I prefer to think of regional cuisine in terms of what Cook and Crang call "geographical knowledges," in which globally extensive flows of food, people, and knowledge are mediated locally.[5]

The chapters of this section provide a broad overview of the main culinary regions of Canada as I experienced them. These chapters are not meant to be comprehensive, since each region can easily provide material for a book. Where such books exist, I've directed the reader who wants a more detailed fill of recipes and history toward them.

Regional cuisines in Canada, however, are not immutable and inevitable, and some amount of continuous invention and reinvention is present almost everywhere across the country. For this reason, I tend to shy away from the French word *terroir*, linked to the tasting properties of a specific landscape, which Trubek defines as the Earth considered from the point of view of agriculture.[6] Linked most closely to wine, the concept of *terroir*—and its oceanic cousin *merroir*—speaks of culinary products encrusted with the patina of history, and in much of Canada (there are exceptions) culinary products are still in flux. Our great culinary regions are in some ways still to be discovered, waiting for the right combination of chefs, journalists, producers, and promoters to bring them to life. I don't really believe that the great culinary regions of Europe were any different; it is just that labour is long under way, leaving a culinary landscape that seems both inevitable and immutable. As might be gathered from the previous chapter, the constant flow of ingredients and techniques in a multicultural world stimulates what Evan Fraser and Andrew Rimas describe as promiscuity in foodstuffs that is a fundamental part of human nature.[7] This ongoing change is present even in Canada's oldest and most established settler culinary region: Quebec.

117

# QUEBEC

Why had I eaten so much? My good friend Toby and I walked quickly along Rue St. Laurent, the cold seeping into our clothes, the dirty rime of the week's snow shattering beneath our feet. We had just enjoyed a meal that was far too large and far too rich, and we held out faint hope that a brisk stroll across Montreal's Plateau District might do us some good. We passed bustling restaurants, lively bars, and shuttered specialty food shops that the next day would be busy with shoppers. Depanneurs brimmed with local beer and wine for carry out, and *casse-croûtes* served up late-night snacks of poutine and Montreal *steamés*. Montreal is one of the world's great food cities, a jewel in the province that dominates Canada's culinary imagination. It is impossible to go to *la belle province* and not come away with the strong sense that here is a place where people care about food. Overindulging is a pleasurable risk.

Quebec's rise as a culinary powerhouse has deep roots. The early explorers and settlers of New France brought with them the cuisine of *l'ancien régime*, still ringing from the revolutionary changes introduced by Catherine de' Medici and her court. The influence of medieval France can still be felt in Quebec; Julian Armstrong notes lingering medieval flavours and techniques, for example the use of spices such as cloves and cinnamon and the use of roux as a thickener.[8] Early explorers and settlers brought this culinary heritage to a land of exotic flora and fauna. Victoria Dickenson, in her descriptions of the experiences of Cartier and Champlain, describes how suspicion of New World ingredients (Cartier's men attempted to maintain a French diet from their ships' stores) gave way to experimentation and incorporation.[9] This slow mixing of classical French cuisine and New World ingredients is well noted in Driver's catalogue of Quebec cookbooks. At first, the French influence was strong, and then Canadian twists gradually began to appear. The first cookbook to feature truly Canadian recipes, *La cuisinère canadienne*, appeared in 1840 and boasted twenty-two recipes labelled as "Canadian style."[10] A true Québécois cuisine developed, bringing together the best of Canada's ingredients with the expertise of French techniques.

The fortunes of cuisine rise and fall, and Québécois cuisine is no different. The foods of Quebec developed largely in the home and on the farm, and the fever for modern packaged foods and shifting labour patterns led to a turn away from the heavy and complex dishes of Quebec's early days. The nadir for the cuisine was likely the 1970s, when North American foodways in general were mired in a deep malaise. However, Quebec's foods were buoyed by the rise of Quebec nationalism. As restaurants in Quebec followed the general pattern of rapid increase in number seen across North America, they became hubs of francophone culture in the province. Stephen Gazillo's study of old-town Quebec City's restaurants showed that they rose in number from twelve in 1900 to eighty in 1979 and that by the 1960s they were predominantly named in French, even though in 1945 half of them were named in English.[11] The rise of Quebec nationalism would occur, at least in part, over a good meal.

It is difficult to pinpoint exactly when the Quiet Revolution began, though it is usually attributed to the election of Liberal governments in Quebec, first during the 1960 provincial election and again in successive political cycles. However, the wide appeal of campaign slogans promising change indicates that social and cultural change had already begun; perhaps the political changes lagged behind the true revolution. The Catholic Church had dominated education in Quebec and had held a primary role in the provision of health care and social services. In contrast, the provincial government held little responsibility for social development in Quebec, a situation that changed drastically under the Liberal government of Premier Jean Lesage. Important state infrastructure was developed during the 1960s and 1970s, including a socialized education system. The provision of health care, education, and social services was subject to modernization and secularization; along with expansion of the role of the state in Quebec society came concomitant expansion of the infrastructure of a political nation.

These social changes went hand in hand with the rise of the Quebec sovereignty movement. Relations between English and French Canadians have been the cause of tensions in both the social fabric of central Canada and the political landscape of the entire country. Hugh MacLennan's renowned novel *Two Solitudes* has become emblematic of this fraught relationship. The novel, set in the interwar period, explores the intricacies of identity in a divided landscape.[12] Quebec nationalists argue that the province has a unique cultural identity, distinct from that of the rest of Canada. Proponents of Quebec sovereignty argue that the predominantly French-speaking population of Quebec is at risk of assimilation into the overwhelmingly anglophone linguistic and cultural

119

identity of the rest of Canada. So nationalists have made cultural protection an important goal, along with preservation of symbols of their differentiation from the rest of Canada. In part, this effort has entailed attempts to gain sovereignty for Quebec; the Parti Québécois, a provincial political party, was formed in 1960 with a platform advocating national sovereignty. Following its win in the 1976 Quebec election, the Parti Québécois formed a majority government with a mandate to pursue Quebec sovereignty. However, its proposal was rejected by a majority of the province's population in a 1980 referendum. Despite this narrow defeat (and an even narrower defeat in 1995), the nationalist movement succeeded in making French the only official language in Quebec and in adopting legislation protecting and promoting Quebec culture. As well as through regulation, though, nationalists have sought to define a unique culture and to inculcate a national identity in Quebec. To that end, the promotion of folk culture and the creation of distinctly Québécois traditions have become central elements of the nationalist movement, on par with linguistic protection.[13] The idea of a distinctly Québécois identity is transmitted, in part, through traditions, festivals, and different events centring on food and drink.

The culinary heritage of Quebec became a rallying point in the 1970s for a group of Montreal chefs who worried that the traditional dishes of the province were in danger of disappearing. They gathered recipes into a grand cookbook, *Cuisine traditionnelle des régions du Québec*,[14] and began promoting the foods of Quebec's regions. The tide didn't entirely turn until the 1990s. There was widespread opinion that the traditional dishes were too bland and too fatty,[15] and in 1990 Edward Behr had a difficult time finding Québécois cuisine in Quebec City,[16] though he did note the existence of Aux Anciens Canadiens, which presents a wonderful array of classic Québécois dishes. Housed in the 300-year-old Maison Jacquet, this fifty-year-old restaurant is a culinary museum where one gets to eat the exhibits, but its menu also hints at the sea change in Québécois cuisine. Specials include bison bourguignon with a blueberry gravy, as well as a wapiti sausage dish. It also acknowledges the twentieth century with a poutine. Such dishes are familiar since they exhibit the larger properties of Canadian cuisine, and they fit well within the larger movement of *la cuisine régionale au Québec*.

The efforts to revitalize cuisine in Quebec have paid off in striking ways, and their culinary stars lead the country. Hashimoto and Telfer describe the changes as a culinary revolution, a shift to local products grown and developed in Quebec. They note that the creation of a cuisine that celebrates local production is a noble manifestation of Quebec nationalism.[17] *La cuisine régionale au Québec* is both a style and a formal association fostered by the Ministries of Tourism and Agriculture. To qualify for membership, a restaurant must have 70 per cent of the food on its menu sourced from Quebec, and 50 per cent must come from the specific region. Quebec also has its own formal designation of origin given to valued local products. Armstrong sums up the current state of the cuisine as based upon the classic techniques of French cooking, with the finest of ingredients.[18] The ongoing diaspora of Québécois chefs to other regions of the country has embedded this style firmly in the national culinary imagination.

A few hours before my wanderings on Montreal's Plateau District, my friend and I sat down to a meal at one of the temples of the new Québécoise cuisine, Au Pied de Cochon. Chef Martin Picard was an early convert to the new Quebec regional cuisine, and he is a tireless supporter of the importance of food within the province's culture. His restaurant is a warm and cozy nook, a long, thin room with the exposed kitchen along one side, filled with a controlled chaos. The smell is intoxicating, a promise of culinary excess. As we dug into the house-baked baguettes, we pondered our strategy. The menu is daunting; even the starters span a wide range from codfish fritters to herring to bison tongue. There are nine foie gras starters, including the signature poutine, a melting ambrosia of crisp french fries cooked in duck fat, cheese curds, foie gras lobes, and a delicate foie gras foam. The restaurant is

121

North America's largest consumer of foie gras,[19] though many of the province's other restaurants also make liberal use of the buttery duck liver. There is no controversy over foie gras there despite outright bans of the product that have appeared in other regions as concerns over animal welfare grow. The appetizers are like a meal, but in the name of research we ordered a shoulder of beef. Other mains include guinea hen and the famous duck in a can or an entire pig's head for two. By the time that we made our way through the main course, the idea of dessert was daunting, but true to form I had a dessert in mind. Au Pied de Cochon is well known for a dessert representative of the changes to the province's cuisine: Picard's take on *pouding chômeur*.

A basic cake batter topped with caramel or syrup before baking, *pouding chômeur* is an everyday dish whose name translates into "Employment Insurance pudding" or "unemployment pudding." It has humble origins as a simple, cheap dish. The lore of the dish suggests that it originated in 1929 as cash-strapped female factory workers crafted a simple but satisfying dessert using butter, flour, milk, and brown sugar. For most of its history, it was a treat served at home or as an easy snack at *casse-croûtes*. I found such a version at the canteen of the Quebec City Public Market, a rich, sugary snack that cheered my morning. The version of *pouding chômeur* on offer at Au Pied de Cochon is much more in line with the tenets of *cuisine régionale*. Rich with cream, and with maple syrup replacing brown sugar, the warm, cloud-like pudding was both buttery and sweet, and it carried us out into the chill of the night on a burst of maple steam. Throughout the twentieth century, many of Canada's cookbooks shunned this simple dish, though I do like the version in *From Pemmican to Poutine* by Roy and Ali. *Cuisine régionale* has elevated something everyday into something sublime.

Catherine Turgeon-Gouin frames the cuisine of Au Pied de Cochon as a gentrification of traditional Québécois cuisine, with haute ingredients replacing common ones. Picard might agree; he argues in one of his beautiful yet surreal food books that maple syrup should have its own designations of origin taken as seriously as those for wine.[20] Other chefs are busy advancing the same vision. *The Art of Living According to Joe Beef*[21] is equally eclectic, and the food is equally visionary. The rotating menu includes rabbit, trout, horse, and a foie gras parfait. Armstrong prefers Toqué as a representative Montreal restaurant, with its venison carpaccio, fried fiddlehead salad, and smoked sturgeon. These chefs draw heavily on the fresh ingredients that Armstrong calls the *"cuisine du marché."*[22] The markets of Montreal will receive more attention in Chapter 10.

Montreal is a multicultural city, of course, and has deep culinary roots beyond the French influence. Some of the best-known Montreal foods stem from the city's large Jewish community, which includes English-speaking Ashkenazi Jews and French-speaking Sephardic Jews. Perhaps the best-known such food is Montreal smoked meat, most often associated with Schwartz's, a deli founded by Reuben Schwartz, a Jewish immigrant from Romania. Smoked meat is a kosher-style beef brisket salted and cured and then hot-smoked. The cure varies and is kept secret, but it can involve garlic and coriander and other spices. It is popular as a sandwich, served on rye with mustard and sour dill pickles. It is usually quite fatty and is steamed before serving. Schwartz's is iconic, centrally located on Boulevard Saint-Laurent , but other delis are just as popular, such as the lovely Snowdon Deli West of Mont Royal.

123

Montreal is also well known for its bagels, and the two best-known bagel spots are only a block apart. I tend to go to the one that happens to have the shorter line at the time. St-Viateur has operated since 1957 and is open twenty-four hours a day. Its bagels are blanched in honey water, giving the faintest kiss of sugar to the final product. Fairmont Bagels also uses a wood-burning oven and hand rolling, and it too is always open. Montreal bagels are heavy and ropy and smoky, perfect with cream cheese or lox.

One other Jewish institution of note is Wilensky's, a strange hole in the wall opened in 1932, famous for its "special." It is a grilled sandwich of egg bread filled with salami, bologna, and mustard, with an option for Swiss or processed cheese. It is, however, a sandwich with rules. Customers are strictly forbidden to ask for a sandwich without mustard or to ask for it to be sliced in half. It is famous for being mentioned in a Mordecai Richler novel, *The Apprenticeship of Duddy Kravitz*,[23] though in my mind it is even more famous for its taboos. I have no information on what happens if one asks for the sandwich bisected, but I'm not going to risk finding out.

The above is the barest introduction to the wondrous culinary wealth of Montreal. The city sports thousands of restaurants spanning every possible origin and price point, and that diversity continues to grow rapidly. Not everything interesting in Montreal is at the top of the price scale; Montreal is home to Canada's largest Lebanese population, most of whom are new arrivals. There is a corresponding bounty of good Lebanese food available at all hours. Montreal also has a vibrant

124

Figure 7.1. Fairmont Bagels in Montreal

microbrewing community, with popular nightspots such as Dieu du Ciel! (Sky God!) brewing their beers on the spot. Even the city's fast food is interesting from a culinary perspective: poutine aside, Montreal is also home to the *steamé*, a soft and tasty hotdog finally being recognized; the first-ever *steamé* week was held in January 2015. Montreal's *steamé* is, as one might imagine, steamed, giving the hotdog a soft texture, but the more interesting variation is that the buns are cut from the top rather than the side, creating a pocket for exotic toppings. They can include the usual mustard, onion, and ketchup, or cheese and bacon, but the additions become rather elaborate, such as with the Michigan dog. It is topped with spaghetti sauce and optionally includes onion and mustard, a combination also found in New Orleans po' boys. My favourite *steamé* spot is the half-century-old Decarie Hot Dog in Montreal. *Steamés* sit particularly well after a few microbrews.

Downriver from Montreal, Quebec City looms above the St. Lawrence River. One of the oldest cities in North America and the only fortified city remaining north of Mexico, Quebec City seems a place out of time. It is difficult to walk the ramparts of its walls without imagining the waves of history that have washed over this cold, grand landscape. It was here that British General Wolfe defeated French General Montcalm on the Plains of Abraham in 1759. Four years later the French would cede their North American colonies to the British. It was also here that American revolutionaries lost the Battle of Quebec, preventing the formation of a unified North American nation. When I think of Quebec City, I am always struck by the fact that, as a city founded in 1608, most of its history occurred before Canadian Confederation.

Quebec City is at the heart of Québécois nationalism. It is a profoundly French city, and its cuisine reflects this. The old city has many restaurants for tourists, but one can still enjoy a good bistro meal with a nice glass of red wine for a reasonable price. And *la cuisine régionale au Québec* is increasingly well represented; Chez Boulez is one of the best restaurants in the province, serving dishes such as Gaspé Peninsula crab in blue honeysuckle with smoked king trumpet mushrooms, Arctic char with cattail hearts, and salmon tartar in fir tree essence and birch syrup. The restaurant is billed as a bistro boreal, and indeed there are strong links between New Nordic cuisine and the innovations happening in Quebec. The chefs of Quebec City enjoy the best ingredients, and the lovely market is explored in Chapter 10. My memories of Quebec City are rich with culinary encounters. The city has the oldest grocery store in North America, Épicerie J. A. Moisan, an excellent place to source a picnic. It offers a wonderful array of Quebec cheeses, including one of my favourites, Saint-André, and the iconic Oka, a semi-soft, washed rind cheese developed by Trappist monks late in the nineteenth century. On a cold and foggy night, the depanneur near the Chateau Frontenac was offering an excellent *tarte d'érable*; this dense flan is similar to pecan pie but without the nuts and with maple syrup as the sweetener. I munched on a slice as I prowled the old quarter, content to be out in the falling snow.

126

Ringing Quebec's major cities are the venerable sugar bushes of the province and the *cabanes à sucre* mentioned in Chapter 6. As March brings at least the promise of spring to central Canada, urbanites flock to the awakening woods to enjoy a day watching the sugaring-off. A meal at a *cabane à sucre* is a quintessential Canadian culinary experience. Near Montreal, Quebec City, and Ottawa (there are a few near the ski destination of Mont Tremblant as well), most *cabanes à sucre* are within an hour of the cities. They are not quite rural; instead, they are an excellent example of cuisine on Canada's urban-rural fringe. A classic *cabane à sucre* menu is a good introduction to the foods of Quebec's countryside. Érablière Charbonneau offers pea soup, the pork spread known as *cretons*, pancakes, maple sausage, baked beans, the rich meatball stew known as *ragout de boulettes* usually simmered in a tomato base, *tarte au sucre*, a creamier version of *tarte d'érable*, and of course *tire d'érable*, the toffee made by pouring boiling syrup onto clean snow. *Cabanes à sucre* are also part of *la cuisine régionale au Québec* movement. Picard runs a sugar shack with changing menus that acts as a laboratory for his culinary creations. He offers up dishes such as eggs cooked in maple syrup (they really are amazing), a classic *creton* spread, *grands-pères*, a rare dish of dumplings cooked in blueberries and maple (they are a version of Nova Scotia's blueberry grunt), and *trempette*, bread soaked in syrup hot from the evaporator mixed with cream and then fried.

Beyond the *cabanes à sucre*, beyond the city, the Quebec countryside is rich in culinary tradition. Some of the more unusual Québécois dishes are found in rural areas, and it is the heartland of one of the province's best-known dishes, the tourtière. This French Canadian meat pie has been popular for centuries. Tourtière is usually based upon ground pork, but it can include other meats and varies in shape and spice depending on the region. It is common at Christmas and New Year's Day, but it can be found year round and is often sold as an easy, ready-made meal. It is unclear where the name of the dish came from, though the now extinct passenger pigeon, once common in Quebec, was known as a *tourte*. Round or rectangular, the tourtière is a fairly deep-dish pie and a substantial meal. Jean-Pierre Lemasson, in his treatise "The Long History of the *Tourtière* of Quebec's Lac-St-Jean," describes the pie as a winter dish. He notes that the Saguenay pie is particularly deep and flavoured with cinnamon and cloves.[24]

127

Each region of rural Quebec boasts its own specialties. Montérégie is carpeted with orchards and is known for its ice cider. The Bas-Saint-Laurent region is known for smoked fish, sturgeon, and eel. Saguenay is also home to the soup known as *gourgane*, made from broad beans. Charlevoix's pastures create a variety of delicious cheeses, and Chicoutai is known for cloudberry liqueur. Out on the Gaspé Peninsula, one can find a variety of seafoods, including salt cod, and for some reason it is the region where I found *pâté chinois* still available. Basically, it's a shepherd's pie, but its origins are lost in history. Stewart notes the continued use of *herbes salées* on the peninsula, as well as the unique cuisine of the Magdalen Islands (Îles de la Madeleine) Islands, rich with wild food and seafood.[25]

# ONTARIO

I was sitting in Toronto's Woodlot restaurant with an old friend and a new friend, sipping my Merlot and pondering how to capture the foods of Toronto in words. I spent seven years in Toronto, living in Kensington Market in ramshackle student housing, listening to the spice vendors call out to the fishmongers. I wrote my doctoral dissertation hidden away in the library of the University of Toronto's Hart House, watching the snow tap against the leads of the windows. I often miss Toronto: the smell of the subway, the clang of the streetcar, the hot, putrid days of summer, and the cleansing thunderstorms. As I sat with my friends, I wondered if I could write about a city that I knew so intimately. Toronto and I, as they say, had a history.

Canada's largest city is a place apart, the hub on which the rest of the country revolves. Toronto is the fourth largest city in North America, and its greater metropolitan area sprawls along Lake Ontario. A full quarter of Canadians live in this "golden horseshoe," and it is the heart of English Canada's culture. Toronto is written about, loved, hated, and fretted over. It is home to Canada's national newspaper, George Brown's beloved *Globe and Mail* (Brown lived and died for his paper; he was shot in his office by a disgruntled employee). The city was founded in 1793 by the British, and Toronto was barely established when it was captured and burned in 1812 by the Americans. The town bounced back to grow steadily, absorbing surrounding towns. This process of urban sprawl gave Toronto a strong set of neighbourhood identities, heightened by the deep ravines that cut through the city. When I was in Toronto, I knew some neighbourhoods intimately, and others I barely passed through. The experience of Toronto changes block by block, a sensation heightened by the over 200 nationalities present in what is one of the world's most multicultural cities. Toronto is home to the foods of the world, and there isn't space here for a full exploration of everything that the city has to offer. I will focus on one facet of the

Toronto experience: the role of the city as an arbiter of what it means to be Canadian.

I was at Woodlot since it is one of several fairly new restaurants that brand themselves as Canadian. It is designed around a wood-burning oven, and it crafts what it calls creative Canadian comfort food using fresh local ingredients. We certainly enjoyed the evening; the menu that day included wood-fired hen o' the woods mushrooms, an interesting sourdough ravioli in a balsam fir butter, and a wild Lake Erie pickerel with fiddleheads. The room was warm and cozy with plenty of dark wood. We left with complimentary loaves of bread; if this was Canadian cuisine in 2014, then it was fine by us.

Even ten years earlier, to find a classic "Canadian" meal, one had to go to Canoe, the venerable and expensive restaurant perched high above Toronto's downtown on the fifty-fourth storey of the TD Bank tower. Views aside, Canoe still provides some interesting dishes, including a wild leek soup, available occasionally, and a lovely butter tart with smoked vanilla cream and ginger ice cream. But these days Canoe has a lot of company; Bannock might not have the view, but it offers poutine, bannock in various presentations, haddock fish and chips, a fried bologna and egg dish, and of course a butter tart. Farther afield in the rapidly gentrifying Roncesvalles neighbourhood, Hopgood's Foodliner offers dishes with a maritime twist, including smoked mackerel, Halifax donair, Digby scallops, and a wonderful butterscotch bourbon pie. Boralia takes Canadian cuisine even further, drawing on historical trends and recipes. It offers Red Fife bread, chop suey croquettes, perogies, pigeon pie, and bison poutine. Both a history lesson and a geography lesson, as well as a meal, Boralia offers up everything that a scholar of Canadian food could want, save for a Charlotte Russe. Freshwater fish play a strong role in Ontario's cuisine and appear on a wide variety of menus. This speaks to the importance of the Great Lakes to the region as transportation routes and larders.

These restaurants speak to Toronto's (and Ontario's) role as the most populous part of Canada and the historical dominance of what was once

129

Upper Canada. Driver noted that Ontario has a huge number of cookbooks, more than the rest of the country combined.[26] Trends formed in Ontario diffuse to the rest of the country; consider Penfold's doughnut, as discussed in Chapter 6. Although doughnuts aren't entirely a national food, their ubiquity in Ontario almost assures their continued spread. Another interesting example is Canadian bacon, an unsmoked, wet, cured pork loin rolled in yellow cornmeal, though historically dried yellow pea flour was used. Also called peameal bacon, this supposed "Canadian food" is found almost exclusively in southern Ontario. If one wants to try it at its best, the sandwiches served up at St. Lawrence Market are excellent.

In some cases, foods are so well loved and so deeply associated with a place that it is assumed they must have originated there. Several Torontonians have suggested to me that red velvet cake must be Canadian, more specifically that it was invented by Lady Flora Eaton, the daughter of Timothy Eaton, who founded the department store chain of the same name. Timothy Eaton was indeed famous, and the restaurants in his department stores were definitely leaders in cuisine. This is well documented in *Lunch with Lady Eaton*.[27] The authors describe grand dining rooms serving thousands of meals a day, offering a seasonal national cuisine tailored to middle-class women. They featured simple dishes, such as berry pies, new potatoes, corn on the cob, pancakes and maple syrup, and the roast beef so closely associated with Ontario's British heritage. The Georgian Room in Toronto's flagship store prepared box lunches with mock chicken, potato salad, and a butter tart. Several people whom I interviewed recounted taking these little lunches to the lakefront on picnics. Eaton's was famous for a dark Christmas fruit cake, as well as for the red velvet cake that Lady Eaton had introduced, though she hadn't invented it. The Eaton's restaurants, which included Vancouver's Marine Room and Toronto's iconic Round Room at the College Street store, introduced many new dishes to Canadians. Conveniently, they were also popular enough that new dishes made the news, literally, and thus we can date the introduction of red velvet cake to Canada in 1961. It emerged elsewhere much earlier, however. The cake recipe was used as a vehicle for selling food colouring as early as 1940, has served as a "groom's cake" at weddings (the "bride's cake" is traditionally vanilla almond), and has enjoyed waves of popularity, including that started by the Eaton's dining rooms. Red velvet cake is popular once again and can be found widely in Canada, but it is not Canadian.

Sometimes a food product becomes so associated with a new region that it is adopted into a national cuisine. Such a product can be found on the Niagara Peninsula, the beautiful region of farms and vineyards southwest of Toronto. The culinary branding of Niagara is part organic and part engineered; certainly, the region is well suited to food and wine production. The Niagara benchlands enjoy moderate winters, are well watered, and have a long, warm growing season, perfect for wine grapes. David Telfer describes how the Taste of Niagara has built the region into a tourist destination through an alliance among producers, chefs, and the tourist industry.[28] Poor grape cultivars have been replaced by classic, high-quality grape cultivars, and wineries have opened their doors to tourists. This shift began in earnest in the 1990s when two wineries, Vineland Estates and Cave Spring Cellars, opened restaurants as part of their branding. Tasting trails and culinary tourism now flourish throughout the region.

The best-known product of the region is Canadian icewine. This sweet dessert wine is created with grapes frozen on the vine and was first produced in Germany, but has really been brought to excellence in Canada. It is an expensive wine that pairs well with cheeses and desserts, and it is produced in small areas of Canada where the proper conditions are present. Exacting temperatures and weather patterns are needed to produce the proper flavour and yield. Icewine dates back to the eighteenth century in Germany and was introduced in Canada in the 1970s by German immigrants. A successful industry was thriving by the 1980s, and today Canada is the largest producer globally.[29]

131

Its status as a cold country works in its favour, for it is only in Canada that a yearly crop of icewine can be guaranteed. Counterfeit icewine is a real problem globally, but in Canada icewine must be produced from grapes naturally frozen on the vine. To date, only British Columbia and Ontario have produced icewines that meet the exacting standards of this product. Icewine is produced in Niagara, on Pelee Island, on the north shore of Lake Erie, and in areas of British Columbia's Okanagan and Similkameen Valleys. Experts argue that, along with soil quality, the wild yeasts of these regions are particularly suited to the production of high-quality wine.

One of the better places to sample the best of the Niagara region is in the town of Niagara-on-the-Lake, a safe distance downriver from the bright lights and crowds of tourists at Niagara Falls. Niagara-on-the-Lake has a solid collection of restaurants in the popular farm-to-table venue with solid local wine lists; when I passed through town, the restaurant Treadwell was making good use of fresh greens and foraged mushrooms paired with local wines. Niagara-on-the-Lake is also a good place to experience the British influence on Canada since the town has several places to enjoy tea. Tea is served in Canada as a light meal with sandwiches and dainties, usually on a tiered plate, and is called high tea, even though it is more akin to what the British would call afternoon tea. Tea can be enjoyed in the grand railway hotels across the country, but it is especially popular in the towns of Stratford and Niagara-on-the-Lake. Victoria, British Columbia, was once the centre of Canada's British tea culture, but as we will see in the next chapter that has changed somewhat. I prefer the local wines when in Niagara, but I never say no to a selection of small cakes.

North of Niagara, the Kitchener-Waterloo region is home to a significant population of Canadians of German descent, including a large number of Mennonites who came to Canada in the 1900s. I have fond memories of buying maple syrup and freshly baked pies from the Mennonite farmers at St. Jacobs Market. Their lovely black horses would stamp and shuffle impatiently beside the stand as the men sold their wares. Kitchener's German influence is proudly on display at the annual Oktoberfest, which draws three-quarters of a million people to enjoy foods such as bratwurst, *spanferkel, rollbraten, sauerbraten*, schnitzel, sauerkraut, and strudel.[30] Beer is also a popular local product, as are Germanic desserts. I have a personal attachment to the apple fritters soaked in maple syrup served at St. Jacobs Market.

The central region of southern Ontario is also a great place to become familiar with the butter tart. This sweet treat is one of the few absolutely Canadian recipes, and it is available in most parts of the country, though it is most common in Ontario. Butter tarts are filled with butter, sugar, syrup, and egg, and they are baked until semi-solid with a crunchy top. Additions to the filling are common and include nuts, raisins, currants, and coconut, among others. The origin of the tart is unclear, but a recipe in the *Royal Victoria Cook Book* produced by the Women's Auxiliary of the Royal Victoria Hospital from Barrie, Ontario, dates to 1900. Butter tarts have spawned an interesting array of tourist experiences, including a butter tart festival in Muskoka, the Best Butter Tart Festival in Midland, a food trail in Wellington, and a butter tart tour in the Kawarthas. The latter two groups had a fairly serious dispute that fortunately was peacefully resolved; apparently, there is enough butter tart tourism to go around. Butter tarts are very sweet and provide an impressive wallop of calories since the best tarts are fairly large. One way that I enjoy them is as an impromptu roadside treat. I was once driving on the rural highway from Peterborough to Ottawa with a friend, and we came across a small stand selling various baked goods, including the most perfect butter tarts. Maybe it was the warm weather, maybe it was that we were hungry, but somehow the tarts were the perfect mix of sweet and filling, of runny and flaky. This was many years ago, but when I asked my friend about that trip the tarts were the first thing that she mentioned.

As one heads north from southern Ontario, farmland gives way to cottage country, the lake-dotted forest where the moderately wealthy

133

and very wealthy come to escape from the city. The iconic symbol of this landscape is the canoe, a form of transportation that has a firm hold on the Canadian imagination. A colleague of mine, Bruce Erickson, wrote a lovely book, *Canoe Nation*,[31] that explores how the canoe is a keystone of Canadian identity. He argues that the lore of the canoe is also part of an attempt to legitimize a particular and dominant vision of the nation. Cottages are similar; in certain circles in Toronto, there are those with cottages and those without them. Cottage country is a landscape of amenity, a cool, quiet retreat from the heat and noise of southern Ontario's cities, which become extremely humid in the summer. Roy Wolfe describes the cottage as a "divorce" from the urban environment, ideally located in a weekend leisure zone.[32] Steven Svenson notes that 70 per cent of cottaging in Canada is done in Ontario and Quebec and that the cottage is a strong part of upper- and middle-class Canadian folklore.[33]

134

The culinary geography of cottage country is of interest since cottages don't tend to spur a strong restaurant landscape, for cottagers tend to bring their own food for picnics and barbecues, and they use local towns as supply depots. I didn't have much first-hand experience of cottaging; I suffered through Toronto's blast furnace summers in my non-air-conditioned rented room by staying up late and then catching a little sleep on my roof. But my few trips into cottage country bolstered some recent interviews suggesting that the best cottage meal is eaten outside. In fact, many a Canadian meal is eaten outdoors. Pauline Morel describes our long-standing love of the picnic, remarking that Canadian foodways are heavily marked by wilderness, and an outdoor commensality is a common Canadian culinary element.[34] In the days of John A. Macdonald, campaign picnics were popular, catered by local women's groups. Food served included cold chicken, cake, strawberries, and lemonade, a meal that wouldn't be out of place in today's cottage country. Gougeon describes these events in her *Original Canadian Cookbook*, noting that they sometimes attracted thousands of people, an impressive picnic.

Today cottage fare ranges from fairly simple food cooked outdoors to elaborate meals prepped in the showpiece kitchens of million-dollar cottages, though on my few trips into cottage country classic hotdogs, hamburgers, and other picnic dishes were served. And almost everyone I've talked to about cottages mentions drinking a beer on the dock at dusk, when the loons are calling on the lake and the breeze is rustling the trees, and they smile when they think of it.

As one heads north from the golden horseshoe, the beautiful farm fields and deep hardwood forests of cottage country fall into the rear-view mirror, replaced by the scrub forest, bare rock, and brooding lakes of the Canadian Shield. This landscape rolls north right to Hudson's Bay. Driving north along Lake Superior is one of the few times that I've become frightened by the emptiness of a place. At the end of this vastness sits Thunder Bay, a city of great beauty and worthy of culinary mention. Thunder Bay also hosts the largest community of people of Finnish descent outside Scandinavia. The Finns arrived in the late nineteenth century and settled to work in the timber industry. This Finnish presence is apparent in Thunder Bay, best experienced at the 105-year-old Finnish Labour Temple and in its basement restaurant, the Hoito. As a Finnish Canadian, I found visiting the Hoito very comforting; the waitress hailed me in Finnish, and the accents reminded me of home. The Hoito serves up classic Finnish pancakes and other specialty dishes, such as *mojakka*, salt fish, and *karjalan piirakka*. The long communal tables are a great place to enjoy a meal. Economic survival is difficult for businesses in rural regions, though, and as I write this the Hoito is in financial trouble, and it is uncertain whether it will continue to operate. Its loss would mark a sad end to an icon of Canada's culinary culture. Thunder Bay's other foodie claim to fame is the Persian, a popular roll frosted in a pink icing and found only in the city. Pronounced *Persh-an*, the confection is similar to a cinnamon roll, unlike similarly named treats in the United States based on doughnut batter. The origin of this treat is unknown, though it might have its

135

roots in Finnish *pulla* bread. There is a running debate over whether the icing is strawberry or raspberry flavoured; when I had one at the Persian Man, it wasn't clear.

In the far eastern corner of Ontario, Ottawa looms over the river of the same name. As national capitals go, Ottawa is a bit of a puzzle; it is hard to get to, and even though it is a fairly large city it feels as if a Gothic fantasy of Parliament fell from the sky into a small, rough lumber town. Ottawa's destiny changed forever on New Year's Eve in 1857 when Queen Victoria herself chose the settlement as the future capital of Upper and Lower Canada. She made this unlikely choice on the ground that remoteness protected the capital from invasion; its large cliffs were easily fortified, and it was at the confluence of the Ottawa River and the newly constructed Rideau Canal. Ottawa was also the only town of any size on the border of Upper and Lower Canada, and it housed a mixed population of French and English. Today Ottawa still feels rather remote, but it is marvellously bilingual. I spent several years in Ottawa, and, though I never quite adapted to the blazing and humid summers and the astoundingly cold winters, I did marvel at the rather tranquil nature of the place and the amazing show put on every autumn by the changing colours of the maple leaves.

Ottawa has its share of good food, but one culinary icon that requires explanation is the Beavertail™. This long, flat doughnut doesn't contain the flesh of our national animal; rather, it resembles the paddle-like tail of our resident dam builders. The Beavertail™, now a registered trademark, was created by Grant and Pamela Hooker in the town of Killaloe, near Algonquin National Park. They quickly opened a stand in Ottawa's Byward Market and have expanded to many of Canada's recreational landscapes. The toppings vary, and they are best eaten hot. I like both the lemon glaze and the classic maple topping. The Hookers claim that the recipe was made by their family long before they opened the stand.

I ate my first Beavertail™ on the Rideau Canal. I was, to put it mildly, having trouble managing with Ottawa's harsh winters, so I decided that it was time to adapt or flee. I rented some skates and attempted to glide along the canal. I'm not particularly suited to skates and spent most of the day sliding from snowbank to snowbank, but eventually I anchored myself next to the Beavertail™ shack and enjoyed a hot pastry drenched in maple topping. I was bruised, cold, and exhausted, but I did feel a bit more of a connection to central Canada. Canadians live in a cold country, and in our capital, hidden away in the wilderness by Queen Victoria herself, we celebrate that reality in food and deed.

137

## 8

# ALBERTA AND
# BRITISH COLUMBIA

## ALBERTA

Alberta is a vast landscape of open prairie, eroded badlands, northern boreal forest, and soaring mountains. Famous—or infamous—for the oil and bitumen extraction that has drawn hundreds of thousands of workers and raised the ire of environmentalists, Alberta is driven by the paradoxical combination of resource extraction and tourism. It is one of only two provinces without a coastline, and historically it had strong ties to the American west. The stereotypical association of Alberta with cowboy culture, right-leaning political views, and stronger religious affiliations still has some grounding in reality, but today's Alberta is a cosmopolitan place, with 80 per cent of its citizens living in the Calgary-Edmonton corridor. In most previous explorations of Canada's cuisine, Alberta has been included with the other two prairie provinces, but this is no longer a sufficient way to encapsulate the diversity and robustness of the foods found there. Alberta has been a wealthy province, both from its oil and from its international visitors, who have come for the high mountain resorts and the foothills ranching culture, and this wealth has driven a unique cuisine that embraces both prairie and mountain. I call this culinary style big sky cuisine.

It begins with beef. The Alberta cattle industry produces 60 per cent of Canada's beef, and local chefs highlight the province's high-quality cattle. Steak is the most popular beef preparation in the province, but Alberta is also a great place to find a high-end hamburger. Cattle were introduced to the province in 1876 from the United States, and from the beginning the industry was successful, for the land that once sup-ported vast herds of bison was well suited to supporting cows. As Henry Klassen has explored,[1] ranches were often medium to small in size and owner-occupied. Entrepreneurial in its scope, the industry helped to feed the raging demand for beef in Britain; export has always been a large part of the Alberta industry. Today Alberta has roughly 5 million head of cattle, and 31 per cent of the province's farmland is pasture. The story of beef, however, is also a story of excellence in marketing and lobbying. Blue captures this well in her 2008 essay "If It Ain't Alberta, It Ain't Beef," which explains Alberta beef culture as an outgrowth of the province's sense of exceptionalism, a feeling that the rest of Canada doesn't understand or value the west and its way of life. James Careless, who gave us the best insight into the life of George Brown, explored this concept as an example of core-periphery power relations deeply rooted in Canada's historical development. Because political power in Canada rested in Ontario and Quebec, Alberta was an agrarian outlier, always feeling slightly excluded and misunderstood.[2] By the late 1980s, ongoing resentment in the region led to the rise of the Alberta-based Reform Party, a federal political party that campaigned on the slogan "The West Wants In." By the time Calgary hosted the 1988 Winter Olympics, the mood was right for the emergence of a distinct identity for Alberta.

The branding of Alberta beef as the best beef in Canada mirrors the province's increasing importance in Canada. Alberta's fortunes cycle with the price of oil, and it remains to be seen if the influence of Alberta

139

will be sustained as commodity prices fall. But what is certain is that, as Blue explains, "cattle production and beef consumption are not natural, inevitable, or politically neutral."[3] The success of linking Alberta and beef required the mediation of pre-existing values and the lionization of a cowboy culture that existed in the west for only a short period in the late nineteenth century.

The branding of Alberta beef began in earnest in 1969 with the creation of Alberta Beef Producers, a lobby group established to advance the interests of cattle ranchers. By the 1980s, it was positioning Alberta beef as an important Canadian cultural product, and the effort was very successful. A study conducted in Quebec found that, though Alberta beef producers are more distant from Quebec than suppliers in Ontario and the United States, restaurateurs, wholesalers, and retailers in that province prefer Alberta beef.[4] Its popularity increased even after the United States banned Alberta beef after a bovine spongiform encephalopathy (BSE) scare. The advertising campaign at the time made the consumption of Alberta beef into a patriotic act, and Canadian consumption increased, an effect that one blogger called "mad cow nationalism."

Today a visitor to Alberta has many opportunities to enjoy beef, most of which is grass fed and then finished with corn on feedlots to create the marbled fat preferred by the North American palate. Steaks and hamburgers dominate and are usually grilled, and when the weather permits this grilling is often done outside. Prime rib roasts are also popular, as are hot sliced-beef sandwiches. Another interesting preparation is ginger beef, deep-fried strips of beef in a sweet sauce with fresh ginger, garlic, and hot peppers, usually with a few carrots and onions, served on rice. Invented in the mid-1970s by George Wong at the Silver Inn in Calgary, ginger beef can be found at most Chinese Canadian restaurants in Alberta and indeed across the country. Barbecue is also popular, particularly in Edmonton, where meaty beef ribs are often served with biscuits and coleslaw. In addition, fried bull testicles, or "prairie oysters," are served.

Alberta's cowboy culture is at its most flamboyant during the annual Calgary Stampede, a rodeo, festival, and exhibition billed as the "Greatest Outdoor Show on Earth." The beginnings of the stampede trace to early agricultural exhibitions in the province, but as an annual spectacle it began in 1923. Although the rodeo and chuckwagon races are the best-known (and most controversial) elements of the stampede, food has always played a large part in the activities. The chuckwagon breakfast is at its best during the stampede, an all-you-can-eat feast of pancakes, bacon, and coffee. Chuckwagon cooks were traditionally well-paid members of the ranching community since they had to cook for a large group under difficult conditions and often doubled as ranch doctors. Their wagon-bound kitchen put strict limits on what they could produce, so simple dishes such as pancakes and baked beans were popular. Today these breakfasts pop up around the city during stampede time. Another dish from the chuckwagon, son of a gun in a sack, isn't seen as often these days; it is a pudding of suet and molasses cooked in burlap. Later in the day during stampede time, the barbecue pits take centre stage. Long grills serve up steak sandwiches and hamburgers. The stampede is also an excellent place to experience Canadian midway food, which has traditionally involved deep frying and adventurous eating. The 2015 menu promised crocodile sliders, deep-fried Cheezies (Cheezies are a Canadian snack food made of corn meal and cheddar, invented in Ontario in the 1940s), deep-fried doughnut cheeseburgers (the doughnut is sliced to replace the bun), *papri tot* (a mixture of tater tots, tamarind, and chili), a poutine burger, a turkey dinner poutine, and, tame in comparison to the other dishes, an elegant-sounding red velvet doughnut.

Although one can't rope and ride a bison, it is an increasingly popular source of protein in Alberta. Bison has been mentioned elsewhere in this text, mostly in a historical context, but there is a growing bison industry in Canada, and half of that production occurs in Alberta. Bison have much to recommend them: they are adapted to life on the prairie and

141

don't need to be brought inside in the winter. They are even capable of gathering water from snow as they graze the winter prairie. Bison meat is lean and now appears on many menus across the country. One can also find beefalo in Alberta, a hybrid of cattle and bison, though it has fallen out of favour as the full-blooded bison gains popularity.

A few other dishes of interest can still be found in Alberta, including a pair of desserts that developed during times of scarcity. The first, the flapper pie, was developed during the First World War and uses a crust of Graham crackers. The pie is a plain vanilla cream dessert topped with meringue. Vinegar pie is older, a dish born from a shortage of lemons during settlement of the Prairies. It is a faux lemon pie, using vinegar to replace lemon juice. An older food seeing a bit of a revival is fried porridge, long a standard breakfast dish. It might seem unlikely, but Calgary is seeing a mild form of porridge renaissance; Diner Deluxe serves a version fried in maple syrup and then topped with lemon curd.

142

Two particular groups of settlers have left lasting imprints on Alberta's cuisine. Ukrainians, mentioned further in the discussion of the remaining Prairies, were actively recruited from the late nineteenth century until 1914 because it was believed that they would be excellent farmers capable of surviving the harsh environment of the Prairies. With the outbreak of the First World War, immigration stopped, and many non-naturalized Ukrainians found themselves placed in internment camps since they were still citizens of the Austro-Hungarian Empire. After the war, many more arrived, and they brought with them dishes that would be adopted widely across the Prairies. The most popular, still widely found today, are borscht, cabbage rolls, kielbasa sausage, and perogies. Edmonton boasts several places serving excellent Ukrainian food, including the Ukrainian Heritage Village near the city.

Edmonton's culinary scene has expanded rapidly to serve workers in the nearby oil sands. Bistro Praha serves up a variety of schnitzel and its well-known *cikanska jehla*, a skewer of ham, beef, and vegetables. Elsewhere in the city, steak and Newfoundland cuisine are also popular choices.

Other groups have since joined Ukrainians on the Prairies. Vietnamese are much more recent arrivals to Alberta, but they have also left a culinary mark on the province. Eight thousand people came from Vietnam between 1975 and 1985 to settle in Alberta; fleeing the communist government in Vietnam, they were often sponsored by church groups and community associations, sometimes in small towns. Many of the new arrivals started restaurants, adding to the diversity of food in Alberta.

The province's culinary identity is most easily accessible in Calgary, a sprawling metropolis at the confluence of the Bow and Elbow Rivers, about an hour away from the Rocky Mountains. A young city of a little over a million people, Calgary began in the late nineteenth century as a base for the North West Mounted Police, but it didn't really thrive until the Canadian Pacific Railway arrived in 1883. A hub of the booming ranching industry enabled by arrival of the railway, Calgary was well positioned to develop as the corporate heart of the oil industry. With its sweeping suburbs, tangle of corporate skyscrapers, and broad freeways, Calgary feels very different from most Canadian cities. The latest burst of growth, which mirrored the boom in oil sands production, has created a vibrant restaurant scene. I visited Calgary often in the 1990s, and that culinary scene was really nowhere to be found. Instead, what I saw then was basically what Gail Norton and Karen Ralph note in their book *Calgary Cooks*: until recently, Calgary was a city of steak houses, Greek pizza joints, and Chinese Canadian restaurants.[5] There were also a few perogies, blintzes, and latkes sprinkled in for good measure. This is no longer the case; Calgary now boasts hundreds of excellent restaurants, creating dishes that sit well within the emerging shape of our national cuisine. Beef might be king, and the steak house certainly still dominates, but in my travels I found a hearty elk lasagna at Cucina, rhubarb-glazed scallops with braised bacon and cabbage at Catch, a wild boar carbonara at Bonterra Trattoria, and a strangely vibrant brunch culture, perhaps second only to that of Toronto. But then maybe I was just beguiled by Beltliner's chocolate milk French toast. Several of Calgary's restaurants

143

embrace a commitment to local foods despite the challenges posed by prairie winters, including Rouge, which offers an elk tartare with mustard greens. Canada is one of the world's largest producers of mustard, a fact seldom celebrated in restaurants.

I wanted to highlight one of the early pioneers of Alberta's young cuisine, Sal Howell's restaurant River Café, but the literal river stopped me from eating there. The flood of 2013, which inundated much of downtown Calgary, closed River Café for fifty-six days. Happily, the restaurant was restored once the water receded, and the mayor of Calgary spoke at the reopening. I was disappointed to miss eating there. The restaurant has the philosophy of using the best regional ingredients, with the goal of strengthening the sustainability of the restaurant industry through the economic and social support of local producers and the environmental benefits of sourcing locally. Graduate student Kristi Peters, colleague Dr. Chris Ling, and I studied the "foodprint" of River Café in 2007 and found that the environmental impact of the restaurant fell by half in the summer months when food could be sourced locally. The menu is resplendent with bison, Alberta beef, locally raised boar, and the best of British Columbia's seafood, including Sunshine Coast sturgeon (the only tank-farmed sturgeon in Canada). The winter menu has to be creative with vegetables; the restaurant offers beets and parsnips and hummus from prairie lentils. The humble lentil isn't often associated with Canada, but lentils are grown in rotation with wheat to recharge soil moisture, and they are exported in great quantities. They are just beginning to appear on Canadian plates. River Café's dessert menu features a maple wild rice pudding that several friends have recommended to me; a return visit to Calgary, this time without a flood, might be in order.

As one drives west from Calgary, the Rocky Mountains suddenly appear over the horizon, a great icy wall stretching as far north and south as the eye can see. To the early explorers attempting to cross to the Pacific Ocean, the sight must have been beyond disheartening, but today it ranks as one of the greatest views in Canada. The mountains are coated with mist and loom over the traveller as the road winds its way up and up and up. And the mountains, and the tourists whom they draw, host an interesting culinary sub-region. Although the hubs of dining activity in Alberta are in the two major cities, big sky cuisine is also heavily influenced by the fine dining offered in the resorts of the Rocky Mountains. The snow-capped peaks, alpine meadows, and emerald waters of the Rockies are one of Canada's top tourist attractions, and fine dining has been on offer since the days of the great railway hotels, when the finest ingredients were whisked into remote parkland locations on the trains. Banff is the oldest and best known of the mountain recreational landscapes, but nearby Lake Louise, Jasper to the north, and Radium Hot Springs to the south all boast sophisticated culinary landscapes that draw on the brash flavours of Alberta yet incorporate elements from the Pacific coast. It is an edge region, a boundary region, shaped by the vision of the grand railway hotels, the brainchild of railway industrialist William Van Horne.

Van Horne spent much of his working life on the rails, and by 1888 he had risen to the post of president of Canadian Pacific Railway. He was thus in the right place at the right time to oversee construction of the first Canadian transcontinental railway, linking British Columbia to central Canada. Van Horne also oversaw the sea transportation division of the company, which began regular service between Vancouver and Hong Kong in 1891. He was thus concerned that the rail journey to his distant Pacific seaport also be a luxury experience, but this wasn't an easy goal: the trains of the time couldn't pull heavy dining cars over the Rocky Mountains. The trip, though much faster and safer than the wagon trips of old, still took days. Van Horne set out to build a chain of luxury hotels along the line, and several of them remain the grandest in Canada, from the Chateau Frontenac in Quebec City, to the Chateau Laurier in Ottawa, to the magical mountain palaces of the Banff Springs and Chateau Lake Louise. Travelling Europeans and North Americans fell in love with this rugged wilderness, the prospect of clean air, and unparalleled hiking and mountaineering. Even today the view of Lake Louise's emerald water feels magical.

The food at these great hotels had to match the expectations of Van Horne's most elegant guests. Van Horne hired French chefs and overcame the thorny problem of supplying raw ingredients by having his station masters and switch tenders grow small, track-side gardens and send fresh food down the line as needed. Even in the 1890s, before the hotels reached the height of their opulence, traveller Henry Finck wrote in *The Pacific Coast Scenic Tour* that the station stops for meal breaks featured waiters and full menus and ample time to enjoy relaxed meals.[6] The great hotels remain today, gently weathered against their mountain backdrops. The towns around them filled with restaurants that serve the waves of visitors who come to experience the mountains. The cuisine of the mountain parks builds on the flavours of Alberta beef but also incorporates plentiful seafood from the Pacific coast. At Fiddle River in Jasper, Arctic char and Newfoundland cod cakes share the menu with elk meatloaf, bison lasagna, and candied salmon. Back in Banff, Eden offers partridge and sturgeon and braised Alberta beef cheeks. It is hard to imagine leaving the mountain towns hungry.

## BRITISH COLUMBIA

Farther west, past the wall of the Rocky Mountains, wave after wave of jagged, ice-capped peaks fall toward the Pacific Ocean. British Columbia is an incredibly vast province; its fjord-carved coast boasts 6,000 islands and 27,000 kilometres of coastline, much of it inaccessible and sparsely populated. But British Columbia can also feel strangely small, since 75 per cent of the province is mountainous, and only about 10 per cent is suitable for farming of any kind. Life in British Columbia takes place in the lush but small valley bottoms surrounded by steep and forbidding mountains and the deep green of one of the Earth's greatest temperate rainforests. The towns of British Columbia are strung along rivers and coastlines, connected by long drives and ferry trips. These valleys and coastlines contain a wealth of culinary *terroir*, including the wine and fruit country of the Okanagan-Similkameen, the agricultural heartland of the Fraser Valley, the maritime riches of Vancouver Island, the near-Mediterranean climate of the Gulf Islands, and the cosmopolitan centres of Vancouver and its smaller cousin, Victoria. British Columbia is home to Canada's take on Pacific coast cuisine, which shares commonalities with other cuisines found on the Pacific Rim, and life in British Columbia draws heavily on the cultures of China, Japan, and India. Canadian creole is at its most prominent in Vancouver, and the heavy use of local ingredients is taken to great extremes across the province. Pacific coast cuisine is rooted in the land and water of its region. The province's cuisine has also been called Cascadian cuisine, a nod to the imagined country of British Columbia, Washington, Oregon, and, depending on the author, the northern part of California. Although British Columbia is unlikely to break away to join this Cascadia, there is a great deal of north-south exchange. The key to understanding Pacific coast cuisine is to understand that British Columbia looks west and is heavily influenced by the cultures of the Pacific Rim. Europe is largely a fading memory lost behind the mountains in the rear-view mirror.

The coast and rivers balance the ubiquitous mountains, and this stunning landscape overflows with wild marine life and supported the largest precontact populations of Indigenous peoples in Canada. And for many of those peoples, the keystone species in their food systems was salmon. British Columbia's cuisine is about much more than salmon, of course, and I occasionally despair when Canadian cookbooks fixate on this signature fish, but there is no escaping salmon's importance. Salmon played, and plays, a central role in both the cuisine and the culture of the West Coast. The Indigenous villages of the Pacific coast were largely oriented to the inland seas and great rivers, and salmon played a critical role in the organization of communities. Settlements on rivers and streams allowed heavy annual fish harvests, whether through the use of weirs, traps, nets, or spears. Salmon were smoked and dried, and they formed the cornerstone of the large communal meals served up and down the coast. As D. Bruce Johnsen notes, "the importance of salmon to the native economy cannot be overstated. Most tribes' livelihood revolved around the yearly cycle of salmon runs that began in early summer and continued late into fall."[7] Inland, fisheries focused on rivers, and salmon were traded as far east as Alberta.

Salmon is more than food. It has been central to the cultures of the Indigenous peoples of the West Coast. The Sto:lo, on whose traditional territories much of this book was crafted, still celebrate a first salmon festival at the beginning of each year's run. The first salmon of the year is served to the community on a cedar plank draped in cedar bows. The bones are then given back to the river. In some groups, the first salmon has been honoured as the chief of salmon and ceremonially placed with its head facing upstream so that other salmon would continue and not turn back to the ocean. Today dishes such as smoked salmon are extremely popular along the West Coast, as are creole dishes incorporating salmon into other cuisines. Salmon has been branded as a traditional Canadian food, and it has been used to represent British Columbia on many menus. Next to maple syrup, salmon is the most recognized Canadian product. Perhaps the best example of its ubiquity in the food culture of British Columbia comes from the BC roll, a popular type of maki sushi that features barbecued or grilled salmon along with cucumber and a sweet sauce. This roll is extremely common in Japanese restaurants on the West Coast, as is salmon sashimi.

Although the salmon remains king, Vancouver's cuisine is about much more than its signature fish. Seafood is plentiful and of high quality; standouts include the sablefish (once known as black cod), which has emerged as a central menu item. Sablefish is at its best smoked, its oily, flaky texture protecting it from becoming dry. At Tojo's, it is smoked and then steamed, wrapped in brown paper. Halibut remains popular as

148

well, along with clams, oysters, and crabs. Lobster, though available in restaurants, isn't found in BC waters.

Two crustaceans merit special note: the geoduck and the spot prawn. The geoduck is a baffling creature: its clam-like shell can be twenty centimetres across, and its long siphon, or "neck," can be up to a metre in length. They bury themselves deep into tidal flats, where they live extremely long if rather uneventful lives. The geoduck is highly prized in China, and in British Columbia it is most often found as a component of sushi; the neck has an unusual, crunchy texture and a light, refreshing flavour. In Japan, the geoduck is seen as inferior to the horse clam, but it has become highly prized in Vancouver's sushi bars. The spot prawn causes a kind of madness to descend on Vancouver when it comes into season. Spot prawns are the largest prawns on the West Coast, fished primarily in the Salish Sea between the Lower Mainland and Vancouver Island. They can be as long as twenty centimetres, are red with distinctive white spots, and have light and sweet flesh. Ninety per cent of the commercial catch is sent to China and Japan, but a strong marketing effort, and their intrinsic quality, have made them popular in Vancouver. They are celebrated in a spot prawn festival each year and command a high price.

Vancouver has a love affair with cuisine that goes far beyond seafood. Next to Montreal, Vancouver is Canada's most food-obsessed city, and the chapter on multiculturalism has already touched on its cuisine. It is the heart of Canada's creole cuisine (recall that Priya Vadi called it a Vancouver creole); it has strong Asian influences, contains the eth-noburb of Richmond, and boasts innovators at all points on the scale from Japadog to Tojo's. There is more to say, however: Vancouver is also the heart of Canada's locavore movement, which flows from broader trends on the Pacific Rim. Understanding Pacific Rim cuisine requires analysis of a number of interwoven threads.

A harbinger of things to come was the opening of Trader Vic's in 1961. It arrived before Vancouver was awash in restaurants and international

149

options. Its Polynesian-style cuisine was an instant hit, and it popularized the idea of drinking with meals. A refreshing change from the stuffy steak houses of the time, it presented for the first time an upscale "Asian" cuisine, and the restaurant hummed with the city's business elite. The Vancouver location was a tiki-style A-frame with its own boat dock, and it was completed with faux carvings and a vaguely maritime, Polynesian collection of decorations. Known for its rum-heavy mai tai, Trader Vic's brought to Vancouver an odd creole that included *saté*, mahi mahi, chow mein, and chicken cordon bleu. The menu included selections inspired by Chinese, Taiwanese, and Indian cuisine, added a French influence, and drew on fresh ingredients. This trendsetter has long since vanished, but it was the first of many restaurants that made dining more accessible and enjoyable. Wolfgang Puck of Los Angeles credited Trader Vic's as an inspiration for future waves of fusion cuisine.

California cuisine exploded onto the scene in the 1970s. It is hard to imagine, but in the 1960s even the fanciest North American restaurants

150

Figure 8.1. Japadog in Vancouver

used ingredients from jars, cans, and freezers. This really changed first in California, specifically in its restaurants, not in its homes. California broke free of the mould before more classical culinary centres such as New York for a number of reasons: it had the climate, the soil, and a multicultural mix of people. As noted in *Inside the California Food Revolution*, it was a break with Eurocentrism.[8] In the 1970s, chefs began playing with fresh seasonal products and flavours and often had to go directly to the farmers. Alice Waters is the best known of these chefs and in some ways the founder of California cuisine, for her restaurant Chez Panisse in Berkeley certainly broke new ground in its simple, ingredients-forward take on classical French techniques. However, Puck's Los Angeles restaurant Chinois on Main deserves mention for bringing fusion to California cuisine, and by the late 1970s this combination of fresh ingredients and fusion dishes was beginning to appear in Vancouver.

Vancouver was an early adapter to the influence of West Coast cuisine, in part because so many Americans moved north in the 1970s to avoid conscription into the Vietnam War and start new lives. This mix of back-to-the-landers, draft dodgers, and hippies had a deep impact on British Columbia, particularly Vancouver and the surrounding rural areas and islands (as well as Nelson in the interior). The expats who settled in the Kitsilano neighbourhood on 4th Avenue (known at the time as Rainbow Road) brought new thoughts on dining.

Canada does not have a particularly strong tradition of vegetarian and vegan diets; only about 4 per cent of Canadians identify themselves as vegetarian or vegan. One Tuesday evening in 2014, it seemed as if most of them were in front of me in the line to get into The Naam, the oldest continuously operating vegetarian restaurant in Vancouver. It emerged at a time when members of the hippie counterculture were turning to the teachings of Eastern philosophical traditions such as Hinduism and Buddhism, and this search for spiritual enlightenment raised interest in natural, ethically produced foods. However, few such options were available at the time, and in 1967 the Golden Lotus (now closed) was born. The Naam was an early spin-off restaurant and has drawn a bustling crowd ever since. Rates of vegetarianism are much higher in coastal British Columbia than elsewhere in the province, and there is general interest in a more vegetable-heavy diet.

The deep commitment to fresh food in Vancouver is also manifested in the locavore movement. The term "locavore" was coined in northern California by a group of women who committed to eating locally after reading Gary Nabhan's 2001 book *Coming Home to Eat*.[9] However, it was a couple from Vancouver, Alisa Smith and Jamie MacKinnon, who popularized the term with their book *The 100-Mile Diet*.[10] Local food has become a watchword of Vancouver cuisine, from the urban farming practised by Soul Food, an organization that grows food around the city and vends at Granville Island and local farmers' markets, to the fanciest restaurants in the city, such as the new and popular Farmer's Apprentice.

*The 100-Mile Diet* and locavorism seem to have done little to curb Vancouver's enthusiasm for coffee. Starbucks outlets abound, but the city also brims with high-end coffee shops offering vacuum brewing, individual pour-overs of single-source beans, and rare coffees such as Jamaica blue mountain. These spaces are also coveted as quasi-public meeting places or places to work for Vancouver's many self-employed urbanites. Vancouver coffee shops favour an exposed brick and polished wood aesthetic, and they are part of the coveted urban lifestyle of walkable neighbourhoods. A fair portion of this book was written in such places, fuelled with strong dark coffee and the odd sweet treat. Food at Vancouver's coffee houses is very much an accompaniment, but several offer a few baked goods or simple sandwiches or perhaps an artisan doughnut.

The spread of upscale urbanity in Vancouver has a dark side. As one of the world's most expensive cities, Vancouver is quickly evolving in such a way that makes life difficult for lower-income households. As Katherine Newman has discussed in her work on consumption and gentrification in Vancouver's Downtown Eastside, the huge increase in the number of new high-end restaurants in traditionally lower-income neighbourhoods can hurt existing residents. She notes that the influx of trendy restaurants and bars into the Downtown Eastside is associated with the displacement of lower-income and marginalized residents, and this can mean that these vulnerable groups are displaced from the city entirely.[11] Municipal efforts to protect lower-income housing are often undone by retail gentrification. Chefs come to the Downtown Eastside because of lower rents, and customers are willing to enter the "edgy" neighbourhood, changing its dynamics. Newman points out that gentrification in this case is packaged as urban regeneration, but the social mixing that occurs quickly excludes lower-income residents. Vancouver's dynamic food scene is too often available only to a subset of residents. Returning to the idea of sitopia, it is important to remember that culinary spaces can be exclusionary. Lower-income customers can be discouraged by high prices and upscale decor or staff attitude. Vancouver prides itself on being a sustainable "green" city, but often this label doesn't take social sustainability into account.

153

Vancouver sits at the mouth of one of the world's great rivers, and east of the city the river has created some of the richest farmland on the Earth. The Fraser Valley has an excellent climate, wonderful delta soil, and plentiful water. The university where I teach sits in the middle of this agricultural landscape, providing me with wonderful opportunities to conduct research. The combination of rich farmland and nearby metropolis has led to some interesting agritourism niches. The Fraser Valley is famous for its berries, particularly blueberries, raspberries, and cranberries, and farther up the valley Chilliwack is famous for its corn, and Agassiz is famous for its hazelnut groves. Farm markets function like *cabanes à sucre* in Quebec; farm stands in the valley present what has been called an "idyll"[12] or vision of rural life and cuisine. City dwellers can visit markets with petting zoos, u-pick fields, and farm stands serving local specialties. The Fraser Valley is also a popular spot for fruit wines.

Farther east the lake regions of the hot interior valleys are home to tree fruit and wine industries. The Okanagan Valley has evolved in much the same way as the Niagara region, with lower-quality cultivars being replaced by high-quality grape production. The Okanagan boasts a number of award-winning wineries and is still well known for excellent apples, cherries, and peaches.

West of Vancouver, across the Salish Sea, sits Vancouver Island, nearly Canada's westernmost province. This long, mountainous island is half the size of Ireland and was a separate British colony until it unified with British Columbia in 1866 in a somewhat tentative union. Mild and fertile, Vancouver Island has long fostered a strong agricultural industry and an excellent food scene. As in the Rocky Mountains, the island sports significant recreational landscapes, including the sweeping beaches near Tofino, which has swollen in popularity as a tourist destination for storm watchers, surfers, and hikers. The culinary landscape of Tofino highlights the best of Canada's cuisine; voted the best restaurant in Canada in 2014, Wolf in the Fog presents Pacific coast dishes such as a seaweed salad mixing daikon and local sea greens with fresh squid. A Szechuan surf and turf mixes short ribs and octopus with bok choy. SoBo offers elk kabobs, fish tacos topped with foraged forest greens and berries, and a feature salmon planked on alder. The abundance of local waters is highlighted all along the West Coast; at Tofino's sushi restaurant, for an extra fee, staff will walk to the end of a dock, grab a live crab from a pen, and make the freshest possible California roll.

Not all foods fit neatly into larger culinary trends. Farther down the coastline of Vancouver Island, Nanaimo shows few signs of its past as a coal-mining boomtown. It is a quiet place, popular with retirees, and since the 1950s it has been home to an active pulp-and-paper industry. Nanaimo is the site of a culinary mystery, however, and the home of one of Canada's best-known foods: the Nanaimo bar, a three-layer dessert. The bottom layer is an unbaked chocolate cake composed of cocoa and graham crumbs, the middle layer is a distinctive custard, and the top layer is a dark chocolate coating. The bar doesn't seem to fit the model of Canadian cuisine; it isn't fresh, local, or wild, and it's composed of branded products: Graham crackers, Bird's custard powder, Baker's chocolate, Fry's cocoa, and Tropic coconut. It's what Johnston and Baumann call a "norm breaking" food,[13] yet it is one of the best-known recipes that is truly Canadian. The Nanaimo bar is known widely, is identified by Hashimoto and Telfer as a rare example of a Canadian recipe,[14] and was voted the nation's favourite confection in a 2006 survey in the *National Post*. The bar is made in homes and sold commercially across the country. But how does it fit within our cuisine?

The bar does fit within a larger understanding of cuisine in 1950s Canada, particularly in the rural, blue-collar towns where mills and factories brought a level of prosperity and comfort. Quick refrigerator squares became popular in such places after the Second World War, when butter and sugar were once more available. My research team confirmed that the bar originated in Nanaimo.[15] The first known recipe was included in the 1952 cookbook of the Women's Auxiliary to the Nanaimo Hospital; the cookbook has three identical recipes for the dessert, under the names chocolate square (twice) and chocolate slice; the one closest to the modern bar was submitted by Mrs. E. MacDougall.

The bar can be classed as a dainty, a sweet treat served at home or public events such as church suppers, since it fits the model of these sweet, hand-held treats. Sherrie Inness describes dainties as frothy and cloud-like but extremely rich.[16] They grew out of the sweet and complex desserts that anchored the tables of the Victorian era; in some respects, the Nanaimo bar is a descendant of Charlotte Russe. Diane Tye notes in her exceptional book *Baking as Biography* that the dainties of the twentieth century were all similar. She discusses how dainties and baking in general were status symbols in her mother's social circle,[17] an attitude echoed by my own mother: the ability to entertain was expected, and the foods were often fancy and time-consuming to prepare.

The continuing popularity of the Nanaimo bar in an era when kale is an all but necessary menu feature is an open question, but Nanaimo is doing what it can to support its local contribution to Canadian cuisine.

For the past few years, Nanaimo has put together a suggested tasting trail that features over twenty variations of the classic bars. Minnoz restaurant offers a cheesecake version, Modern Café slings a Nanaimo bar martini, and Two Chefs Affair presents an ice cream version. There are gluten-free versions and raw-food versions and a deep-fried version. Island Farms sells a popular ice cream version of the bar throughout the region. Since one probably shouldn't eat more than one Nanaimo bar at a time, the trail can test even the most dedicated foodie, but it is no less calorie laden than Ontario's butter tart trail. And one can't eat kale only.

A trip south from Nanaimo down Vancouver Island takes one into Canada's mildest climates. A sort of foodie wonderland, the region boasts innovative farmers who cultivate non-Canadian exotics such as olives, tea, and lemons. Snow seldom touches the southern tip of Vancouver Island and the surrounding Gulf Islands, and the whole region seems to drift along in a bucolic eternal spring. Attempts at truffle farming are under way; if they are successful, I might have to settle in permanently.

At the southern tip of this special region sits the provincial capital of Victoria, a compact and pretty city best known for many decades as a quaint outpost of the British Empire. However, in the past decade, the Victoria of red phone booths and double-decker buses has given way to a quickly growing cosmopolitan centre. The high cost of living in Vancouver has spurred start-up technology firms to relocate to Victoria, and chefs have followed in turn. Victoria is rapidly becoming a hotbed of culinary innovation, with more in common with Portland than Portsmouth. The British influence still exists for someone looking for it: fish and chips are plentiful, and high tea is still served at the magnificent stone pile that is the Empress Hotel. Van Horne's westernmost hotel still lords over the waterfront, even though one can no longer catch a luxurious steamship for Hong Kong. The new Victoria, however, is much more a creature of Canadian cuisine. Restaurants such as 10 Acres Bistro Bar and Farm offer local ingredients identified by farm source or location of landing for their rich seafood selections, and down the street Little Jumbo has paired local cuisine with a commanding cock-tail selection, part of a strong bartending scene that has helped to fuel the spirit-forward classic bar experience. Other chefs are adding to the Pacific creole by blending local products with flavours from around the Pacific Rim, such as Foo, a small space in a box-like old garage where I ate several lunches while writing this book. Victoria is proof of how rapidly a city's culinary geography can change.

A resurgence of a different sort is occurring farther north. The Haida Gwaii archipelago is a special place with its own flora and fauna since this rugged, sea-swept landscape avoided glaciation during the last ice age. When I visited Haida Gwaii, I was amazed by the incredible rich-ness and beauty of the landscape, from the deep moss full of berries and mushrooms to the wide beaches with tidal pools and clam beds. The Haida Nation is proud of its culinary heritage, and one can find some interesting dishes there, including k'aaw, herring roe on kelp cut into squares and fried. K'aaw, which tastes refreshingly of the ocean, is a delicacy, as is the sea asparagus that grows abundantly on the beach. Other dishes include octopus, halibut, and the razor clams that grow abundantly on the tidal flats. These remote islands far from the bustle of Vancouver's coffee shops show a different side of Canada's cuisine. There is much to be found outside Canada's metropolitan areas, and it is to these less populous regions that I now turn.

157

9

# THE EAST COAST, THE PRAIRIES, AND THE NORTH

Beyond the western and central urban hubs of Canada lies a vast landscape with a varying deep cultural heritage, yet this rich hinterland does not always receive the attention that it deserves. The decline of Canada's far-flung rural regions was an almost inevitable outcome of Confederation as the more populous central regions dominated political and economic decision making. The eastern provinces of Canada were deeply divided over the question of entering Confederation since support was strong for a union of the Maritimes that would have created a robust colony of half a million settlers, but there were definite risks in joining with the much larger colonies to the west. Francophone Lower Canada had over a million citizens at Confederation, and Upper Canada was larger still. Could the East Coast colonies maintain their position in Confederation when they were so badly outnumbered? The centres of power in Canada shifted to the heartland, with Montreal and Toronto emerging as the economic and cultural powerhouses of the country. In the second half of the twentieth century, the resource-rich western provinces surged in population and influence, and now Calgary and Vancouver form a western focal point in Canada's culture. The lopsidedness a century and a half after Confederation is striking: 86 per cent of Canadians live in Ontario, Quebec, Alberta, and British Columbia, and it is understandable that the cuisines of these regions dominate the country. Canadian cuisine, however, is so much more than what is found in these four provinces. The remainder of the country attracts fewer visitors and lacks the economic base of the major cities, but it is home to some of the most wonderful elements of Canadian cuisine. This chapter explores these culinary traditions, many of which are quietly vanishing along with the towns and small cities that have supported them. This journey across vast distances begins in the far east, in a land of rock and mist, in the last province to join Canada: Newfoundland.

## NEWFOUNDLAND

As a researcher, I try to maintain a neutral approach to my fieldwork, but I must admit that I adored Newfoundland from the moment that I drove off the ferry in Port aux Basques. It is a harsh place, a cold and damp land of bare rock and dark, stunted forest. Everywhere the tortured coastline cuts deeply into the landscape. This vast and thinly populated island is a culinary outlier in Canada; with a homogeneous population, little immigration, and little agricultural production, Newfoundland maintains a "fortress cuisine," the term used by Duruz,[1] and it has changed little since the days that cod was jigged from small dories. This cuisine has deep roots and reflects the trade patterns of earlier empires in other centuries. The modern era of Newfoundland settlement goes back as far as 1497, when John Cabot landed at Cape Bonavista. The land itself was of less interest than the vast shoals of cod in the waters offshore, which might explain why the British didn't formally claim the island itself until 1583. Meanwhile, cod was taken in vast amounts and processed in seasonal camps, dried on wooden racks known as "flakes." These onshore "rooms" were not settlements but sites of temporary labour populated by the Basques, French, Portuguese, and of course British. By the mid-seventeenth century, the British, who preferred "dry cure" cod to "wet" cod processed shipboard, had settled the island and begun trading dried and salted cod with colonies in the Caribbean and ports in southern Europe.

Cod remains a defining feature of Newfoundland cuisine, though its dominance was shaken by the collapse of the fishery. Driver found that Newfoundland's early recipes were dominated by berries and cod, page after page of loving preparations for these simple local ingredients.[2] In my travels in Newfoundland, I enjoyed cod prepared many ways, beginning before I ever set foot on land. On the ferry, the dinner special was a delicate stuffed cod, a perfect white fillet wrapped around a savory bread stuffing. Little did I know how much of the herb savory I would encounter on the island! Beginning my first evening on the island I ate my share of one of the best-known Newfoundland dishes, cod tongues and cheeks, when I found the dish amid the gently decaying grandeur of the Glynmill Inn at Cornerbrook. Cod tongues are usually served with a side of tartar sauce, and despite the name no actual tongue is involved; rather, three fatty pieces of meat from the head of the cod (called the tongue and cheeks) are fried and served with scruncheons, small cubes of fried salt pork. Cod tongues appear again in more detail in the final chapter, but it is worth noting here that they are the sort of dish that develops in a society in which nothing goes to waste, and they weren't the only Newfoundland dish based upon the leftovers from the industrial processing of cod. The roe also has little value as an export product and is fried into a dish known as britches. Perhaps my favourite preparation was cod and brewis, also called fisherman's brewis (pronounced "broos"), a mix of rehydrated salt cod and soaked hardtack ship's biscuit drizzled with molasses. Cod is so popular in Newfoundland that often it is simply called "fish."[3] The quintessentially British dish of fish and chips is also widely served. Cod is a simple fish, though, and all of these dishes speak of a harder time, a cuisine based upon trade goods with long shelf lives and local products. Newfoundland traded salt cod for molasses, and though the sticky syrup is eaten on several dishes it is also brewed into the province's strong rum.

Fish dominates Newfoundland cuisine for a reason; farming is extremely difficult in the cold climate, particularly on the northern peninsula. In this region, some of the last incipient agriculture on the Earth is practised; along the highway, small pockets of rich soil are used to grow small patches of crops. The owners of the patches return occasionally to tend the lonely plots of vegetables. Mostly cold weather vegetables are grown; turnips, carrots, and a blue potato popular in the area for its hardiness. Angelica is also grown and was likely cultivated there by the Vikings, who first came to the northern tip of the peninsula at L'Anse aux Meadows. John Omohundro documents in *Rough Food* a lasting attachment to the starchy Newfoundland blue potato; his interview subjects preferred it even when other potatoes were widely available.[4] If vegetables are in short supply, berries certainly are not. Besides the widely used wild blueberry, the two best-known berries are the bakeapple, a delicate yellow berry with an astringent flavour, and the partridge berry, a small red berry known as lingonberry in Europe. Bakeapples are the most famous Newfoundland berry, though they are a northern berry and thrive in Labrador as well, where an annual bakeapple festival is held. At Auk Island Winery in Twillingate, I tried a light orange bakeapple wine, though I preferred the Sedna vodka made with water melted from icebergs. Farther north the crowberry appears; black and the size of a wild blueberry, this low bog berry has a deep and spicy flavour. At breakfast, I was served touton, a flat fried biscuit, with a good dollop of berry jam and a little molasses for good measure.

As I moved north, I encountered a selection of traditional foods. Moose is a popular meat in most parts of Newfoundland and often bottled and served in stews. These massive yet gentle animals were introduced to the island in 1904, and now they are almost too plentiful, the cause of regular traffic fatalities. Less common now are flipper pie and bottled seal flipper. This controversial food was a critical element of the early diet of Newfoundlanders since the seal hunt provided fresh meat, and thus vitamin C, during the coldest months of the year. Seal meat and seal products can be purchased at Bidgood's, likely the world's only large grocery store to specialize in Newfoundland food. It was there that I confronted the mystery of Newfoundland's summer savory head on; the store had a commanding display of the herb that I had been encountering across the island. Savory is often mixed with dried bread to create a dressing and then sprinkled onto everything, including poutine. No one could tell me why that particular herb is so popular in Newfoundland, other than it grows well there. In 1977, Pamela Gray noticed the same strange prevalence and could come to no more under-standing than I did.[5] Some food mysteries are deeply rooted, and the origin of Newfoundland's fixation on savory remains for a future food theorist to unravel.

162

When I wasn't eating, I was walking the streets of St. John's admiring the tidy wooden houses in every shade of pastel and taking in the vistas of the harbour and the bare rocks of the surrounding hills. I visited the Newman Wine Vaults where, for 300 years, port wine was brought from the Old World to be aged and bottled, a strangely long and arduous production chain. What I didn't find easily was the signature dish of Newfoundland, Jigg's dinner. I spent the better part of three weeks look-ing for it. It is a wondrous dish designed to maximize scarce resources. A boiled meal, it consists of salt beef, cabbage, carrots, and potatoes, or perhaps a turnip, and pease pudding, a solid mush of yellow split peas. It can also contain blueberry duff, a popular local pudding, and all of these ingredients are slowly boiled together in one pot, minimizing the need for cooking fuel. Jigg's dinner is usually made on Sunday, and it is extremely popular outside St. John's. One Sunday as I drove across the island I found (and smelled) Jigg's dinner cooking at several small gas stations that also served as tiny restaurants, but I was several hours early. I finally did have a premade Jigg's dinner at Bidgood's, though eating cold salt beef balanced on my lap in the rental car didn't quite capture the elements of a home-cooked meal. But, for the most part, it hasn't occurred to people that tourists might want to eat such a thing, and Everett noted that for a long time Newfoundland food was seen as unfit for tourism.[6] I finally managed to eat Jigg's dinner again on the boat to Labrador, and the meal was as promised: hot, filling, and deeply comforting. It helped that it came with a few slices of fried bologna, another interesting item in Newfoundland cuisine.

Until recently, Newfoundland's cuisine has garnered little attention outside the province. As Everett explains, the island's remoteness and late entry into Confederation has left Newfoundland with a marginal position in our national identity.[7] However, this is changing, and I might well have a better chance of finding a Jigg's dinner in northern Alberta.

163

Figure 9.1. A packaged Jigg's dinner at Bidgood's

This is largely because of the migration of Newfoundland residents to other areas of the country, particularly Alberta and Saskatchewan. Collapse of the cod fishery led to widespread unemployment, and many Newfoundlanders relocated to Alberta to work in the oil industry. As described in an excellent article by Sara Keogh, the population of Fort MacMurray is 30 per cent Newfoundlander and was growing rapidly until the recent downturn in oil prices. These workers miss their home ingredients; Fort MacMurray offers several Sunday Jigg's dinners, and there is an outlet of the Newfoundland chicken chain Mary Brown's, which offers chips with dressing. As Newfoundland chefs disperse further, foods once encountered only on the island are slowly appearing elsewhere. Thanks to a Newfoundland chef, cod and brewis have become available on Vancouver's Granville Island at the Culinary Canada restaurant, though the side of cabbage was raw, not boiled. As I write this, falling oil prices are slowing the flow of Newfoundlanders west, yet Newfoundland cuisine has at long last captured the world's attention. Raymonds in St. John's has won several awards, including *EnRoute* magazine's 2011 best new restaurant prize. And, true to the region, it serves cod.

## PRINCE EDWARD ISLAND

Time and fortune change all things, and by the time I reached the Maritimes they had long since ceased to be the centre of colonial life in British North America. When I visited Province House in Charlottetown, I largely had the grand building to myself, and I could almost imagine that little had changed since 1864. I had the feeling that the Fathers of Confederation had simply stepped out to attend another luncheon. Prince Edward Island is a dreamy place of small towns, long, windswept beaches, and stunningly red-soiled potato fields. There are strict limits to farm sizes on Prince Edward Island, keeping farm numbers high with nearly 1,500 individual farms. Potatoes account for over

164

half of farm-gate sales in the province. The potato is important nationally, of course, both as the supporting role in fish and chips and as the main ingredient of poutine. The potato is also the base for ketchup potato chips, an oft-cited example of Canada's culinary prowess. I decided to stop at the Canadian Potato Museum in O'Leary, which highlights the history of the potato and the evolution of the industry on the island, and it even has a hall of potato diseases. The highlight, though, was potato fudge, an all-around pleasant confection that deserves wider fame.

Potatoes and *Anne of Green Gables* might come to mind when one thinks of Prince Edward Island, but it is also a truly excellent place to experience Atlantic seafood, including lobster. Lobster is an iconic food of the entire region, but in Prince Edward Island it is both cooked to perfection and presented as a critical tourist encounter. Lobster is one of those strange luxury foods: it is a crustacean with a long body and muscular tail that does not immediately appear to offer much hope of a good meal. It has five sets of legs, the front set overdeveloped into fierce claws, and it is heavily armoured with an exoskeleton. This armour ensures that most tourists have to work hard for their lobster and usually leave a fair number of edible pieces behind. Lobster is only good fresh and is best steamed and boiled. The shells make a nice colourful and flavourful bisque. They are caught using traps that play their own role in the Maritime landscape, particularly the older wooden traps, often stacked rather picturesquely along docks and beaches.

The popularity of lobster has risen sharply over the years, though tales of lobster used as fertilizer on farm fields or as food for the poor are hard to verify since they are largely anecdotal. Tye explores the history of lobster in depth and notes that in the Maritimes lobster is largely the food of tourism.[8] Tasting a lobster is deeply associated with having experienced the "real" East Coast. Lobster sales exploded when the shipping of live lobsters replaced the canning industry—canned lobster is a weak substitute for the fresh version. Lobsters are caught in a two-month season, and Prince Edward Island brings up over 20 million pounds each year. Eating lobster may be a culinary rite of passage for many tourists; locals, on the other hand, tend to eat lobster in bursts. There are several regional lobster festivals and places where "feeds" are held. At such events, lobsters are usually served steamed with butter and no other accompaniment. As Tye writes, everyone eats more than one with the goal of satisfying her or his taste until the next year. Lobster suppers for tourists are much more elaborate; they usually feature lobster and butter, chowder, rolls, potatoes, vegetables, and pie. Sometimes potato salad and coleslaw are also served. Lobster suppers are very popular on Prince Edward Island and have become important fund-raising instruments. Potato museums aside, I spent a lot of my time on Prince Edward Island eating lobster and walking on long, sandy beaches. The lobster poutine at Charlottetown's Brickhouse restaurant was particularly well done, with a thick lobster bisque instead of the usual gravy.

## NEW BRUNSWICK

Lobster looms large on the mainland in New Brunswick as well, one of the least visited of Canada's mainland provinces. This is a shame, for it is a pretty place of rolling forests and particularly charming river valleys and coastline. The Bay of Fundy shore is captivating, and the lobsters there particularly sweet, perhaps because of the clean and cold water. Seafood dominates New Brunswick, as does small-town life. The small cities of Fredericton and Saint John are charming places. Canada's only truly bilingual province, New Brunswick draws on both French and British influences, and as a maple producer it offers a lovely maple pecan pie.

Some of New Brunswick's culinary highlights are covered elsewhere in this text, including the dulse of Grand Manan and the grand public market of Saint John, covered in Chapter 10. The seafood of the region deserves mention here, however. The coasts are known for their tiny Beausoleil oysters that grow in sheltered bays, and for Arctic char, salmon, haddock, trout, sole, crab, clams, and mussels. Scallops are also particularly large and sweet in New Brunswick thanks to the extreme tides of the Bay of Fundy and the nutrient-rich water that they provide. The land offers a few iconic dishes as well, including the fiddleheads mentioned in Chapter 3, made into an interesting local soup or more traditionally served with butter and a bit of vinegar. Less traditionally, they also pair well with quinoa. Land and sea come together in a salad of cattail hearts and shrimp that can still be found occasionally in the far south of the province. Near the resort town of St. Andrews, far down the Bay of Fundy coast where Canada abuts Maine, I stopped at Ossie's Lunch, a roadside diner offering fresh seafood since 1957. The lobster roll, buttery and sweet, came across as a weird hybrid of road food and high cuisine. Composed of fresh lobster meat mixed with a salad dressing and served on a white bun, lobster rolls are common across the Maritimes, and they are a popular tourist snack. Pies are also a common New Brunswick dessert; the slice of fresh rhubarb pie that I had at Ossie's Lunch was a wonderful mix of sweet and tart.

167

The Bay of Fundy shore is also an excellent place to sample one of Canada's lesser-known regional cuisines, that of the Acadians. The second of Canada's two groups of francophone settlers, the Acadians, in contrast to settlers in Quebec, were largely from urban areas of France. Settling first in Port Royal in Nova Scotia in 1605, these newcomers traded freely with the Indigenous populations, and many Acadian families have Mi'kmaq ancestry as well. Acadians settled widely from Newfoundland to Prince Edward Island, but their stay in the future Canada was not to be a peaceful one. In the 1640s, the Acadian colonies in Port Royal and Saint John were in a civil war, barely settled when France and England themselves went to war in 1654. English occupation of Acadian lands lasted until the Treaty of Breda was signed in 1667. The Acadians would enjoy their greatest period of expansion, though it was not to last.

The Acadians and their allies the Mi'kmaq resisted British rule whenever possible, but the British presence eventually overwhelmed the smaller population of Acadians, and in 1710 the British conquered

Acadia. The full-scale *grand dérangement* or "expulsion" of Acadians began in 1755; three-quarters of the population were forced from the colony. Some moved to the east coast of the United States, and a large number fled to New Orleans and surrounding regions, where they became known as Cajuns and established a distinctive cuisine. Others went back to France, some blended into Mi'kmaq communities, and many died in the chaos. Resistance was fierce and bloody; Louisbourg would fall in 1758, and its 3,000 inhabitants were deported to France.

At the end of the Seven Years War in 1763, Acadians were allowed to return to Nova Scotia in small numbers, though not to their former capital of Port Royal. Some returned to New Brunswick, where their influence is still found today. The Acadians drew heavily on Mi'kmaq ingredients, brewing spruce beer and crafting distinctive dishes such as *poutine rapée* (big potato dumplings filled with salt pork), chicken fricot (a stew of vegetables and chicken), and the common rappie pie (a casserole of crispy shredded potatoes, sometimes filled with clams). Rappie pie is a popular snack food in much of rural New Brunswick. A tourtière similar to that of Quebec is also found in Acadian areas. Another interesting dish is *poutine à trou*, a square pastry filled with cranberries, raisins, and apples. Interestingly, there is no evidence that the word *poutine* in Acadian culture is related to the word in Québécois culture. They seem to have evolved independently. These dishes can be scattered about New Brunswick and Nova Scotia, along with houses sporting the five-pointed nautical star that symbolizes Acadia.

168

# NOVA SCOTIA

Nova Scotia is defined by its coastline, a convoluted, windswept expanse dotted with picturesque settlements and long-standing culinary traditions. In the centre of the province's main peninsula sits Halifax, the largest city in the Maritimes and the cultural heart of the region. Established in 1749 to help cement Britain's hold over Nova Scotia,

Halifax is home to Dalhousie University, one of Canada's largest universities, and to many of the federal and provincial services for the region. Halifax has a cosmopolitanism not found in the rest of the Maritimes, and as a major port city it feels less isolated from the larger world. It also boasts more restaurants than the rest of the region combined. The culinary scene in Halifax is overwhelmingly centred on seafood, including lobster and scallops as mainstays, but also a generous array of haddock dishes, one of the few places where I've seen that fish given a chance to shine. The seafood rests with dishes that would be familiar to major cities and Canadian cosmopolitan cuisine, including fresh local seasonal vegetables, with influences from Asian and Middle Eastern cuisines. The aptly named Chive Canadian Bistro is an excellent example of this sort of take on Canadian cuisine. Halifax is overwhelmingly populated with people of British, Scottish and Irish descent, but there is also a significant population from the West Indies, and the occasional jerk dish and roti restaurant provide jolts of spice to the city.

169

Halifax is a lively city, known for music of all stripes played in small venues. On Friday and Saturday nights, the streets downtown are filled with students, locals, and tourists hopping from bar to bar and venue to venue. Such a place calls for an informal food that pairs well with nights of liquor and music, preferably something that can be eaten on the street. Enter Halifax donair. This well-known dish is the brainchild of Peter Gamoulakos, who opened the King of Donair in 1973. As a newly arrived Greek immigrant, Peter wanted to offer something reminiscent of his homeland, but he realized that East Coast Canadians were unlikely to appreciate the traditional Greek gyros, particularly the gaminess of traditional lamb. He created a new version of beef, spices, and breadcrumbs, retained the spit roasting and presentation in a pita, but also replaced the tzatziki with a mild sweet sauce based upon condensed milk; this sauce is the critical element in making a Halifax donair.

The donair has spread across the region, and variations such as donair egg rolls, donair pizza, and donair poutine are common. I even tried a vegan version based upon *seitan* at the Wooden Monkey. As promised, Halifax donair pairs well with beer, and after a few days of music, ale, and donair I was ready to head out along Halifax's coastline to experience life in the old and picturesque seaports that beguile many visitors to the province. Compared with Halifax, the rest of the province is sedate though rich in culinary history. Down the coast from Halifax, Lunenburg offers a few distinctive culinary experiences, along with a peculiar dialect of English. Although the town is now a quiet place, its history is long and filled with conflict. It was the first major Protestant settlement on the south shore, intended to drive out remaining Acadians and their Mi'kmaq allies, breaking treaties established between the Mi'kmaq and British. Lunenburg was raided repeatedly during this early period. During the War of 1812, the town became a centre for privateers commissioned to raid the Americans, and several bands set sail from the port. Later the town turned to the more stable yield of the offshore fishery, and it became renowned for the wooden boats built there.

Today Lunenburg is a popular tourist destination. The town is dominated by lovely wooden architecture and serves up its own set of local dishes. I went to Lunenburg to finally get a proper blueberry grunt, a dessert made by boiling sweetened blueberries in an iron pan on the stove and then adding biscuit dumplings. It might sound like a dessert best made in an oven, but the stovetop method took advantage of heat from the ever-present wood stoves in the area. Modern chefs toss the pan under a broiler to brown the biscuits a little, but boiled grunt is still popular. It is particularly good with ice cream. Also still popular is Lunenburg pudding, a large coil of beef, pork, and organ meat. Lunenburg sausage is smaller and sometimes served with sauerkraut and boiled vegetables. What I couldn't find available was perhaps the most famous Lunenburg dish, Solomon Gundy, pickled herring and onion. Interestingly, a dish of the same name is available in Barbados, though there it is a pickled fish pâté. Herringless, I ended my time in Lunenburg with a visit to the Ironworks distillery, set in an old blacksmith shop; it produces a truly wonderful blueberry liqueur, among other things. The renaissance of distilling and brewing is a recent phenomenon in Canada, and a rapidly emerging food trend across the country, and Nova Scotia was an early leader in this field.

Across the causeway in Cape Breton, one returns to Acadian influence, along with a heavy Scottish presence. I had my best piece of Acadian butterscotch pie at the truck stop in the middle of the causeway to the island; the thick custard was caramelized enough to cut the sweetness of the dish slightly. At Chetticamp, one can find Acadian *fricot* (a chicken and vegetable soup) and *chiard*, a roasted mix of potatoes, salt pork or bacon, carrots, and dumplings. This hearty food got me ready to drive the Cabot Trail, one of Canada's most scenic coastal routes. At the other end of the trail, I encountered another local oddity, the Cape Breton pizza burger, a hamburger bun with tomato sauce, cheese, processed sliced meat, and any other pizza-style topping handy. It has a lovely story of origin that might be apocryphal, involving hungry foundry workers toasting these little snacks on the edges of hot iron kilns. It is more likely that it was popularized by Paul's Food Factory in Sydney, which prepares them for sale in gas stations and corner stores, where they are purchased and then microwaved on the spot. The pizza burger is often washed down with a can of pineapple crush, a popular regional soda.

There are many other Nova Scotia food experiences worth noting. Tangiers is famous for *kat*, a type of pungent smoked eel, as well as finnan haddie (cold-smoked haddock), and in the amazingly beautiful harbour town of Digby one can enjoy the Digby scallop in its fresh state. Scottish oatcakes abound in bakeries and cafés, though I didn't encounter *clapshot*, the Scottish mixture of chives, turnips, and potatoes. Digby sits at the southeastern end of the Annapolis Valley, a sheltered region that once exported apples to all corners of the British Empire, an industry still celebrated in the annual apple blossom festival. Farming in the valley is again on the upswing, helping to fuel the fresh elements of the cuisine of Halifax. It is hard to say why the cuisine of Nova Scotia is so incredibly diverse; perhaps the convoluted coastline spurred these innovative yet local culinary creations.

## MANITOBA AND SASKATCHEWAN

Best known for their endless expanses of farmland, the Prairies host a subtle cuisine grounded in plains culture. A close look at the plains reveals a land shaped by the forces of great rivers: Saskatoon is bisected by the South Saskatchewan River, and Winnipeg sits at the confluence of the Red River and Assiniboine River. These rivers were the highways of the prairie region for Indigenous populations and settlers alike; at the point where those two rivers meet sits the Forks, a gathering place for thousands of years and now the site of a public market, a public orchard, the Canadian Museum for Human Rights, and other attractions. The rivers still dominate the space; as I walked along the river at the Forks Market, the great sheets of water slid by, passing north toward Lake Winnipeg. The market offers a good introduction to the foods of the prairie region, dominated by wild ingredients of the region and influenced by waves of settlement on the land.

The best-known prairie food aside from pemmican (discussed in Chapter 3) is the Saskatoon berry. A rich purple berry resembling a large blueberry, it has a deep nutty flavour when ripe. It carries some astringency that can be challenging at first, and thus the berry is best at its ripest. It grows on a large woody shrub and was a critical food for the Indigenous peoples of the plains. They ate the berries fresh and dried them into blocks, and they brewed the leaves into tea. The dried berries were reconstituted in the winter or used for pemmican. Today the berry is used for jams and pies, and most recently it has been marketed as a superfood rich in fibre and antioxidants. The city of Saskatoon is named after the berry, which gets its name from the Cree word *misāskwatāmin*.

We don't tend to think of water when we think of the Prairies, but the boggy riverlands and countless lakes of the region host other food species as well. The chokecherry is similar to the Saskatoon, though significantly more bitter, and it is best mixed with sugar as a jelly; in Manitoba, it is used to make a distinctive fruit wine. Cattail hearts take time to gather and are served as a delicacy that tastes rather like hearts of palm, and the most common fish encountered in the region are lake fish, particularly pickerel and goldeye. Manitoba is one of the few places in Canada where one can actually try pemmican, and bannock burgers (bannock with a slice of pemmican) are rising in popularity in the region. Bannock also appears in the unusual dish section 29, a beef stew with chunks of bannock mixed into it. On the Prairies, a section is a measure of land (one square mile), but the name is a bit of a mystery. In the prairie numbering system, sections 11 and 29 were designated for school buildings, so perhaps the dish began as a school lunch.

The Prairies were a popular destination for many different groups of immigrants early in the twentieth century. The Ukrainian influence on prairie life is still felt in many aspects of regional culture, including cuisine. The ninth largest ethnic group in Canada, the Ukrainians were encouraged to come to the Prairies in the late nineteenth century since the government thought that immigrants from a strong agrarian background were likely to succeed at carving farms out of the raw landscape. The immigrants brought standard fare such as perogies, cabbage rolls, and borscht. These staple dishes can still be found at local restaurants and in regional grocery stores, and they are popular at local festivals. Church groups often provide Ukrainian food at local fundraisers, and many events on the Prairies are scented by frying onions. Pickling also plays a large role in Ukrainian cuisine on the Prairies; sauerkraut and pickled cucumbers often accompany meals.

Another huge influence on the development of Manitoba resulted from the eruption of a volcano. On March 29, 1875, Mount Askja in Iceland shuddered to life, and the eruption that followed poisoned

173

farmland and killed animals. Nearly a quarter of Iceland's population left the island, and many of those people settled on the shore of Lake Winnipeg, in what was then Rupert's Land. The colony struggled through some hard winters but settled into a thriving life of farming and lake fishing. In effect a free state, though never a completely independent republic, New Iceland was eventually incorporated into Manitoba, and the town of Gimli remains the cultural centre for Icelandic Canadians. Even today, though they are largely dispersed, there are more people of Icelandic descent in Manitoba than anywhere else except Iceland. The Icelanders brought with them a love of strong coffee and a taste for pickerel. In Gimli, one can sample *fiskibollur*, or "fish balls," at Kris Fish and enjoy *kleinur*, a sugared doughnut, at the Reykjavik Bakery. And each week Ammas Tearoom serves *vintatarta*, a prune and cardamom cake that is perhaps the best-known Icelandic Canadian recipe. Every year Gimli hosts the *Islendingadagurinn*, a festival celebrating Viking and Icelandic history. At the festival, smoked goldeye and pickerel abound, and the *kleinur* come complete with sour cherry sauce.

174

Not all culinary influences on the Prairies have come from newcomers. The role of the Métis in Manitoba in particular is also represented in the cuisine of the region. The Métis arose out of marriages between French, British, and Scottish fur traders and Cree, Ojibwa, and Saulteaux women, predominantly in the Red River region of what is now Manitoba. The Métis manufactured pemmican for the fur trade, hunted buffalo, and traded furs themselves, and the women often cooked for the various European forts in the area. The Canadian government bought what the Europeans called Rupert's Land from the Hudson's Bay Company in the mid-nineteenth century and aggressively began to intrude on the Métis way of life. Through a series of rather one-sided treaties with Indigenous groups (but not the Métis), the Canadians took control of almost the entire region. The anti-French and anti-Indigenous British sparked fear and hatred, and rebellion came in 1869, spurring creation of the province of Manitoba. Métis leader Louis Riel fled into exile in the United States but returned in 1885 only to be defeated in the Northwest Rebellion. Life for the Métis under Canadian rule was hard, and they faced widespread prejudice that lingers today. Despite this adversity, they maintain a distinctive cuisine particularly evident in Manitoba; the annual Métis winter festival features tourtière, pea soup, pork and beans with bannock, and plentiful maple syrup.[9] Elements of each of these cuisines appear in small-town fowl suppers, public meals that highlight ham, roast beef, chicken, salads, pickles, and pies.

## THE NORTH

Canada's portion of the Arctic looms large over our national consciousness. Over 40 per cent of our land mass is contained in the three northern territories, northern Quebec, and Labrador, together forming an area larger than India but populated by less than half of 1 per cent of Canada's population. The North is also the only region of Canada where most communities have Indigenous majorities. Remote and nearly unvisited, the North boasts a culinary heritage still largely hidden from outsiders. However, as the world climate shifts and resource-hungry interests move north to the warming Arctic, the isolation of much of the North is changing, and protecting the foodways of this region in the future will require a concerted effort. Few visitors to Canada ever reach the North; the only easy ways to visit it are the train to Churchill, Manitoba, where polar bear viewing and aurora watching drive a small tourist economy, and flights to Yellowknife or Whitehorse. Accessing most other regions of the North is expensive and time consuming. Nunavut, the newest and most sparsely populated territory in Canada, has no road links at all to the rest of the country.

During my time travelling in the North, one glaring outcome of the remoteness of this vast region became all too obvious: food is scarce and expensive in many communities across the region, creating hardship for those who live in them. Fresh fruits and vegetables are often completely missing, and staples such as milk and eggs are very hard to come by. The North is a hard place in which to live: in many of the towns that I visited, the water was unsafe to drink, the weather can be extreme at any time of the year, and during certain seasons the insects can be intense. On one trip north, I stopped in Enterprise, Northwest Territories, only to be attacked by a cloud of two-centimetre-long, fly-like insects that the locals call "bulldogs." They bite large chunks out of the skin, leaving the victim bleeding and sore. Covered with blood and crying at how unprepared I was for the landscape, I retreated to my tent for a dinner of cold beans and beer. In the spring and summer, the North is filled with blackflies and mosquitoes, almost guaranteeing that the visitor contributes to maintaining the local ecosystem. The North is intensely beautiful, however, and worth a few insect bites. It is a place of vast horizons and sparse but grand landscapes. Wildlife is plentiful, and little sign of human habitation clutters the landscape. The cuisine of the North builds on the experiences of numerous groups of Inuit and Indigenous peoples who lived off the harsh landscape for thousands of years and incorporates a small number of southern innovations brought north by early settlers. Despite the hardships, my experiences exploring the coast of Labrador, James Bay, and the Northwest Territories are priceless. Northern Canada, at its best, offers one of the last great wild cuisines.

176

Yellowknife might not quite be above the Arctic Circle, but in summer there is so little darkness that one is almost always blinking under a vast bath of sunlight. The drive north skirts Great Slave Lake, crosses the Mackenzie River, and passes through the last free-roaming bison herds on the Earth. The animals meander along the road, backing up traffic. Giant ravens perch in tiny trees. The city itself is a great entry into northern cuisine, highlighting the dominant wild flavours. The best food that I ate in the North was in Yellowknife, and most of it was wild. At Bullock's, perhaps the best known of the Yellowknife restaurants serving local cuisine, one can choose from eight types of local fish, including the iconic Arctic char. Char is a delicate pink with a texture reminiscent of salmon but with a firmness that speaks of extremely cold water. Pike and pickerel are also on the menu. The "surf and turf" equivalent features a choice of muskox, bison, or caribou, and the restaurant offers a "stewtine" that pairs these exotic meats with french fries. Nearby, the Wildcat Café serves a few local items, including a selection of lake fish and fresh bison burgers in a heritage log cabin with communal tables. If the food sounds heavy, it is: a reminder of the sheer calories needed to survive in such a harsh climate.

In addition to the meats mentioned above, seal still plays a huge role in northern life and is often eaten as *quaaq,* semi-frozen meat sliced very thinly with an ulu, the curved knife used in the Far North. Muktuk, cubes of epidermal fat from the bowhead whale, was traditionally also eaten frozen, but now it is often deep-fried. In a nod to globalization, it is also often dipped in soy sauce. Zona Starks describes *quaaq* as likely to vanish, along with other high Arctic fare such as willow leaves in seal oil.[10] In the mid-Arctic, particularly in former gold rush centres such as Whitehorse, the influence of California gold miners still resonates, particularly in the presence of sourdough bread. In Whitehorse, one can also find the slightly resinous and sour pickled spruce tips, a food eaten fresh by Indigenous groups in the area.

The cuisine of the high North was often met with disdain by many Europeans, a pattern repeated in many areas where survival was difficult and communities poor and marginalized. As Lisa Markowitz describes in her work on the foodways of the Andes,[11] neglected subaltern foods can be used to distance poor and rural populations. This distancing cuts both ways, however; in the early twenty-first century, Edmund Searles documented how the Inuit of the newly formed territory of Nunavut use food to distinguish themselves from people of European descent. Those Inuit who live in town trade fuel and ammunition to those who hunt, sharing desired bush foods. Searles found that the foods thought to be most "Inuit" gave warmth (often they had a high fat and caloric content). One of his interviewees described eating walrus gar as the equivalent of "doing steroids."[12] One exception is bannock, which appeared in the region in the 1950s but has been adopted by both Inuit and Europeans.

Another interesting expression of marginality is the strange silence surrounding the role of the chest freezer in northern life. During my travels in the North, I was struck by how much of the food consumed there is either imported from the South prefrozen or harvested from the wild and then frozen. The ubiquitous presence of the freezer in rural Canada and the North in particular was noted by Martin Hand and Elizabeth Shove, who describe it as an orchestrating node around which multiple aspects of consumption and provision converge.[13] In the North, the freezer might contain seal, caribou, berries, or chicken fingers and french fries from the South. Rural Canadians use the freezer as a key tool for food storage, particularly in areas where trips to the store are difficult or where food is barged in only a few times a year. I like to think of the freezer as a grocery store of last resort, the place where one can find a meal when the weather is too bad for travel or when money has run short.

Interest in northern cuisine is growing in Canada, even though few people ever venture north of the Arctic Circle. The wealth of wild foods in the Far North presents an opportunity for those who seek new products for the broader world market. Most recently, the University of Saskatchewan has been working on improving wild varieties of the haskap, a northern berry harvested from the blue honeysuckle. Shaped like a large irregular blueberry, the haskap is increasingly popular for its raspberry/blueberry flavour and its antioxidant properties.

The North exerts a pull on some people. My time in it has been limited by time and funding and the realities of travelling vast distances in a difficult landscape, and each trip leaves me wanting to go back. I wonder what it would be like to take the train to Churchill, on the shore of

178

Hudson Bay, or to drive the Dempster Highway north over the Arctic Circle. When the heat and noise press in on me, I think of the North and take solace in the knowledge that there are still places at the edge of the map to explore.

179

# PART III
# CANADIAN CUISINE LOOKS FORWARD

·IO

# FOOD AND PUBLIC LIFE

I was sipping a latte at the Java Moose in the Saint John City Market in
New Brunswick, waiting for the fog to clear. Outside, the city played
hide-and-seek in the mist; glimpses of lovely architecture appeared
only to vanish again into the gloom. I didn't mind waiting. The market
and city were quiet and peaceful, and the coffee was good. A great public
market is more than a place to buy food: it's a place to linger, a place
to meet, a place to observe. Public markets are quintessential sitopias,
food places of the highest order. The renaissance of the public market
in Canada corresponds closely to the increasing interest in food specifically and livable cities generally. Although public markets might appear
to comprise a small segment of the Canadian food landscape, the fall
and rise of public markets, farmers' markets, and street food are worthy
of discussion. In Canada in the twenty-first century, the public realm is
once again alive with food. This resurgence is an excellent example of the
living nature of cuisine. In the chapters of this section, I discuss new and
emerging food spaces in Canada and close with a look at what the future
might hold for our iconic foods. However, to understand the presence of
public markets in today's Canada, we must begin in the past.

Built in 1876 in Second-Empire style, Saint John City Market is one of the oldest and most beautiful markets in North America. Well known for its heavy timber roof that resembles an overturned ship from inside, it also has some excellent innovations that make it a great place to sell food, such as the sloping floor easily hosed down at the end of the day. The market operates under an even older charter that runs back to the eighteenth century, to the days when Saint John was a bustling major city. Although the city has quieted over time, the market still has a good selection of cafés, butchers, fishmongers, and green grocers. The market, for all of its loveliness, was threatened with talk of demolition in the 1960s and 1970s, but now it is preserved as a national historic site, daily market bell and all.

The story of public markets in North America largely mirrors the story in Saint John: a tug-of-war between those who love market spaces and those who see them as dated and old-fashioned. This debate has continued for a century at least, but on a longer time scale the marketplace is one of the oldest human institutions. As a public space only loosely affiliated with religion or politics, it has long played a role in the crafting of civilization. Marketplaces serve multiple purposes in a city and provide the opportunity for people to meet and mingle. The key misconception about markets has been that they aren't needed in an era when supermarkets are widely available. The critical flaw with such an argument is that a market's public space achieves other goals besides selling food and sends ripples through the surrounding urban fabric. Unlike a grocery store, a market acts as a public space, an experimental space, and ironically a true culinary space; one can shop and eat at the same time, sampling new foods. A public market is more a sitopia than other forms of food retail. Entire districts take on a culinary air, and command a real estate premium, with a market at their heart. Markets also shape cuisine; they allow for the sale of small lots of new crops and products not yet ready for the massive commitment needed to launch a food product into the global provisioning system. Markets are incubators, and chefs know it;

I often encounter chefs from well-known restaurants browsing markets early in the morning. The pink blueberries under development at Mann Farms in the Fraser Valley, for example, will likely end up debuting at area farmers' markets. Sadly, the knowledge that markets are important to the wider urban fabric came too late to save several of our beautiful market halls, lost to wrecking balls in the urbanist dark ages of the 1960s and 1970s. Some of the best food places are just memories.

Public markets are surprisingly understudied given the rising general interest in them. Linda Biesenthal's *To Market, to Market* notes that the market is a central component of city building; she points out hieroglyphs in a tomb at Sakkarah that depict scenes that would be recognizable in today's markets.[1] Such spaces are found in almost every culture, but Canadian markets are descendants of the golden age of the market town in the fifteenth century, when almost every major British and French centre hosted market days and elaborate halls were erected to host vendors. Since markets occurred on only a few days each week, these halls acted as multi-use spaces; along with churches, they were often the most important gathering spaces in the town. One could hang out at the market without buying anything, and it was a space that encouraged, to some degree, a mixing of classes. As Helen Tangires notes in her seminal work on market spaces, the activity of buying and selling food has shaped our cities and towns for centuries, and even if a market is private it has public goals and creates a public space. She suggests that markets have a "unique spirit and character—qualities that no other form of food retailing has yet been able to match."[2] This spirit of encounter is echoed in the work of Alfonso Morales, who notes that "markets are liminal places where social rules or expectations are suspended or replaced in favour of a variety of experiences inclusive of trade but also where identities are explored and non-economic agendas are promoted."[3] Markets are crucibles of culture.

The role of the market is contested, however. The move to clear markets out of cities predates the supermarket and in North America can

185

be traced to the thoughts of Charles Mulford Robinson, one of the continent's first well-known urban planners. He thought that markets were dirty and obsolete (I suspect that he had servants to gather his food), and by 1910 he was arguing strongly that food was outside the scope of urban planning. He created some tidy but hungry urban landscapes. This attitude was typical of the City Beautiful Movement. Morals of the time were offended by the simple truths of the human animal: to feed ourselves can require spaces of dirt, blood, and death. Markets enjoyed a light resurgence during the war years, but in the 1950s and 1960s they fell to the wrecking ball across North America as cities themselves seemed obsolete. Many Canadian cities lost their markets; in 1968, for example, Mayor of Montreal Jean Drapeau and his council attempted to close the city's six publicly owned (and very profitable) markets. According to the media at the time, council believed that "the large urban market has had its day and is no longer viable,"[4] a thought shared across the continent. Public protest saved two of Montreal's beautiful markets, Jean-Talon and Marché Atwater. The others were casualties of "progress."

As noted by Biesenthal, the rise of the market beginning in the early 1970s was nothing short of miraculous; public markets in many places were at the vanguard of urban renewal. A pivotal moment worth noting was the redevelopment of Seattle's Pike Place Market: in 1973, the market was renovated rather than razed, to great success. This model inspired many other cities, including Vancouver, which built its grand market on Granville Island from scratch in 1979. This interest, however, didn't occur in a vacuum. Markets were resurrected by the ongoing and growing interest in food, particularly in the regional, seasonal, local, and wild cuisine that requires the freshest ingredients.

I have had the great privilege to spend significant research time studying the role of public markets in our urban spaces, and almost without exception Canada's great public markets are urban; one of the few outliers, St. Jacobs Market in Elmira, Ontario, combines elements of a public market and a farmers' market to provide a venue for the purchase of low-priced, bulk farm goods; for many years, I went to St. Jacobs to stock up on dark amber maple syrup and bushels of apples. Sadly, the market building at this interesting site burned to the ground in 2013, but its popularity assures that it will be rebuilt.

St. Jacobs is an outlier in terms of its low prices; one of the few urban markets that still offers good deals on bulk produce is Montreal's Jean-Talon Market, which has an excellent selection of local produce and a surprising amount of wild food. In the years that I have been going to Jean-Talon, prices have been creeping up, and delicious, ready-to-serve food is on offer, reflecting a number of different culinary traditions and backgrounds. Serving a multicultural neighbourhood, Jean-Talon is also one of the few places where one can find bulk local produce more common to immigrant cuisines, such as okra and eggplant or even fresh chickpeas. In her study of this market, Sarah Musgrave found that it reflects the promotion of place as a marker of authenticity.[5] Jean-Talon highlights Quebec's dedication to fresh ingredients. Multiculturalism is accommodated alongside local traditions, such as the use of wild blueberries and ground cherries. On one visit to Jean-Talon, I found the market filled with bushels of Roma tomatoes and basil, waiting to be slowly cooked down into sauce for the winter. The smell was enchanting.

My studies of Marché Atwater[6] represent my first explorations of Canadian cuisine, and this book might never have existed if I hadn't become so enamoured with that grand market hall. I kept going back, watching the seasonal shifts in this amazing public space. Atwater is an astounding building, constructed in the true spirit of the market as a public agora. Built as a make-work project in the early years of the Great Depression, Atwater included a 12,000-person hall above the market where key debates on Canada's role in the Second World War and Quebec's place in Canada were held. The building was designed by Ludger Lemieux in the art deco style, and it is considered one of his finest structures. With two floors of permanent shops, and a large outdoor vendor area, Atwater responds to the needs of its neighbourhood and

187

the seasons, providing spring bedding plants for the numerous backyard gardens in the area and then a rush of lovely seasonal foods. In the fall, an astounding array of pumpkins is available, catering to a long tradition of celebrating Halloween in the once mostly Irish neighbourhood. As Christmas approaches, butchers provide special orders, and most of the neighbourhood heads to the market to get a Christmas tree. In the depth of winter, the market and in particular its bakery serve as an indoor town square. Atwater now caters to a much higher-income community than it once did, reflecting gentrification of the neighbourhood following revitalization of the Lachine Canal. These two grand markets of Montreal, Atwater and Jean-Talon, are keystones in the ongoing invention of Québécois cuisine.

Quebec City's fairly modern public market deserves mention since it is one of the few markets in the country that mainly sells raw food, most of it unprocessed. When I visited it, the market was overflowing with fresh produce, including fresh *gourganes* (fava beans), maple products, wild blueberries, and a plethora of variations of duck. What is amazing

Figure 10.1. Marché Atwater

about this market is its dedication to fresh food despite the huge number of tourists who wander in. The market overflows with fresh oysters labelled by region and maple sugar in blocks, and perhaps it is the only market in North America where one can buy cassoulet for two in a can.

Ontario boasts several excellent public markets. Ottawa's Byward Market building is rather small, with a few interesting restaurants and a good bakery. I lived near Byward for several years, and what I came to appreciate was that it sits in what is likely the best market district in Canada. The streets around the market proper are filled with culinary enterprises, and the streets adjacent to the market building are wide enough to allow for farm stalls that offer fresh local produce in season. The market is an event; people go to shop and then stay to eat a meal or browse surrounding shops. For a long time, Byward was also the only place where one could get a beavertail doughnut in the depths of winter without putting on skates and hitting the canal.

Farther south, Toronto's St. Lawrence Market is a high-end market: the surrounding neighbourhood treats it as a rather fancy grocery store; specialty meats are a centrepiece of it, as are exotic Canadian specialties such as lox and caviar (not to mention the peameal bacon discussed in Chapter 7). St. Lawrence Market is at the heart of a rapidly expanding residential district catering to those seeking a walkable and livable urban environment, and a new north market building is under construction.

189

A couple of prairie markets are worth mentioning. Calgary's new public market is a good place to sample Alberta's big sky cuisine, complete with a focus on excellent and plentiful meats. Rising wealth in Alberta and increased interest in local cuisine have created the customer base needed for this ambitious project. In Winnipeg, the Forks Market is an interesting study in urban renewal; it is built on reclaimed railway land, and it was hoped that it would stir interest in the city's moribund downtown. Cut off from the heart of the city by a railway embankment, the Forks struggled in its early years, but recently it has been invigorated by surrounding construction, including an inn and the Canadian

Museum for Human Rights. And the Forks has always been an excellent place to find prepared foods such as perogies and Saskatoon berry pie and to pick up some wild rice. The market also highlights local grains.

Granville Island Public Market in Vancouver is famous for its seafood and is unusual for its large size and popularity with tourists and locals alike. The market square, open to an ocean inlet, feels a bit like the city's back porch. The market began as a bit of a dream, an attempt to clean up a brownfield site, open up the waterfront, and liven up the city's culinary scene all at once. Karen Johnson called the city a "meat and potatoes" place,[7] but Granville Island changed that. The market opened in 1979 on the disused industrial island to almost immediate success. It introduced the city to fresh bagels, cappuccino, and fresh flowers.[8] The market continues to bring Vancouver a world of fine food; in the past number of months, I have browsed past Canadian caviar, Australian finger limes, fresh *shiso* for sushi, and young ginger perfect for stir-frying. These exotics tend to show up in local restaurants: *shiso* mojitos were popular in 2014. Innovative stores continually pop up on the island. Masa Shiroki makes Canada's only local sake at Granville Island using rice grown in the nearby Fraser Valley.

As Vancouver's premier tourist attraction, Granville Island highlights national cuisine. Smoked salmon and maple syrup are easily available, and the Edible Canada bistro offers poutine, Newfoundland cod and brewis, and other tastes of the nation. This market, once seen as an unlikely experiment, has been described as so iconic that no place epitomizes city life on the West Coast as much as Granville Island,[9] and geographer David Ley states that the market there is the quintessential public space in the postmodern city.[10]

If resurrection of the Canadian public market is notable, resurgence of the farmers' market is nothing short of miraculous. Farmers' markets, which traditionally involve producers selling directly to buyers on an established market day, had all but disappeared in North America following the Second World War. Those that remained were often in

rural areas where they served as sources of cheap, bulk produce. Jane
Pyle summed up the plight of markets nicely in 1971, arguing that the
few remaining markets, propped up by financial supports of one sort or
another, would likely disappear.[11] This seemed inevitable until the rise
of California cuisine changed everything. Suddenly, chefs such as Alice
Waters were seeking out farmers who grew the best and freshest crops
locally, and the idea that the global food system might be sacrificing taste
and quality began to take hold. Small-scale farmers could garner premi-
ums for their products by selling them directly to customers, providing
encounters with rural life along with their vegetables. The exponential
growth of farmers' markets has in turn greatly influenced cuisine by
fuelling interest in fresh, local, and seasonal foods.

Defined as a market at which farmers, growers, or producers from
a defined local area are present to sell their products directly to the
public,[12] the farmers' market has helped to fuel a niche interest in local
foods. The markets spreading across the landscape are not the farmers'

191

Figure 10.2. Granville Island Public Market

markets of old. Now numbering in the hundreds, most farmers' markets in Canada come complete with country musicians, a rectangular hay bale or two for atmosphere (though few farmers still use such bales), foods ready to eat, and non-edible crafts that speak to a rural lifestyle hard to find in the industrial reality of modern agriculture. Farmers' markets are certainly a place to buy and try food, but they also present an Arcadian vision far from the daily reality of most rural citizens.

At their best, and farm kitsch aside, Canadian farmers' markets function as food spaces friendly to small-scale businesses and are filled with people open to culinary experimentation. Markets draw culinary early adopters, and food adventurers have helped to drive the market boom. I have enjoyed many of this country's excellent markets and seen the many ways in which they drive changes in Canada's culinary scene. Nova Scotia's markets offer products from the province's burgeoning artisan distilling industry, and Quebec's markets offer varieties of produce that don't scale up well for industrial production. Toronto has several excellent markets, including the Brickworks, which reuses an abandoned industrial space to offer fresh greens and vegetables. Kitchener's market offers Mennonite-made preserves and baking, and the prairie markets offer the best of the underappreciated Saskatoon berry. In British Columbia, markets offer an array of multicultural dishes made with local ingredients; on Mayne Island, I had an excellent South Indian curry made with kale and a wonderful take on the croissant doughnut. At BC farmers' markets, one can sometimes find Chris Hergesheimer and his hand-ground Red Fife wheat, which makes an excellent biscuit. Foraged food is common at markets across the country.

Farmers' markets have become a necessary piece of street furniture for the global city. I sit on the board of the Vancouver Farmers' Markets, an organization that runs eight markets in the Vancouver area, with a focus on fresh local food. Demand at the markets is relentless, and the new Vancouver Food Policy calls for twenty-three markets, one for each neighbourhood.

I am a great fan of market spaces, but there are problems with the extreme optimism of the potential for market spaces. Markets provide only a small percentage of food in the urban food system. Attempts to scale up regional provisioning run into the rural imaginative space that I mentioned above. Markets are often framed as providing an "authentic" experience for consumers; however, if the ideal of authenticity can only be established and verified by the producer-as-seller entering into face-to-face transactions, then authenticity becomes a limiting concept and a problematic ideal for local producers.[13] Canadian farmers' markets are also not representative of the multicultural nature of our country. As Natalie Gibb and Hannah Wittman note, the local food movement in British Columbia is white and affluent, even though 40 per cent of farmers are people of colour.[14] However, there is also a much older network of roadside stores, initially founded and still predominantly supplied by Chinese Canadian farmers. Prices at farmers' markets are high, bringing into question some of the enthusiastic claims that such markets can improve health outcomes in low-income areas.

Markets are not the only culinary spaces enjoying a resurgence in Canada's cities; street food is also making a remarkable comeback. For much of the twentieth century, the most interesting thing about street food in Canada was its near absence. In cities across the country, streets sported only the occasional hotdog. In a world where many cities are defined by their lively food carts and stands, North Americans in need of a quick meal usually had to turn to a fast-food restaurant. The lack of street food evolved in two waves: the xenophobia and social engineering theories of the early twentieth century created a first wave of street food–hostile bylaws, and the postwar period saw a general separation of uses through bylaws and zoning that made it all but impossible to find food on the street. Street food, however, is a hallmark of city life and a major part of many urban economies.

The growth of street food in Canada is an outgrowth of a larger North American movement originating in the food carts of Portland

and the food trucks of Los Angeles. Street food is an important part of city life and will find a way to exist anywhere that it is not expressly forbidden. Portland now has hundreds of food carts clustered in distinctive pods where people come to enjoy commensal meals. In a study of these pods, my team discovered many factors that help to make Portland a great street food city: the block size is small, the city is walkable and human-scale, and there is a general effort to encourage the creation of an agora. What was interesting was the almost total lack of fast food in Portland: with so many options available, chains can't compete.[15] Much of the interest in street food has come from would-be vendors and consumers, driven in part by mass media. With shows such as *Eat St.* and *The Great Food Truck Race* airing on the Food Network, and the serial *Street Food around the World* on the National Geographic Channel, potential participants are exposed to a world of excellent street food.

Canada's largest cities are working to create a street food–friendly environment, though this effort has been hampered by decades of hostile regulation. Vancouver and Calgary have been the most successful, perhaps because of the west's libertarian undertones, better weather, or proximity to Portland and Los Angeles—two cities that provide good examples on which to draw. Vancouver does require that all menu changes be approved, and it mandates that vendors try to serve healthy local foods,[16] but it has been generous in growing the program, and as of 2013 it established the first Portland-style food truck pod in the downtown core. Initial experiments with food truck festivals and allowing trucks to cluster together at the winter farmers' market were wildly successful, drawing hungry Vancouverites into long rainy lineups. There are now over 100 food carts and trucks on city streets. Occasional food truck festivals draw thousands of people.

Montreal's street food experience is just beginning. A strict ban was lifted in the spring of 2013 to allow a pilot program of food trucks with dishes that, in the words of council, must add to the city's reputation as a high-quality culinary destination. At first, I was skeptical;

even buttoned-down Ottawa has a few trucks selling poutine. However, Twitter reports of the new trucks mention pulled pork sandwiches, foie gras poutine, lobster rolls, and *gulab jamun*. Most of the trucks are run by established restaurants, a pattern common throughout Canada. In Portland, food carts tend to be stepping stones to successful storefront operations, but in Canada it tends to go the other way as well. Time will tell if Montreal's trucks can survive in a highly regulated environment, but the initial results seem promising.

In the country's largest city, street food is becoming more established after a disastrous first attempt at loosening bylaws against street vending. In my five years in Toronto, I didn't really notice the absence of street food; in comparison with the other three largest cities, Toronto is blessed with a stunning array of hole-in-the-wall restaurants serving cheap cuisine from every part of the globe. But there was a general feeling that a diversity of quick, tasty street food would be a good addition to the city. In 2009, Toronto began a pilot project called Toronto à la Cart, which remains a cautionary tale for any city trying to encourage street food. Before Toronto à la Cart, street food was limited to a few hotdog vendors serving rewarmed hotdogs on street corners; the program added a limited number of licences for other foods. The city had its hands in every aspect of the program; it assigned locations, approved menus, and insisted that vendors use large and expensive city-built carts. The licences were $15,000 annually, and the carts were $30,000 each. Designed by committee, the carts weighed 360 kilos and couldn't be towed, yet vendors weren't allowed to leave them in place overnight. Vendors weren't allowed to put up photos of their food, and all menu changes had to be submitted for a lengthy review.[17] Considering that in Portland carts could be built out of just about anything, and had to be mobile only in theory, as well as the fact that food choices there were limited only by the imaginations of vendors and a few basic food safety rules, Toronto's program seemed almost Kafkaesque. Within two years, city staff recommended that the project be cancelled. A consultant called

195

in to conduct a postmortem noted that street food is an entrepreneurial business that cannot be institutionalized. If the city wants to see more diverse food offerings, then it must be prepared to accept the eccentric character of street carts.

Toronto didn't re-enter the world of street food until 2012, when potential vendors and foodies embarked on a social media campaign called the Toronto Street Food Project. This new program is much more promising, though options are still heavily controlled, and rules are still designed from a hegemonic Western perspective that hinders innovation and stacks the deck against foods from other cultures. However, trucks are now allowed to vend on private property, a key element of Portland's success.

Public markets and farmers' markets continue to grow in popularity and will likely continue to drive Canadian cuisine and serve as key tourist attractions in major centres and smaller regions of the country alike. Food systems are never static, however; even Granville Island, arguably Canada's best-known public market, is about to undergo its largest change since its opening as Emily Carr University leaves the island for larger quarters. Reimagining the space will reshape Vancouver's food scene. Farmers' markets continue to multiply, and the real limitation on them will be a lack of farmers producing the products that do well in them. Although there are young farmers hoping to enter the industry, the barriers posed by Canada's extremely expensive real estate market greatly hinder them. Farmers' markets might have to move away from the rural imaginative of each stand being staffed by a local grower.

The future of street food in Canada is less clear; certainly, public demand for street food is there, and the success of Vancouver's program demonstrates that street vending can coexist with the rigid regulations of the modern municipal state and the food safety rules that favour large-scale producers and fixed-location restaurants. No Canadian city is likely to open its street food market to the degree found in Portland, so we will likely continue to see strict government regulations on what can be sold where. Both markets and street food also contribute to gentrification since they are highly desirable pieces of street furniture. This is not to say that we shouldn't develop such enjoyable features of urban life, but they will have implications for neighbourhood affordability.

Another missing piece of the food system that could greatly affect the development of Canadian cuisine is the presence of food hubs. A food hub combines food aggregation from small farms, commercial kitchen facilities, and/or market spaces. Food hubs have become popular in the United States, where they launch many food entrepreneurs by providing both infrastructure and advice. Food hubs can also solve the problem of overtaxing farmers at markets; a food hub that I visited in Ohio connected farmers to consumers through the use of QR codes and a clever mobile phone application. Farmers made occasional appearances and presentations but for the most part stayed on their farms. The United States, however, is very entrepreneurial and has a much larger support structure in the form of the USDA. Several food hubs are now in various stages of operation in Ontario. Alison Blay-Palmer and her colleagues at Wilfrid Laurier University in Waterloo have studied these food hub movements extensively, noting the need to connect people within "communities of food" by providing improved small-scale processing, transportation, and distribution infrastructure.[18]

As I was finishing this chapter, I had the good fortune to attend an unusual event: the opening of a new public market. Victoria's newest food space occupies the first floor of the old Hudson's Bay Company building, which has been reused as a condo development known as The Hudson. The development is typical of a new trend in Victoria, and indeed in other small cities near the country's major metropolises, such as Kitchener near Toronto: young professionals priced out of major centres and retirees wanting a slower pace of life are rejuvenating downtown cores once crime-ridden and nearly abandoned. If this market succeeds, then it will break a century and a half of bad luck with public markets in British Columbia's capital. The first large public market there was built in 1881, when a section of Chinatown was cleared to create a space. The market never thrived, however; farmers preferred selling their produce in the street, and the grand brick building with a glass skylight ended up housing the fire department, a train station, and even, for a while, the city morgue (likely a first, and a last, in the history of public markets). When the building was torn down to create parking in 1959, there was little market activity left. Most Victorians had moved to the surrounding suburbs.

The new Victoria Public Market opened during a time of rapid gentrification and repopulation of the downtown core, and it addresses its audience as a group of refined consumers with money to spend on living well. Stalls sell Saltspring Island artisanal cheese, fresh fish, and expensive cuts of meat, and Sutra, an outlet of Vij's empire, focuses on selling ready-made curries. The mantra of fresh, local, and wild is evident, and condo dwellers upstairs are lucky enough to have a Parisian bakery below their floors. In the alley behind the building, space has been created for the Wednesday farmers' market, thronging with customers when I visited it trying to get a sample of the raclette on offer. Inside, the exposed columns and industrial feel mirror Granville Island, whose runaway success continues to shape market architecture in Canada forty years later.

Response to the Victoria Public Market is a reminder that markets of all sorts are on the rise in Canada. Although they provide only a single-digit market share of Canadian food, they are strong tourist attractions, help to shape the national cuisine, and are growing rapidly. Their role in the sitopia is many-sided. They offer spaces to innovative newcomers, introduce customers to new foods, and provide spaces in cities to bask in the sights and smells of the food system. Once close to vanishing, now much loved, Canada's public markets are keystones in the structure of its cuisine.

## I I

# BETWEEN PLACES

anada is vast, and long journeys to get to work, see a loved one, or enjoy recreation are part of our national psyche. Canada is the second largest country on the globe; 6 per cent of the Earth's land area is Canadian, and our coastlines touch three oceans and are by far the longest in the world. Our status as a large country, however, doesn't really capture why solitude is embedded in our national identity. Most of Canada is a lonely place; its 35 million people have a population density of about 3.3 citizens per kilometre, one of the lowest in the world, and of course they are not spread out evenly. Eighty per cent of Canadians live in a handful of urban areas. The bulk of Canada is a wilderness of hard winters, rugged terrain, and wondrous nature. It is largely unvisited by tourists, save for a handful of specific locations such as the iconic national parks.

Canadians are drivers; a million kilometres of paved and unpaved roads thread across our nation. Only 17,000 kilometres are expressways, and many regions cannot be reached at all without additional trips by ferry, train, or plane. We are a nation that considers a frozen river a reasonable roadbed, and the distances between our cities challenge even the veteran driver. It is 8,000 kilometres from Vancouver to Newfoundland and 5,000 kilometres from Toronto to Yellowknife. Canada's roads are long, remote, and lonely. Yet Canadians, particularly those in rural areas, take to the road readily, routinely making trips of hundreds of kilometres. Many coastal Canadians accept ferry travel as a way of life, and many other Canadians fly between cities on a regular basis. And on these trips travellers must eat. Each modality adds its own elements to Canadian cuisine, and in the interstitial spaces on the road, in the airport, and at the ferry terminal we find another side of Canadian cuisine.

Cuisine on the road is not just a scaled-down version of cuisine in towns and cities. When in motion, we tend to be more conservative eaters, opting for comfort over adventure. We also tend to establish places along routes that we travel regularly that become parts of our sense of place, way stations to fuel ourselves and, in the case of driving, our vehicles. These way stations serve as familiar grounds where we can shed the discomfort of moving through space. If we are travelling on a route for the first time, we might ask others for suggestions of way stations (in person or online), or we might fall back on a chain restaurant. Or, as my father likes to do, we might look for a place with the most long-haul trucks parked nearby. No matter the mode of travel, we need to eat, and sometimes we eat needlessly to pass the time or create some comfort in the vast space that we call our nation. Tim Edensor observes that we quickly gain familiarity with the landmarks on our routes and hesitate to stray from known paths.[1] This might reflect the human need to mark progress through space or just the need to feel as if we are in familiar territory in a strange landscape. Once we establish a way station, we tend to visit it repeatedly.

From a personal point of view, this chapter touches on a reality of my research. To date, I have driven roughly 40,000 kilometres in my exploration of Canadian food; I have spent far more hours on far-flung highways than hours sitting in front of a meal, browsing a store, or exploring a farm. My memory of this travel is oddly fragmented, and bursts of intensity frame the quotidian act of putting kilometres behind me. The travel was punctuated by the surprise of an unexpected encounter, such as a glorious day of driving on the James Bay road, the only paved route to Arctic waters. The landscape is a vast emptiness of rivers and stunted taiga, the road largely empty. I pulled over at a small lake to stretch and get a better look at a well-crafted beaver lodge and found the surrounding hillsides covered in tiny blueberries, perfectly ripe. I picked far more than I needed since there was something magical in such a bounty in such a harsh place. That spot will forever be a place of comfort in my imagination.

As I had small culinary encounters that couldn't easily be tagged to a place other than "the road," I began to see the food of interstitial spaces as contributing in a small way to cuisine. Defined by the *Oxford English Dictionary* as "an intervening space," the word *interstitial* comes from the Latin *intersistere*, which means to "stand between." Our time in the air, on the water, and on the road stands between events in our lives; depending on what awaits us, we usually traverse these spaces with a mixture of anticipation and impatience. Geographers have only recently turned their attention to such spaces, and many have a low opinion of modern spaces of transportation. Marc Augé's work *Non-Places* remains a defining text in this area; Augé coined the term "non-place," highlighting the aura of transience that to him eroded any sense of place in such spaces. He describes non-places as stripped of deeper meaning.[2] He frames modern spaces of travel as "marchlands," drawing on the old term for the blurred boundaries between countries in the time before sharp national borders. Augé's non-space reads as a hostile and alien environment, which might explain why he says so little about people who travel in interstitial spaces as an end in itself and why he says so little about the food found in them. He frames non-spaces as often solitary, "a world thus surrendered to solitary individuality, to the fleeting, the temporary, the individual."[3] Even if we are not alone in these spaces, our interactions are highly circumscribed. And, for the solitary traveller in Canada, one can be more alone than most people on the globe ever become; one can literally spend hours driving hundreds of kilometres from the nearest outpost of humanity. One can find the world and all of its complexities boiled down to the road, the weather, the car, and the self. It is like being at sea, the car a tiny bubble of technology in a sprawling wilderness.

The idea of non-place makes me slightly uncomfortable, though I have to acknowledge the impact of this path-breaking book on the field of mobility studies. The idea of non-place or placelessness is left rather ambiguous by Augé; in some ways, his argument depends on an audience privileged enough to have travelled the geography of roads and air networks that supports modern civilization. The idea that somehow interstitial spaces are not places has been oddly resilient; for example, Daniel Boorstin calls spaces of travel "pseudoplaces," though he then contradicts himself by noting that hotels are used to transgress usual norms of behaviour since they are located away from local entanglements.[4] This might qualify them as places outside daily life, but they still exist as real places, operated by real people living real lives.

Edward Relph delves much deeper into the lack of a sense of place in his 1976 work *Place and Placelessness*. Relph notes that places are experienced not as independent, clearly defined entities but in a context of setting, ritual, people, experience, and other places.[5] This allows the same place to be different to different people and helps to explain one of Tim Cresswell's critiques of Augé,[6] a critique that I share in my discomfort with the term "non-place." The so-called non-place can be someone's workplace or home and thus certainly not placeless. The traveller's gaze doesn't share in the quotidian nature of the truck stop, for example, and doesn't necessarily notice what sort of day the ticket agent in an airport is having. Because we don't tend to encounter service workers at thrilling moments in our lives, we often erase them from interstitial landscapes as well. Even on the open road we likely encounter all sorts of non-human actors, but unless they are particularly charismatic (e.g., I vividly remember the skunk that sprayed my car's front end before it disappeared into the scrub east of Moose Jaw) we edit them out. As Relph notes, being lived in confers some authenticity on even the most trivial and unrelentingly uniform landscapes. However, he hedges his bets slightly, noting that there is a geography of places, and a placeless geography, and that one of these two landscapes is greatly preferable to the other. Jon May and Nigel Thrift continue in this tradition, arguing that non-places are also non-events; things don't happen in them.[7] However, the journey as a whole is often measured in time, and we tend to classify a journey as uneventful, a middle ground in which surprise (both the bad, such as a car accident, and the good, say an excellent roadside meal) doesn't happen. In this model of journey, place is created only when one stops and only if something of note occurs. In this erasure of the interstitial, the foods of these spaces are lost along with everything else. Our presence in the interstitial space gives it a real and personal sense. Our lives don't stop while we are in motion, and interstitial or not, if we spend any amount of time in a space, eventually we need to eat. What I am curious about isn't whether we eat while we journey, or whether way stations are important in our individual lives, but whether road food plays any role in our national cuisine or helps to shape our identity as Canadians.

203

At first glance, most food that one eats in motion seems to fall into the category of fuel rather than high cuisine, but there are glimmers of culinary culture when we enjoy a meal on the road. As John Jakle and Keith Sculle claim in their comprehensive look at North American road food, "the making and remaking of identities takes place in the contact zones along the policed and transgressive intercultural frontiers of nations, peoples, and locales."[8] Between our origin and our destination, we tend to be reflective; the world shrinks to our immediate surroundings and interactions. The foods found in these places reflect this immediacy, this simplicity. And the food at a way station has its own identity, whether the way station is a favourite truck stop, the *casse-croûte* with the best poutine in Quebec, or the Tim Hortons in Whitecourt, Alberta, where I once found a good number of townsfolk involved in a rollicking debate with travellers over local politics. Way stations help us to give form to our disconnected lives.

The narrative of the journey is as old as storytelling, and one popular form of food exploration involves the car as a trope for linking a series of culinary experiences. One of the most popular of these shows is *Diners, Drive-Ins, and Dives*, hosted by chef Guy Fieri on the Food Network. In each episode, Fieri explores three far-flung food experiences, travelling in his red convertible at the opening and closing of each segment, creating a mythic landscape populated by hand-crafted abundance for the clever diner willing to go off the beaten track. Fieri is a sort of high-cholesterol Ulysses whose explorations mesh with the idea of the food trail explored in previous chapters. However, his popularity is also a result of increasing interest in eating on the go. It seems that we are eating more often when in interstitial space; Neil Wrigley and Michelle Lowe note a rise in food in airports, gas stations, and similar convenience landscapes.[9] This might reflect an increase in "grazing" behaviour among travellers or simply entrepreneurs filling a need. In interstitial space, the place-making agent is not always the eater; the person cooking or serving the food also plays a critical role. This can involve creating a unique place, as in the roadside attraction; a cozy and nostalgic place, as in the diner; or even a familiar place, as in the chain restaurant. And many of these spaces are defined by the automobile.

Canada's mobility landscape is currently centred on the car. Although our country was built by the railway, we have turned away from trains and fully embraced automobiles as our central mode of transportation. Car culture and the admittedly brutal architecture that it can sometimes create are not often celebrated, but for better or worse they completely shape modern life. Driving isn't just about people; it can be viewed as an act that moves two bodies, ourselves and our cars, across great distances. When we drive, we become what Mike Featherstone describes as "a hybrid, collective, cyborg organism" of human and car,[10] and that hybridity shapes the geography of convenience offered to us.

The motorized landscape contributes to our sense of place, and roadside cafés, truck stops, and diners add to our sense of national identity. In the early days of the highway, motorists ate at the occasional roadside inn or tearoom, or they took their chances with restaurants in towns on the way. However, this need to chase down food didn't mesh with their vision of the car. As Featherstone notes, an early draw of the car (given that towns were walkable) was freedom from the constraints of socially structured time and space, allowing spontaneous picnics in the woods, for example. The car is also associated with speed, of course, a speed that the early trains simply didn't have. Driving off the highway to hunt for a place to eat didn't fit well with the ideal of the human-car hybrid, and an entire geography of convenience arose around the rest stop, where human and car could both find fuel and perhaps a little sleep. Ideally, these spaces were located near towns but not in them to allow for the greatest flow of traffic. However, a town had to be nearby since rest stops required workers. Darrell Norris wandered the interstates to study what he called "numerous anonymous places."[11] In his study of "exit morphology," he found that roadside rest areas have to balance convenience with choice and ease of access. In Canada, rest stops can be random conveniences or more orchestrated collaborations among large chains to provide fuel, food, and lodging.

So what forms do way stations take? In general, they can be divided into the categories of roadside stands, truck stops, diners or drive-ins, roadside spectacles, and chains. The stand is provisioning at its simplest, a small shack or lean-to selling some food item. One of my favourite areas for shacks at their most basic is on the Gulf Islands in British Columbia. Numerous small shacks sell home baking and fresh produce to passing motorists. Larger stands have kitchens and larger menus; I stopped at Ossie's Lunch near Bethel, New Brunswick, on a windy day to see if it could possibly have "the best seafood in North America," as its sign boasted. The cod and chips and the lobster roll were good, and the fresh pies were excellent; the rhubarb pie had a freshly baked perfection.

I spent a good part of the meal trying to weigh down everything on the picnic table with small rocks to protect it from the wind, another typical Canadian roadside experience.

In Quebec, the *casse-croûte*, which translates roughly as "snack bar," is a small stand that typically serves roadside food. Usually named after their owners, these stands are found on secondary roads, and sadly they are not as common as they once were in rural areas. *Casse-croûtes* often encourage mixing between locals and travellers, for they serve as open-air town squares in some small towns. On rare occasions, they offer traditional dishes, though in general the menu leans toward heavy, fatty, comfort food, perfect for calming the nerves on a strange highway. Some of these stands are near local attractions, such as lakes and playing fields, thus drawing on two ready sources of business.

A much more organized business model is the truck stop, which needs special mention since long-haul trucking is so central to the movement of goods in Canada. Many of the major fuel companies operate truck stop restaurants, including the Irving chain, Petro Canada, and the now-vanished Voyageur restaurants with their signature red roofs operated by ESSO. In the Prairies, Husky stations are known for their hearty hamburgers and generous portions of pie. The truck stop at midnight is an oasis of light in a sea of darkness, a place to grab food and coffee before moving on.

The next common form of Canadian road food is the diner, in many ways similar to the truck stop. In many cases, the only real distinction is that a truck stop is usually attached to a fuel station. As discussed in Jakle and Sculle's seminal history of roadside dining, the diner is a product of the road, rising out of the soda fountain and drugstore lunch counter. They argue that diner food has roots in fairground food, which must be fast, cheap, and easy to eat.[12] Diners have dropped in number greatly with the rise of fast-food chains, but a significant number hang on, serving a standard fare that draws heavily on nostalgia for the early age of the intercity highway. They present a version of home cooking deeply

206

associated with comfort, along with a bright environment of plenty. My favourite diner in Canada is tucked into the Chilliwack Regional Airport, just off the Trans-Canada Highway. Its slogan is "I Fly for Pie," and its dozens of flavours of pie have lured more than a few pilots over the years. It rotates through all of the classic pies, from the berry pies, to the cream pies, to the pecan and pumpkin pies. It also serves an all-day breakfast and a range of diner meals such as hamburgers and sandwiches, and it even roasts its own turkeys. Diners draw heavily on an earlier cuisine largely scorned now; salt, fat, and sugar are the dominant flavours. The Airport Coffee Shop is a single restaurant, and some diners are part of small regional chains of a few outlets. Other chains are larger, such as the Irving chain on the East Coast, though they might also be considered truck stops. The Irving cafés offer regional cuisine, and I had a lovely Acadian butterscotch pie at the Irving station on the causeway to Cape Breton, and for many years the Jigg's dinner served on Sundays at the St. John's Irving station won high acclaim from travellers.

The diner has retreated under the advance of chain restaurants, which now dominate our major highways. Although it has been mentioned earlier in the book, I can't discuss Canadian road food without discussing our best-known national chain, Tim Hortons. Recall that Penfold described doughnut shops as "a passing-by kind of business,"[13] which captures the nature of a way station well. Tim's began in Hamilton, also a crossroads for traffic between Canada and the United States and a convenient stopping point on the way to and from the Niagara region. However, Tim's doesn't fully control the roadside market.

In British Columbia, the White Spot chain remains popular. This burger chain is a Vancouver icon, from the mysterious "triple 'o' sauce" on its burgers to the small cardboard "pirate paks" that it offers children. White Spot was founded by culinary entrepreneur Nat Bailey, and the first stand-alone store in 1928 was also the first drive-in restaurant in Canada. Cars were becoming widespread by then, but eating in a car was still a bit of an adventure. The White Spot drive-ins were popular

207

throughout the 1950s and 1960s, particularly among teenagers looking for a dating venue away from supervision. Bailey is credited with the invention of the car-hop tray, which allowed the drive-in diner a little extra comfort.

As suburbanization spread, so did White Spot restaurants, but full-scale franchising did not occur until the 1990s after the boost of Expo '86, where White Spot was the host restaurant of the BC pavilion. The presence of such a strong local chain limited the penetration of international chain restaurants in British Columbia, and White Spot remains a popular spot on road trips. And no one has yet figured out for sure what is in the sauce.

Finally, Canada has a few unusual roadside way stations, a phenomenon found in North America and Australia almost exclusively. Jakle and Sculle also note that there have always been "whimsical" roadside stops,[14] though they have been few in number. These sites serve as way stations, and there is a small collection of them across the country. In Ontario,

Figure 11.1. I enjoy a White Spot burger in my car.

the Big Apple near Colborne has been drawing people off Highway 401 since 1987. Aside from the world's largest fibreglass apple, the site offers a tasty apple pie served to those passing through. The Big Apple is a rare spot of interest on what might be one of Canada's most monotonous highways; almost all of the food available on the trip is provided at international chain restaurants located in service centres far from towns. The Big Apple provides a reasonable place to stretch and grab a quick jolt of sugar. Apple pie is better known, of course, as a central part of American culture, but apples are also a staple of cooking in Ontario. In the Prairies, there are a surprising number of oversized attractions, including the world's largest Ukrainian Easter egg in Vegreville; on the West Coast the beaches of Tofino are a popular weekend getaway, and many people stop for a quick lunch on their way at Coombs. A sprawling tourist attraction there is known as the place with goats on the roof. It also claims to have invented the pastry known as the "bee sting," a honey-drenched Bavarian cream concoction. But the main draw is certainly the sod roof and its curious residents.

209

For remote coastal communities, travel on Canada's ferry fleets is a way of life. British Columbia's ferry system is the second largest in the world, serving forty routes that vary from short crossings to two-day voyages into some of North America's most rugged and remote coastline. East Coast ferry routes are just as critical; ferries join Newfoundland's road network to the rest of the continent with long crossings, and other ferries connect Newfoundland to outlying islands and the east coast of Labrador. Ferries also supplement the bridge to Prince Edward Island and connect remote islands such as Grand Manan and Anticosti to the rest of the country. As places to eat, these ferries and their terminals are part of Canada's foodways. They are also, of course, lifelines for shipping, and often they are critical links in the food security of small communities.

The main routes of the BC ferry system link the region around Vancouver with Vancouver Island, and these routes are popular with tourists visiting the more accessible regions of British Columbia. For visitors and residents alike, these runs with their crossing times of an hour and a half to two hours provide another outlet for Canadian cuisine. Although the main cafeterias are run by White Spot, they also feature local specialties such as salmon, fish and chips, poutine, clam chowder, and the Nanaimo bar. The Vancouver-Victoria run features a much more elaborate buffet service that specializes in "West Coast cuisine," with salmon, British-style roast beef, and fusion dishes such as sweet-and-sour spare ribs and butter chicken. What is interesting is that many locals eat on the ferry, even though they could bring their own lunches if they wanted. The cafeteria is a way station, used as a refuelling stop and a floating commensal space. White Spot burgers on board have strengthened this ritual; they are familiar since White Spot has a sense of familiarity developed by the chain over the years.

In the case of Canada's ferry systems, both the waiting areas and the

210

Figure 11.2. The Big Apple

boats themselves serve as way stations on one's journey. Phillip Vannini writes extensively about the role of BC Ferries in coastal life in *Ferry Tales*. He notes that the ferries are not just a means of conveyance but also a means to a unique way of life.[15] Eating on the ferry, he claims, is an example of travel as performance, an embodied expressive action and interaction. This is another good example of eating separately together, when a large group of strangers in a confined space unite into a temporary group of "ferry travellers" before going their own ways once again. The food helps to ease the shift in mode from the freedom of the car to the confinement of the ferry.

Although less explicit in their desire to serve regional cuisine, the ferries of the East Coast provide similar experiences. On the six-hour crossing to Newfoundland from Sydney, Nova Scotia, a good way to spend the time is to enjoy the high-quality food served in the restaurant. The stuffed cod and scalloped potatoes were a good introduction to the cuisine of Newfoundland; other travellers write of cod tongues, Jigg's dinner, and cod and brewis on the crossing. I did notice that on the Newfoundland boats the locals tend to bring their own food, except for the truckers. On the crossing to Grand Manan, the ferry cafeteria was serving clam chowder, a moose stew, and a rather interesting deep-fried clam bar.

The ferries of Canada shape cuisine in other ways as well. In British Columbia, the ferry system's hub-and-spoke model creates what Cresswell calls "mobility constellations."[16] Because boats don't travel between minor islands, each island tends to have its food specialties. Less food likely moves between islands than in the time before the ferry system. In some cases, the ferry dominates the food system. Vannini describes one such run. In Ocean Falls, which has only one store, most people have to order their groceries in bulk to be shipped in on the weekly ferry. This greatly limits the role that fresh vegetables play in the food systems of these communities. The same ferry serves the town of Klemtu on Swindle Island, which is particularly food-insecure. When the ferry pulls in on Sunday locals board en masse to enjoy a hot meal, eat fried chicken, and load up on milk and fruit from the cafeteria. The recent downgrading of this ferry run threatens food security in these far-flung communities.

In the case of the ferry system, the terminals where the boats dock are interstitial spaces as well, places that regulars on the ferries know intimately. Some of the terminals are located in towns and shape the local retail landscape to reflect the need for quick meals. In Horseshoe Bay near Vancouver, some people phone for pizza delivery, and in more remote locations people prepare food on camp stoves while waiting. In many of the better-serviced locations, small businesses sell food at the terminals themselves; these services include a small public market, a food court, a bakery, and espresso bars. On the East Coast, the major terminals have small restaurants to serve customers as they wait for several hours to board the Newfoundland ferry. One of my favourite parking lot food experiences occurred on Mayne Island in the Gulf Islands of British Columbia. In the ferry parking lot, Village Fare operates out of a steel shed, offering excellent barbecue and pies, along with retail sales of smoked meat to islanders. The owner also owns a similar stand on Galiano Island and commutes between his two enterprises by speedboat.

One of the more remote crossings in Canada ties Labrador to Newfoundland and is a lifeline bringing food to the communities there. As I waited to make the crossing, the hamlet of St. Barbe, Newfoundland, filled with transport trucks lining up to board the MV *Apollo* for passage across the Strait of Belle Isle. Drivers, many of them tired from epic journeys from shipping terminals in Halifax, lazily drank coffee or beer as I waited to be directed to the dock. The feeling of the frontier was real; none of the usual tourist niceties was on hand, and locals rolled their eyes as I fumbled for tickets. All around me, people with tasks more critical than academic exploration were consumed with moving as much food as possible back home to a hungry population. Private vehicles were filled to their roofs with flats of canned goods and sacks of flour; a trip to the big island was an opportunity to avoid the extreme cost of food on Canada's farthest frontier.

The MV *Apollo* is an interesting study in the creative reuse of resources. Built for the run between Finland and Sweden, the ship is ice-hardened, critical for the Labrador crossing. However, it is much larger than is really needed for the run: it can hold well over 1,000 people, and most trips across the strait serve a few hundred at most. The lounges are strangely empty, while the staterooms are filled with broken and discarded furniture. The decor speaks of a different place and age, the disco and main dining room shuttered and silent. The small cafeteria was hopping, though, and since it was Sunday I got a chance at last to eat a hot Jigg's dinner. Most of the families brought extensive lunches, but the truckers and I got a heaping plate of potatoes, boiled peas, carrots, cabbage, salt pork, and a little shredded turkey, all swimming in salty gravy. The boat limped across the strait (one engine was out of service), and whales and icebergs drifted past the windows.

213

For southern Labrador, this crossing is serious business. Almost all of the region's food is brought in on the MV *Apollo* in the summer or on the icebreaker that makes the winter crossing from Cornerbrook only once a week. Aside from these few runs, the south shore is linked to the rest of Canada by air and the Trans-Labrador Highway, 2,000 kilometres of rough gravel through one of the world's most remote wilderness regions. I ate my salt pork slowly, watching icebergs slide by the boat, marvelling again at the vast regions of Canada strung together with fragile links of steel and asphalt.

Before the roads, Canada was linked by rails, and though the train and its cuisine no longer play much of a role it is worth considering how central trains once were to Canada's culinary landscape, both as a means of moving food and as a place to eat regional cuisine. One catches glimpses of a time gone by on Canada's few remaining long-haul train runs, including the "cross-country" *Canadian*, which, sadly, crosses only from Vancouver to Toronto. I recall having a pleasant trip on the

*Canadian*, mainly because of the commanding views from the dining car, ever changing but always grand. The cuisine of the railways was mentioned earlier in the text and is mainly an element of our history. However, "silver and blue" class on the *Canadian* still carries some elegance (it's equivalent to first class but named for the colour scheme in the cars), offering regional cuisine and wine as the great expanse of the wilderness slides by.

For most Canadians, a continental crossing is done by air, and conditions in the country's airports have improved markedly. Early in my career I suffered through an unfortunate snow delay in the Winnipeg International Airport. I wasn't actually going to Winnipeg; I was on one of those interesting flights that crosses the continent in a dreaded "milk run" of multiple hops. So, through the whims of weather, I was stuck at YWG overnight, with the meagre collection of restaurants long closed. It was a hungry and lonely night as I crammed myself onto a hard bench, famished, a howling, snowy darkness between me and the rest of humanity.

The change in global airports since that night has been remarkable. Although food on the plane has faded from laughable to non-existent, airports themselves, in many cases, have settled into what Justine Lloyd calls a "postfunctional" focus on making them pleasurable places to spend time.[17] The food in these new spaces can be quite good and is often carefully crafted as part of a larger regional branding strategy. The revamped non-place is presented as a useful place for leisure and work. In *Aviopolis*, Gillian Fuller and Ross Harley claim that airports are gradually forming a global archipelago, new spaces cut loose from national borders.[18] As part of this international grey zone, Canada's airports can be seen as gateways and thus offer interesting sites of presentation for Canadian cuisine. This opportunity is still only partly realized, but airports do help to drive the iconic status of maple syrup and vacuum-packed smoked salmon. Many a traveller has landed back in her home country with a box of maple-leaf-shaped syrup cookies wedged

214

into her luggage. On my previous few trips overseas, I noticed that the racks of duty-free items now offer a selection of berry products as well, and I suspect that this variety will continue to grow.

Eating in the airport is also evolving, and in major centres it is no longer something to be dreaded. Celebrity chefs are opening establishments in major airports, and Canada is expanding its offerings. In a 2013 Daily Meal contest identifying the best airport restaurants around the world, Vancouver's Globe@YVR made the top twenty-five. It is located in the Fairmont Hotel inside YVR and specializes in Pacific Northwest cuisine. The current seasonal dinner menu features wild mushroom soup, Qualicum scallops, cedar-roasted salmon, and Fraser Valley duck breast, among other specialties. The dessert menu features a chai-spiced carrot cake, the Fairmont's traditional sticky toffee pudding, and a selection of BC cheeses. Its fish and chips are beer-battered, and the beer comes from a local brewery. Globe@YVR is a far cry from the vending machine meal that I made do with in Winnipeg, and though it is an extreme example airport food in general in Canada is trending in the same direction. YVR also boasts outlets of several Vancouver chains and plentiful sushi. In Toronto, YYZ, once a notorious food desert, has opened new terminals with a dozen or so passable food options. In Montreal, visitors to the airport can enjoy a branch of the well-known Brûlerie St-Denis and the Quebec fast-food chain St-Hubert. The day might come when the airport offers a passable representation of the nation's cuisine.

The food that we encounter when travelling continues to evolve. Although such meals might seem to be a minor part of the culinary landscape, because our country is large and our centres of population are widely scattered, culinary way stations can define a particular route for generations of travellers. Diners will continue to be nostalgic favourites, and the power of Tim Hortons to promote regional foods nationally will continue to shape our cuisine. Although food choices along the major highways are largely dominated by chains, the demand for higher-quality food will likely shape what is available in roadside

215

service centres as well. After all, even ten years ago, the idea of eating a good meal in an airport would have been laughable. Way stations contribute to the national cuisine, and this link is becoming stronger. They can be spaces of waiting, or places of refuge and refuelling, but in general they serve comforting food that eases the sense of being alone in a vast landscape; to go back to the idea of eating separately together, we take comfort in knowing that we are travelling with others, even if all we share are a few moments together eating poutine in a windy parking lot.

# COMING HOME TO AN UNCERTAIN FUTURE

On September 12, 1864, George Brown was in a low mood, slightly ill and missing his bride. His letter to Anne that evening barely mentioned the hospitality showered on the delegates as they argued for Confederation in Halifax.[1] The weather was likely not helping: the *Morning Chronicle* of the next day noted that "the rain fell in torrents." The paper also commented, however, that the "choicest edibles and the best viandes" were presented to the visitors,[2] and the *British Colonist* from a few days later called the dinner at the hall of the Halifax Hotel one of the most successful banquets in the history of the city, a meal "got up in excellent style."[3] Today we would call the actions of the founding fathers networking, and as momentum for a broad union grew their efforts were increasingly met with warm receptions. Each banquet brought the idea of Canada closer to reality, and the evening in Halifax was one of the grandest of all. Although largely skimmed over by a pining Brown, this banquet was notable in one other way: he kept the menu.

I learned of the existence of the Halifax banquet menu near the end of my travels and immediately wanted to see it. Printed on fine linen, the menu had managed to survive the ages among Brown's letters and papers and had been given to his biographer, James Careless, by the Brown family as a gift. Careless had then passed it on to Massey College at the University of Toronto, where it hangs in the small formal dining room. There it played a part in Canada's literary history. Robertson Davies, the founding master of the college, got into the habit of telling a ghost story each year at the college "gaudy night," and one year he drew his inspiration from the menu, creating what is probably the only culinary haunting in Canadian history. In his story "The Charlottetown Banquet," Davies sits down to a spectral recreation of the meal with none other than John A. Macdonald and then is so distracted by the food that he forgets to ask the founding leader of our country anything of importance.[4]

On a sunny afternoon in the small dining room of Massey College, free from ghostly influence, I could see why Davies was distracted by the spread of dishes summarized in the menu. There are over thirty items of food listed, enough for hours of dining, all matched with different types of alcohol. The bill of fare begins with mock turtle soup and then moves into a fish course featuring salmon and mackerel sauced with buttered lobster. There are six entrees, beginning with *petites bouchées à la reine* (a puffed pastry usually topped with mushrooms), followed by dishes featuring veal, rabbit, lamb, and fowl, and ending with *timballo di macaroni*. As if this list could somehow leave a founding father wanting, yet other items follow: sirloin, mutton, turkey, chicken, ham, and corned beef, then a second course of partridge, wild duck, lobster salad, galantine, plum pudding, jelly, blancmange, Italian cream, genoise, a pastry assortment, ice cream, plum cake, and, yes, Charlotte Russe. As the librarian and I replaced the menu in its place of honour on the wall, we both wondered if lunch might be in order.

Although undeniably grand, the Halifax banquet is immediately identifiable as belonging to a different age. Turtle soup is no longer the height of culinary fashion, and the entire meal provides far more meat than the

218

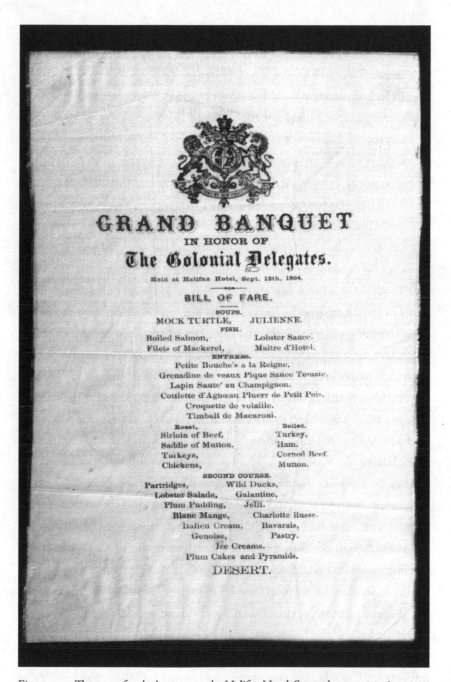

Figure 12.1. The menu for the banquet at the Halifax Hotel, September 12, 1864, is now displayed in the dining room at Massey College. Courtesy of Massey College.

modern Canadian would desire. The fresh wild fish would likely still be appealing, but the macaroni would seem out of place at a formal event. The desserts would likely come across as overly fussy and sweet, and the overall feel of the meal would seem to lack a certain cosmopolitan multiculturalism. The amount of food would likely seem excessive instead of sumptuous, and except at the most formal occasions we would likely choose items from the spread as we circulate about the room rather than sit for hours at a time. Meals and styles change, and the food researcher treats culinary culture as unchanging at her peril. This point was made in a lovely but obscure article by Charles Perry in a small hand-published journal series called *Petits propos culinaires*. In "The Oldest Mediterranean Noodle," he reminds us that "it is our romantic habit to believe the popular foods of a culture are eternal."[5] In his exploration of the role of pasta in Italian cuisine, he looks at how we tend to imagine some foods as unchanging pillars with robust histories. This is one reason that I've stuck largely with an exploration of culinary properties in this work. Although maple syrup has a long and well-established history in Canada, for example, poutine didn't exist seven decades ago. The next expression of Canada's food culture, the next poutine, is likely still brewing in some chef's imagination, but the themes of wild, multicultural, and the like are more lasting. As Perry notes, "time and chance and fashion rule cookery as they do the rest of our social behavior."[6] It isn't always obvious what is a lasting cultural shift and what is a fad, yet, as the previous chapters suggest, cuisine is influenced by far more than the whims of fashion. It is a conversation between a land and its people, and like a conversation the intricacies and complexities of cuisine change over time. The prediction of individual future food trends is nearly impossible, but what about larger trends driven by cultural shifts and landscape-level changes? Are there changes at the landscape level or cultural level that are likely to influence cuisine? This chapter summarizes some of the potential future impacts on Canada's cuisine, some good, some bad, beginning with the most potentially disruptive: climate change.

When I think of climate change, I always think, for a moment, of that first trip on the Rideau Canal in the bitter cold. I think of taking photos in Calgary when it was forty-four degrees below zero only to find that some critical component of my camera wouldn't function at such a ridiculous temperature. I think of maple syrup on snow and the texture of the sand that the streetcars in Toronto drop onto the tracks to provide traction in winter. I now live in the one tiny corner of the country where winter is optional, but if my years in central Canada taught me anything they taught me that Canada is a cold country and that our cuisine is a cold cuisine. Much of our culinary history is grounded in preparing for and surviving winter, and many of the foods highlighted in this book make sense only in the context of deep, prolonged cold that must be endured both in body and in spirit.

Climate change threatens the balance between culture and cold that once led folk singer Gilles Vigneault to declare *"mon pays, ce n'est pas un pays, c'est l'hiver."* Several of our iconic foods are threatened in some way by the "one-two punch" of climate change: increasing temperatures coupled with more frequent extreme weather events. Canada, particularly in the North, is warming more quickly than most places on the planet, with higher winter temperatures and warmer overnight lows causing concern. Extreme weather is increasing as well and will have increasingly negative impacts on Canada's iconic foods. Losing those foods and the cultural capital that surrounds them would leave a noticeable hole in our culture. The impacts of climate change are wide-ranging but not entirely understood, yet a few examples suggest a frightening trend.

Let's begin with maple syrup. Standing in a sugar bush, it's hard to imagine that anything could threaten the giant and serene maple tree. Maple syrup production, however, is particularly sensitive to climate change. The tree roots themselves are vulnerable to freezing since they lie close to the surface of the soil and require a blanket of snow to protect them from the cold. In recent winters, that blanket has been less certain, and freeze-thaw cycles can coat the roots with an armour of damaging ice. The syrup season itself, lasting only four to six weeks, requires a delicate balance of crisp, cold nights and warm, sunny days to draw the sap from the roots. This stable weather is no longer guaranteed to arrive, and in the past fifteen years syrup production has fallen as spring temperatures have risen. Projections suggest that production will decline by about one-fifth in the next four decades in Canada, more in some southern regions.

Extreme weather is also a threat, even to something as solid as a grand old maple tree. The 1998 ice storm damaged wide swaths of forest in Quebec and Ontario, destroying 12.5 per cent of the maple taps in eastern Ontario and dropping syrup production by 25 per cent.[7] Maple syrup itself won't vanish, and the industry can move north over time, since 17 per cent of Quebec's forests are sugar maple and only a tiny portion is used for syrup production. However, the beloved landscape of small farms with sugar bushes and *cabanes à sucre* located close to major centres such as Montreal will struggle with these new climatic conditions, fraying the cultural fabric that surrounds our most iconic food. This would be a great economic and cultural loss, and if those small farms cannot survive without the early season return from maple syrup their contributions of fresh local product to the food system will vanish as well.

Maple syrup might be the best known of Canada's iconic foods, but several other economically and culturally important products face an uncertain future as the climate shifts. Beef might be much more difficult to produce in Alberta as it becomes both hotter and drier. Water shortage will be the principal impact of climate change on Alberta's beef industry since cattle require a great deal of water, and that water must be clean if they are to gain weight. Contaminated water can put a cow off its feed, and in today's markets larger cows provide the meat marbled with fat most prized on many kitchen tables. However, declining snowpack in the Rocky Mountains and declining rainfall threaten both fresh water and ground water in Alberta, challenging cattle production directly and

222

indirectly through the rising cost of feed grain production. Adapting to this second impact can be addressed by switching from grain-fed beef to pasture-fed beef, but retailers and consumers often object to the yellow fat produced by cattle finished entirely on grass. The flavour of grass-fed beef is quite different from that of grain-fed beef, and is not immediately embraced by the public, though forage beef is healthier and has less of a climatic footprint. In the long run, forage beef is certainly more sustainable than grain-fed beef, both in environmental impact and in overall water use, so in the future we will likely have to pay more for Alberta beef and get used to it tasting more like, well, beef. Beef producers might have to go back to raising beef on the small-scale farms that once defined the industry. The predicted scarcity of both the fresh water and the nutritious foods required to finish cattle can be mitigated in part by decreasing the number of cattle raised in Alberta. In some ways, this result is both healthier and more ecologically friendly, but it will provide economic challenges to Alberta's beef industry and might well end the numerous barbecue pits in the province.

223

The impact of climate change doesn't stop at our plates; what we pour into our glasses is also at risk. Icewine grapes are also a cold-reliant crop, and only a small number of locations have climates suited to the growing and harvesting of these grapes. Temperature and water supply are critical for all wine production, and changes in them pose risks to icewine production.[8] Growers of icewine grapes will have to wait longer into the winter for the necessary cold to freeze the grapes, and this extra time on the vine increases evaporation and predation by birds and rodents. On the bright side, wine regions in Quebec and Nova Scotia might have warm enough summers to begin production of icewine grapes, though these regions will still be marginal since they will be prone to extreme winter events. In regions such as Niagara and the BC interior, longer waits for harvest and the increased likelihood of vine-damaging storms will punish established producers. Icewine production is a high-risk form of agriculture, in particular because of the specific temperature range that icewine grapes require and because of the industry preference for multiple cycles of freezing and thawing. Climate change will make a hard job harder. The production of icewine is already inherently more difficult than the production of other wines: since icewine grapes must be pressed while frozen, the juice harvested from them is only between 15 per cent and 20 per cent of what the same grapes would have produced if destined for table wine. As with maple, extreme variability in climate poses a particular threat to icewine. Both extreme cold and exceptional warmth can damage grapes and vines. The complex and valued flavour of Canada's icewine is evoked through freezing and thawing, and disruption of this pattern poses the greatest risk to both volume and quality.

The most serious threat of climate change to Canada's culinary identity goes beyond declines in production and increases in disruption. BC salmon, our most important iconic food in the west and the base upon which both Indigenous foodways and settler foodways were built, could vanish with warming water. As the child of a fishing family, I find this deeply upsetting; if British Columbia loses its salmon, then many of us will lose a part of ourselves. The particular threat is to the salmon's anadromous nature. Salmon live most of their lives in the ocean, but they begin and end their lives in fresh water. And in both the ocean and the rivers, they face temperature changes, and in the rivers in particular they also face reduced summer flows, increased winter flooding, and greater sedimentation. Human impacts don't help the situation. Rivers must provide water for electricity, human habitation, and agriculture. They carry far too much waste and are mined, dammed, and stripped of cooling vegetation. Vancouver sits on one of the greatest river deltas in the world, yet the Fraser River is barely on the radar of most Vancouverites, save as an irritating barrier to traffic flow. We might love our salmon, but we don't love our rivers, and in the long run our love of the fish might not be sufficient to overcome our damage to their habitat.

Ocean temperature is the ultimate factor in the Pacific salmon's range, and temperatures either too high or too low are lethal. Salmon can adapt to temperature changes only slowly. Temperature affects them differently depending on the stage of their life cycle, though they are most vulnerable in fresh water. Many streams that once had large salmon runs are now at lethal temperatures; salmon are considered extinct in 142 watershed systems throughout British Columbia where they were traditionally found.[9] Higher temperatures also lead to higher infection rates and more virulent fish pathogens, weakening salmon as they fight to reproduce. Flow rates are also critical, and reduced winter snowfall is leading to decreased summer flows in rivers, which leads to warmer water that is harder to navigate. The salmon is a miraculous fish, but it does need water to survive. Paradoxically, increased winter water levels from more frequent extreme weather events damage spawning habitat and kill young fish. Changes to flow rates even continue to impact salmon after death; decaying carcasses release organic matter into rivers, which influences the nutrients available to the next generation of salmon as well as the bacteria in the water.

The long-term projections for Pacific salmon are extremely poor. Although the salmon's fate will ultimately rest on the global success or failure to control climate change, in the short to medium term British Columbians need to love their rivers. Rivers and streams can be shaded with vegetation to provide calm, cool water, and wetlands can be restored to improve habitat. In the future, water use in British Columbia will need to take salmon into account, and forestry practices must protect streams. The salmon is a resilient fish that will thrive if given the slightest chance; there is a stream near my house in East Vancouver, little more than a drainage ditch really, that thanks to a little effort now sports a salmon run for the first time in nearly a century. It is odd to watch these fish splash past parking lots and industrial buildings, but their presence gives hope that it isn't too late to save them.

It is too early to say with certainty how climate change will impact Canada's cuisine. The worst-case scenarios above could be balanced by longer growing seasons and an influx of crops never before part of the Canadian culinary experience. On the Gulf Islands in the south-west corner of British Columbia, I found farmers experimenting with new crops such as tea, olives, and even pomegranates. Our wine regions might become better suited to the more tender reds, and production in the North might rise, reducing the chronic food insecurity in our remote communities. However, climate change is only one part of the larger story. There are other potential challenges to Canada's cuisine.

At the heart of my lab is a map. It dominates one wall, and as my team works on projects to better understand our region's culinary culture we never forget that it is the farmland that keeps us there. The map shows all of the farming regions surrounding Vancouver in a soothing green, and the farmland that has been lost to urban development is highlighted in a shocking purple that a previous postdoctoral scholar thought max-imized the contrast. We occasionally amend the map, but ultimately it is more a totem than a practical part of our workspace. It reminds us where our food comes from.

Across Canada, such farming regions are under threat from urban sprawl, that creature of the second half of the twentieth century, fuelled by the development of freeway systems, postwar prosperity, and separa-tion of residential and industrial land uses. The idea of everyone having a nice house on a small slice of land has always sounded rather bucolic to me, but the reality is a demonstration of the law of unintended con-sequences. Suburban development brought long commutes, alienation, and destruction of small farms that provide cities with fresh seasonal food that forms part of the backbone of Canada's cuisine. Around the world, sprawl has consumed farmland—often the best farmland—at a shocking pace. It might seem ridiculous in the second-largest country in the world to speak of land shortage, but very little of Canada's soil is able to support the intensive production of a wide variety of crops. Only about 8 per cent of Canada's vast area is farmed, and 80 percent of that land mass is in the Prairies. Of the remaining fraction capable of the sort of crop diversity that supports a culinary culture, over half is found in the areas surrounding Montreal, Toronto, and Vancouver. It makes historical sense that our major cities are located amid our best farmlands, but it poses a problem; as the cities grow, our best lands vanish. According to Statistics Canada, nearly 4 million hectares of prime farmland have been lost since 1971, an area larger than Vancouver Island.[10]

Such widespread decline in farmland began raising significant alarm in Canada's urban regions, leading to attempts to slow or stop the conversion of farmland into urban development. The first such effort was made in British Columbia, 90 per cent mountainous despite its lush reputation. Both cities and farms are constrained to the warm, fertile valley bottoms, and by the 1970s thousands of hectares of land per year were being taken out of farm production. In response, the government created the Agricultural Land Reserve, placing 5 per cent of the province's land off limits to development. Of particular importance, over half of the lush bottom lands near Vancouver were placed under protection, in effect containing urban sprawl. Although not perfect, and subject to tremendous pressure from developers, the Agricultural Land Reserve has created a landscape of intensive farming, small mixed farming, and urban development. This strict set of regulations slowed development immensely; my team found that land loss to development fell by a factor of twelve near Vancouver once the Agricultural Land Reserve was in place. Quebec followed suit in 1978 with its *Loi sur la protection du territoire et des activités agricoles*. These two examples of strong legislation have had profound effects on farming. Secure in the knowledge that their farm regions wouldn't be eroded by urban development, farmers near Montreal and Vancouver have been more likely to invest in expensive infrastructure and upgrades. These farms produce high-value, intensive crops for nearby urbanites and strengthen the availability of fresh local food. In British Columbia, my research team continues to study this example of agricultural bootstrapping: farmland fuels the culinary industry, which supports local farmland, which innovates for the culinary industry. Without this leadership in land protection, the cycle would be broken.

227

Pressure continues to build on farmland in British Columbia and Quebec despite strong legislation, but the most worrying farmland loss in Canada continues in the golden horseshoe region surrounding Toronto. Home to a quarter of Canadians, the vast urban regions of southern Ontario threaten Canada's most-varied and highest-yielding farmland. In the late 1990s, the area around Toronto was losing 1 per cent of its farmland per year to sprawl, threatening diverse crops, including the fruit and wine country of Niagara. The provincial government introduced greenbelt legislation in 2005, protecting over 7,000 square kilometres of land. The threat of urban development of farmland is constant and growing across Canada, and lovers of all things culinary would be wise to support the preservation of local farmlands.

If the farmland loss of Canada's near-urban landscape is a reflection of too much population growth in a region, ironically the decline of culinary richness in Canada's remote regions reflects too little population growth. Although Canada is a growing nation, that growth is almost entirely urban; the number of rural Canadians is only 6.3 million, and though Statistics Canada notes that the number is relatively stable it hides a steep decline in remote residents as near-urban regions grow.[11] In the time of George Brown, nine of ten Canadians lived in remote regions, yet now only 19 per cent do, one of the lowest rural population percentages in the developed world. As I travelled Newfoundland's remote coastal villages, I saw the impacts of rural catastrophes such as the 1992 cod moratorium first-hand. By 2001, populations were down 20 per cent, and small cafés and grocery stores were closing their doors in large numbers. Displaced populations often lose their food traditions since they are cut off from local landscapes, wild foods, and long-established cultural patterns. Deprived of the cod, and then of the people, rural Newfoundland foodways are shrinking. Similar losses are happening across Cape Breton, in northern Ontario and Quebec, and in small farming towns of the Prairies. Many of the mainstay Chinese restaurants of the rural west have disappeared as prairie farms grow larger and

228

populations dwindle. And in British Columbia, where access to remote communities can involve long and expensive ferry trips, populations in remote regions have also fallen sharply. I felt a particularly sharp pang when the population of Sointula, a remote community on Malcolm Island, fell 3 per cent according to the last census. Sointula was populated by Finns seeking to form a utopian community and escape the harsh mines of Robert Dunsmuir, a BC coal baron. They carved the remote community out of thick wilderness at the turn of the twentieth century and prospered despite several disasters and a general disillusionment with communal living. The town still boasts the country's oldest cooperative store, and Finnish *pulla* bread similar to my grandmother's recipe is still offered at the Upper Crust Bakery near the ferry dock. Finnish can still be heard spoken in the streets, where—for some unknown reason—dogs have the right of way over cars. The forces drawing people away from such places are strong, but over time they leech diversity out of the countryside, taking oddities such as *pulla* bread, Persian doughnuts, or the dulse of Grand Manan with them.

A cuisine is a language that exposes the soul of a place, and in a country such as Canada, where our foodways are so closely linked to wild stocks, the ecological systems of our landscapes can't be separated from the people. The decline in human population in Newfoundland and Labrador followed the decline in cod population: it was on the backs of the cod that the local culture rested. I have been asked numerous times why this book is titled after cod tongues rather than a more popular or iconic Canadian food. The answer is as complicated as the story of the cod itself. Since I began this project, I have been haunted by the story of cod tongues. If cod tongues could speak, then what would they say about Canada as a place? As a people? What secrets would they reveal? Cod are by no means extinct, and cod tongues are still available in Newfoundland restaurants. A luxurious version piled high with scrunchions still greets visitors at the grand Fairmont Hotel in St. John's. But no longer do people gather for a scoff from a battered iron pan over a gas burner behind the processing sheds of the small coastal towns of Newfoundland. Fresh cod tongues hot with pork fat aren't served in brown waxed paper hours after being harvested. Those times are gone, perhaps forever. When I talk to Dean Bavington about cod tongues, anger tints his voice. What was once a dish of the people processed and eaten on the docks from the by-product of a major industry is now served only to tourists as a "freak food" or "zoo food." Cod tongues are a monument to the fragility of culinary cultures grounded in wild stocks. What endured for centuries under seasonal hook and line, and then year-round net fishery, was finally broken by industrial draggers that drove cod to its vulnerable status as a red-listed (somewhat endangered) species. No chef would admit to me where the cod tongues served today in Newfoundland actually come from, but by following the trail of wholesalers it is likely that they now come from Norwegian cod, and the processing is done in China. They are shadows of what they once were. And they are not the only wild food in Canada under threat.

In the spring of 2014, I had the good fortune to be in St. Catharines, Ontario, just as the forest stirred to life. While hiking the rocky, watery wonderland of the Niagara Escarpment, I spotted a great number of wild leeks, also known as wild garlic, wood leeks, or ramps, lovely green shoots stark against last season's fallen leaves. I resisted the urge to pick a few to spice up my evening salad or omelette. Wild leeks are delicious, both sweet and pungent, particularly the bulbs. However, they are also becoming rare since they are extremely slow growing and increasingly desired by food-savvy citizens. I settled on taking some pictures and left them be. The wild leek is similar to the fiddlehead in that its appeal is partly because of its early arrival when fresh local food is in short supply, but in my opinion it packs a much greater flavour punch. Sadly, as Jacob Richler reminds us, increased demand is damaging the leek beds, for plucking the bulb kills the entire plant.[12] They come back only slowly since the seeds take two years to germinate and then must grow for several years before they seed and spread the species. To maintain a patch, most of the bulbs must be left behind; a sustainable harvest rate is perhaps 5 per cent of what is present. In Quebec, the taste for wild leeks led to a ban in 1995, and the plant is listed as threatened in the province. Bans also exist in several places in the United States, and the species is on watch lists in the Maritimes. In Ontario, leeks can still be harvested, but for how long is unclear. Hopefully, they can be sustained in the wild, for they really do liven up a spring omelette.

Another example can be found on the West Coast, where the northern abalone can be found hiding on rocks in cold water at the lower intertidal zone. I vaguely recall the sweet taste of the abalone from my childhood, and I remember the entrancing colours in the nacre inside their shells. They are herbivores and feed on the kelp that also provides them with shelter from predators. A traditional food of Indigenous groups who harvested them by hand in small numbers, these shellfish were no match for the advent of scuba gear and a hungry world market. The commercial dive fishery of the 1970s and 1980s saw harvests drop by 90 per cent as populations plummeted. The abalone is now the only species on the BC coast completely closed to harvesting, but it is extremely vulnerable to poachers: there is a high demand on the black market, it is located close to shore, and it is a sedentary creature with little ability to flee from a scuba diver. A public awareness campaign to control poaching will be critical if Canadians are ever to enjoy eating this traditional food again. Extinction is still a real possibility.

231

These threats to Canadian cuisine, when listed together, can seem overwhelming. However, the future of Canada's foods is also likely to be filled with new and exciting flavours and thrilling innovations. After all, our cuisine is in the middle of a renaissance, fuelled by thousands of dedicated and passionate people rediscovering old flavours and inventing new ones. Examples of culinary innovation in Canada could fill a book of their own, from the chefs creating our cuisine, to the farmers providing ever-fresher and more varied products, and to the myriad food studies programs springing up at universities across the country (at the University of Guelph, food has become a focal point, and the university has made culinary expert Anita Stewart its first laureate of food). A few examples paint an optimistic vision of Canada's culinary landscape.

Cuisine is always changing as waves of innovation match our ever-shifting appetites. This innovation isn't confined to Canada's urban centres; not all rural communities passively accept falling populations, even on the remote shores of Newfoundland. The island of Fogo is a harsh but beautiful windswept landscape, an isolated settlement in an isolated province. Populated in the eighteenth century by Irish and English fishers, Fogo boasts the oldest Irish graveyard in North America and dialects found nowhere else on the Earth. The rocky coastline is dotted with towns sporting names that sound as if they are in a Tolkien novel. Visitors to the island can explore Tilting, which hosts a museum of the island's strong cooperative movement, and the clustered towns of Seldom, Little Seldom, and Seldom-Come-By. Local history is deep, love of community is strong, and for a remote place that has lost half of its population over the past few decades the sense of place is thick. In the 1950s, the Joey Smallwood government suggested relocating the communities of Fogo to the mainland, a suggestion soundly defeated by the locals, who would rather get by on their remote island. Collapse of the cod fishery posed a much starker threat, but one of the locals who had lived the bulk of her life "away" returned to spearhead a movement to strengthen the island's economy and help to secure its future. Zita Cobb made her fortune early in the technology industry, and she dedicated part of that fortune to stemming the flow of people from Fogo to the world and working to bring the people of the world to Fogo instead. Her Fogo Island Inn juts grandly from the rocky coast, and her organization, the Shorefast Foundation, helps to foster development on the island, primarily through encouragement of the arts and tourism. Food forms a central plank of this endeavour, and the restaurant at the inn, headed by chef Murray McDonald, was voted the third best restaurant in Canada in 2014. McDonald borrows from the New Nordic tradition to blend the local flavours of Newfoundland into modern presentations. Inn guests don't want to eat at just one restaurant, of course, no matter how lauded, and the inn draws a spillover crowd to restaurants such as Flat Earth Coffee and Nicole's Café, both of which offer sophisticated takes on Newfoundland's cuisine. Fogo's culinary heritage is likely to survive and hopefully thrive, preserving a unique point of view on food, culture, and the world. As Cobb noted in an interview, no one wants to live in a world where everything is the same.

Our culinary renaissance touches every province. At the far eastern end of Prince Edward Island, near beaches of sand that sang gently in the wind, Julie Shore and Arla Johnson are part of a wave of craft distilling redefining alcohol in Canada. I marvelled at the massive copper and brass still, sipped their lovely gin, and wondered about the unlikely location far off the beaten path, in a province that held on to prohibition for over fifty years. And prohibition is part of understanding the story of alcohol in Canada, for before prohibition there were hundreds of small distillers, along with abundant local brewers. After prohibition, the alcohol business consolidated to produce rather run-of-the-mill liquor. Now dozens of distillers dot the country, and the movement is growing rapidly. The quest for local products is a help, as is the renaissance of the spirit-forward cocktail. The resurgence of craft-brewing beer is even more stunning. Beer has always been popular in Canada and has been brewed for nearly five centuries by settlers and much longer by Indigenous makers of spruce beer. The first European-style beer was made in Quebec City, and soon most communities were conducting small-scale brewing. In 1786, John Molson established the first large brewery, though most remained local and small. A slow process of consolidation began, and continued until prohibition, which came into effect between 1916 and 1918 depending on the province. Light beer remained legal in Quebec, but most Canadian breweries simply closed. After prohibition, only a few major breweries remained to dominate the landscape with mass-produced and uninteresting lagers. This didn't begin to change until the early 1990s, when Canada entered the age of the microbrewery. This renaissance owes its origin to enthusiasts who fought to relegalize small-scale beer production. British Columbia was an early adopter, with the Horseshoe Bay Brewing Company and Granville Island Brewing Company leading the field. In Victoria, Spinnaker's was one of the first brew pubs in the country, reminding Canadians that beer could be served with a nice meal. Now, in the twenty-first century, microbreweries abound. The microproduction of alcohol was an unexpected twist in Canada's culinary evolution, but when one considers that alcohol is a deeply commensal product it isn't surprising that drinks associated with place would be popular with tourists and locals alike. Wes Flack identified this shift as an important component of a neo-localism that grounds products in place and builds a strong sense of local community.[13]

234

Food builds community and not just in informal commensal settings. Across the country, municipal groups are engaging with citizens to strengthen our neighbourhoods by promoting food. In Toronto, the Food Policy Council has advised city leaders on issues of food security and sovereignty since 1991. This thirty-member advisory board has helped to shape Toronto's urban foodscape. Historically, Canada has encouraged the strict separation of rural production of food and passive urban consumption of it, but food-related activism is on the rise in our cities. The Food Policy Council has helped to build school food and gardening programs, helped to block bovine growth hormone in Canada, encouraged rooftop gardening, and established a Toronto Food Charter to encourage food security. Other cities are now following Toronto's lead. The Food Policy Council was led from 2000 to 2010 by food activist and author Wayne Roberts, one of the people who encouraged me to follow my passion for sustainable food systems. Policy might be outside the scope of this book, but it touches on many of the subjects explored here. Food trucks and farmers' markets require policy to support them, as do microbreweries and small farms. I chased down Wayne

by email (he's a hard man to find in person since he's nearly always moving around) to ask him what he sees as the future of Canada's grassroots
food movement. He echoed this chapter's tension between a sense of
optimism and a concern for the future. Wayne replied that, in his mind,
the food movement is amazing in that it has succeeded even though it
is young and Canada provides little support for such movements. His
only concern was whether the groundswell of support for sustainable
local food systems can offset catastrophic damage from threats such as
climate change.

Wayne isn't alone in his thinking. A lack of federal and provincial
support for farming and food security is balanced by a groundswell of
interest in food at the community level. A new and engaged generation of
chefs, farmers, scholars, and activists is creating a vibrant culinary landscape. In Vancouver, the city's Food Policy Council, many excellent food
non-profit organizations, and dedicated chefs are critical voices against
urban sprawl, and they work with farmers to protect and strengthen the
provincial food system.

One strength of Canada's food movements is the growing ranks of
energetic new participants from all walks of life, and I am privileged to
know several of them. Postdoctoral scholar Lisa Powell is a member of
a growing legion of young academics building their careers on the study
of food and agriculture, uncommon even ten years ago. Lisa brought
her expertise on the interaction of Kentucky's mining industry and agricultural industry to the problems facing British Columbia as it juggles
the needs of a growing population with the preciously small amount of
available farmland. She has grown fond of West Coast cuisine, so we sat
down to a meal at Salmon n' Bannock, one of a new generation of restaurants featuring Indigenous cuisine that has appeared across Canada.
Cozy and comfortable, Salmon n' Bannock serves cuisine drawn from
a variety of nations, including Haida, Cree, and Nuxalt. It serves the
best and freshest fish, and Lisa and I enjoyed a salmon sampler before
tucking into a salmon burger with the house bannock and a side of cedar

jelly. That evening the special was eulachon, a small silver fish highly prized by the coastal peoples, but it rarely finds its way onto Vancouver tables. We left full and happy.

It should be clear by this point that much of Canadian cuisine is Indigenous, though it is seldom recognized as such, but the emergence of Indigenous dishes and restaurants represents a first halting step in recognizing how critical Indigenous culinary traditions have been to our cuisine. In Toronto, Tea-n-Bannock offers salmon, lake fish, and bison, as well as a superb elk stew, but it also serves postcontact dishes such as canned luncheon meat on bannock and blanket dogs made from wieners and fry bread. Bannock bread pudding is also very popular. Near Yellowknife, the Aurora Lodge offers visitors the best of northern cuisine. Small but growing, recognition of the importance of Indigenous cuisine is welcome and long overdue.

I ended my exploration of Canada's cuisine with lunch. My hometown of Roberts Creek is a sleepy BC coastal village, but hidden down its shaded lanes among the sun-dappled blackberries is a vibrant mix of logging families, fishers, American draft-dodgers and expat back-to-the-landers, and wealthy urbanites with summer cottages. There is a good microbrewery that grows its own hops, there is an excellent Thai restaurant that operates out of a converted 1950s drive-in, and the woods are filled with mushrooms that draw foragers every fall. It was in Roberts Creek that I began this project, and I decided to conclude it on a lovely if slightly brisk spring day when the blossoms in my family's orchard had just emerged to bathe in the sun. A two-year project had turned into a four-year project, and I now doubt that I will ever be truly finished with Canadian cuisine. There will always be new twists, new innovations, or new treasures from the past brought back by innovative and passionate chefs. But the time had come to finish writing, return from the road, and gather my thoughts on what makes a Canadian meal. What better way to do so, I reasoned, than serve up a modern version of the great feasts of Confederation, and what better place than on the edge of the Pacific Ocean? I swept a winter's worth of cedar bows off the deck, scrubbed down the picnic table, and set to work.

Friends and family joined me to see what I'd been up to all those months away. We began locally, with Fraser Valley crème fraîche on Ukrainian blintz with northern divine caviar from just up the highway in Sechelt, washed down with Okanagan *blanc de noir*. The caviar was unbelievably fresh and clean-tasting, a product of the cold water that bathes the BC coast. Continuing with an oceanic theme, we moved on to a delicate smoked char with partridge berry, served with local microgreens. The growth of local farm stands selling such greens on the honour system has been a great addition to a region that lost most of its farming activity over the mid-twentieth century. For the next course, I whipped up a rather experimental poutine gnocchi, served with a thin but rich brown sauce and topped with Newfoundland savory. We chased this down with a few bottles of microbrew from Montreal's Dieu du Ciel!, and we moved on to the mains. The first was a side of sockeye salmon roasted in a rhubarb butter glaze and paired with an Ontario Gewürztraminer. The floral overtones of the wine pair well with salmon; the fresh fish has the most subtle berry flavour. With the salmon, I served Alberta ginger beef with some fresh ramps served on rice, paired with some gently steamed *gai lan* that I picked up at the market. By this time, we were already feeling full, but given the wide range of Canadian desserts to choose from I provided a selection of dishes: a *pouding chômeur* with saffron cream and candied sage, individual blueberry grunts, and a plate of traditional butter tarts provided by my mother. We picked at the food and watched the afternoon lengthen. And, as happened in the dining room of the steamer *Queen Victoria*, we found ourselves content with the world and excited by the possibilities that the future offered.

# NOTES

## CHAPTER 1. INTRODUCTION: SIDEBOARD DIPLOMACY

1   George Brown, "Letter to Anne Brown," September 13, 1864, Library and Archives Canada, George Brown Papers, MG 24, B 40, Vols. 5–8.

2   Harry Bruce, "Confederation," in *Canada 1812–1871: The Formative Years*, ed. James Knight (Toronto: Imperial Oil, 1967), 66.

3   Dorothy Duncan, *Canadians at Table: Food, Fellowship, and Folklore: A Culinary History of Canada* (Toronto: Dundurn Press, 2006), 93.

4   Bonnie Huskins, "From Haute Cuisine to Ox Roasts: Public Feasting and the Negotiation of Class in Mid-19th-Century Saint John and Halifax," *Labour/Le travail* 37 (1996), 9–36.

5   Luella Creighton, *The Elegant Canadians* (Toronto: McClelland and Stewart, 1967), 11.

6   *Ross's Weekly*, September 8, 1864.

7   Brown, "Letter to Anne Brown."

8   Julie V. Watson, *Ardgowan: A Journal of House and Garden in Victorian Prince Edward Island* (Charlottetown: Seacroft Books, 2000).

9   Brown, "Letter to Anne Brown."

10  Ibid.

11  Creighton, *The Elegant Canadians*, 13.

12  *Vindicator*, September 7, 1864.

13  Brown, "Letter to Anne Brown."

14  J. M. S. Careless, *Brown of the Globe*, vol. 2 of *Statesman of Confederation, 1860–1880* (Toronto: Macmillan, 1963), 155.

15  Brown, "Letter to Anne Brown."

16  Creighton, *The Elegant Canadians*, 14.

17  *Islander*, September 15, 1864.

18 Creighton, *The Elegant Canadians*, 7.

19 *Ross's Weekly*, September 8, 1864.

20 Carolyn Steel, *Hungry City: How Food Shapes Our Lives* (London: Vintage Books, 2009), 322.

21 Henri Lefebvre, *Rhythmanalysis: Space, Time, and Everyday Life*, trans. Stuart Elden and Gerald Moore (New York: Continuum, 2004).

22 Jeff Miller and Jonathan Deutsch, *Food Studies: An Introduction to Research Methods* (London: Berg Publishing, 2009).

23 Clifford Geertz, *The Interpretation of Cultures* (London: Fontana Press, 1993), 19.

24 Roland Barthes, "Toward a Psychosociology of Contemporary Food Consumption," in *Food and Culture: A Reader*, ed. Carole Counihan and Penny Van Esterik (New York: Routledge, 2013), 23–30.

25 James Daschuk, *Clearing the Plains: Disease, Politics of Starvation, and the Loss of Aboriginal Life* (Regina: University of Regina Press, 2013).

26 Olivier de Schutter, "Report of the Special Rapporteur on the Right to Food: Mission to Canada," presented to the UN Human Rights Council (GE.12-18956), 2014.

27 Richard Hoskings, ed., *Wild Food: Proceedings of the Oxford Symposium of Food and Cookery, 2004* (Devon: Prospect Books, 2006).

28 Sharon Zukin, *Naked City: The Death and Life of Authentic Urban Places* (Oxford: Oxford University Press, 2009).

29 Deborah Lupton, *Food, the Body, and the Self* (London: Sage, 1996), 16–17.

## CHAPTER 2. THE LANGUAGE OF CUISINE

1 David Pimentel et al., "Biofuel Impacts on World Food Supply: Use of Fossil Fuel, Land, and Water Resources," *Energies* 1, 2 (2008): 74.

2 Jean Anthelme Brillat-Savarin, *The Physiology of Taste: Or, Meditations on Transcendental Gastronomy*, trans. M. F. K. Fisher (Mineola: Dover Publications, 2011), 54.

3 Ibid., 74.

4 Maria Polushkin Robbins, *The Cook's Quotation Book: A Literary Feast* (New York: Viking Press, 1984).

5 Priscilla Parkhurst Ferguson, *Accounting for Taste: The Triumph of French Cuisine* (Chicago: University of Chicago Press, 2006), 3.

6 Warren Belasco, *Meals to Come: A History of the Future of Food* (Berkeley: University of California Press, 2006), vii.

7 Janet Davison, "Food Eats Up Less of Our Spending, but Costs Us More," October 7, 2011, http://www.cbc.ca/news/canada/food-eats-up-less-of-our-spending-but-costs-us-more-1.1054574.

8 Zukin, *Naked City*.

9 Lewis Holloway and Moya Kneafsey, "Reading the Space of the Farmer's Market: A Preliminary Investigation from the UK," *Sociologica Ruralis* 40, 3 (2000): 285–99.

10 Pierre L. Van den Berghe, "Ethnic Cuisine: Culture in Nature," *Ethnic and Racial Studies* 7, 3 (1984): 387–97.

11  Aristotle, *Complete Works of Aristotle, the Revised Oxford Translation*, ed. Jonathan Barnes, vol. 1 (Princeton: Princeton University Press, 2014), 2110.

12  Benjamin Jowett, trans., *Dialogues of Plato: Translated into English, with Analyses and Introduction*, vol. 4 (Cambridge, MA: Harvard University Press, 2010), 154.

13  Claude Fischler, "Commensality, Society, and Culture," *Social Science Information* 50, 3–4 (2011): 529.

14  Lenore Lauri Newman and Katherine Burnett, "Street Food and Vibrant Urban Spaces: Lessons from Portland, Oregon," *Local Environment* 18, 2 (2013): 233–48.

15  Josée Johnston and Shyon Baumann, *Foodies: Democracy and Distinction in the Gourmet Foodscape* (New York: Routledge, 2010).

16  Ann Barr and Paul Levy, *The Official Foodie Handbook* (New York: Doubleday, 1985), 6.

17  Pierre Bourdieu, *Distinction: A Social Critique of the Judgement of Taste*, trans. Richard Nice (Cambridge, MA: Harvard University Press, 1984).

18  William H. Whyte, *The Social Life of Small Urban Spaces* (Washington, DC: Conservation Foundation, 1980).

19  Ibid., 50.

20  Benjamin F. Coles, "Making the Market Place: A Topography of Borough Market, London," *Cultural Geographies* 21, 3 (2014): 515–23.

21  Edward W. Soja, *Seeking Spatial Justice* (Minneapolis: University of Minnesota Press, 2010), 1.

22  Ian Cook and Philip Crang, "The World on a Plate: Culinary Culture, Displacement, and Geographical Knowledges," *Journal of Material Culture* 1, 2 (1996): 131–53.

23  David Bell, "Fragments for a New Urban Culinary Geography," *Journal for the Study of Food and Society* 6, 1 (2002): 15.

24  Igor Cusack, "'Equatorial Guinea's National Cuisine Is Simple and Tasty': Cuisine and the Making of National Culture," *Arizona Journal of Hispanic Cultural Studies* 8 (2004): 131–48.

25  Benedict Anderson, *Imagined Communities: Reflections on the Origin and Spread of Nationalism* (London: Verso, 2006), 3.

26  Rebecca L. Spang, *The Invention of the Restaurant: Paris and Modern Gastronomic Culture* (Cambridge, MA: Harvard University Press, 2001).

27  Eric C. Rath, "Banquets against Boredom: Towards Understanding (Samurai) Cuisine in Early Modern Japan," *Early Modern Japan: An Interdisciplinary Journal* 16 (2008): 43–55.

28  Cusack, "'Equatorial Guinea's National Cuisine Is Simple and Tasty,'" 135.

29  Katharyne Mitchell, "Educating the National Citizen in Neoliberal Times: From the Multicultural Self to the Strategic Cosmopolitan," *Transactions of the Institute of British Geographers* 28, 4 (2003): 388.

## CHAPTER 3. FROM A COLD COUNTRY:
## THE CUISINE OF AN IMAGINED WILDERNESS

1  Atsuko Hashimoto and David J. Telfer, "Selling Canadian Culinary Tourism: Branding the Global and Regional Product," *Tourism Geographies* 8, 1 (2006): 31–55.

2  Patricia Hluchly, "Taste of the True North," *Maclean's*, June 30–July 7, 2003, 67–72.

3   Jo Marie Powers and Anita Stewart, eds., *Northern Bounty: A Celebration of Canadian Cuisine* (Toronto: Random House, 1995), 3.

4   Euell Gibbons, *Stalking the Wild Asparagus* (New York: David McKay, 1962).

5   Warren Belasco, *Meals to Come: A History of the Future of Food* (Berkeley: University of California Press, 2006).

6   Joshua Gitelson, "Populux: The Suburban Cuisine of the 1950s," *Journal of American Culture* 15, 3 (1992): 73–78.

7   Ken Albala, "Wild Food: The Call of the Domestic," in *Wild Foods: Proceedings of the Oxford Symposium on Food and Cookery 2004*, ed. Richard Hosking (Devon: Prospect Books, 2006), 9–19.

8   Susan Campbell, "The Hunting and Gathering of Wild Foods: What's the Point? An Historical Survey," in *Wild Foods: Proceedings of the Oxford Symposium on Food and Cookery 2004*, ed. Richard Hosking (Devon: Prospect Books, 2006), 68–78.

9   Steven Kramer, "Tracking the Wild in 'Wild' Foods," in *Wild Foods: Proceedings of the Oxford Symposium on Food and Cookery 2004*, ed. Richard Hosking (Devon: Prospect Books, 2006), 184.

10  Richard Wilk, "Loving People, Hating What They Eat," in *Reimagining Marginalized Foods: Global Processes, Local Places*, ed. Elizabeth Finnis (Tucson: University of Arizona Press, 2012), 16.

11  Elizabeth Finnis, ed., *Reimagining Marginalized Foods: Global Processes, Local Places* (Tucson: University of Arizona Press, 2012).

12  George Colpitts, "Provisioning the HBC: Market Economies in the British Buffalo Commons in the Early Nineteenth Century," *Western Historical Quarterly* 43, 2 (2012): 179–203.

13  Ibid.

14  Daschuk, *Clearing the Plains*.

15  Suman Roy and Brooke Ali, *From Pemmican to Poutine: A Journey through Canada's Culinary History* (Toronto: Key Publishing House, 2010).

16  Taylor A. Steeves, "Wild Rice—Indian Food and a Modern Delicacy," *Economic Botany* 6, 2 (1952): 107–42.

17  Thomas Vennum Jr., *Wild Rice and the Ojibway People* (St. Paul: Minnesota State Historical Society Press, 1988).

18  Margaret Webb, *Apples to Oysters: A Food Lover's Tour of Canadian Farms* (Toronto: Viking Canada, 2008).

19  Mark Kurlansky, *Cod: A Biography of the Fish that Changed the World* (New York: Random House, 2011).

20  Duncan, *Canadians at Table*, 27.

21  Kurlansky, *Cod*, 51.

22  Dean Bavington, *Managed Annihilation: An Unnatural History of the Newfoundland Cod Collapse* (Vancouver: UBC Press, 2011).

23  Kristen Lowitt, "Fish and Fisheries in the Evolution of Newfoundland Foodways," in *World Small-Scale Fisheries: Contemporary Visions*, ed. Ratana Chuenpagdee (Delft: Eburon, 2011), 117.

24 Holly Everett, "Vernacular Health Moralities and Culinary Tourism in Newfoundland and Labrador," *Journal of American Folklore* 122, 1 (2009): 28–52.

25 John Sandlos, *Hunters at the Margin: Native People and Wildlife Conservation in the Northwest Territories* (Vancouver: UBC Press, 2011).

26 Hugh Brody, *The Other Side of Eden: Hunters, Farmers, and the Shaping of the World* (London: Macmillan, 2002).

27 Richard White, "From Wilderness to Hybrid Landscapes: The Cultural Turn in Environmental History," *Historian* 66, 3 (2004): 557–64.

28 William Cronon, "The Trouble with Wilderness: Or, Getting Back to the Wrong Nature," *Environmental History* 1, 1 (1996): 7–28.

29 Judith Williams, *Clam Gardens: Aboriginal Mariculture on Canada's West Coast* (Vancouver: Transmontanus, 2006).

30 Ibid., 78.

31 Sarah Whatmore, *Hybrid Geographies: Natures, Cultures, Spaces* (London: Sage, 2002).

32 Lenore Newman, "Blackberries: Canadian Cuisine and Marginal Foods," *Cuizine: The Journal of Canadian Food Cultures/Revue des cultures culinaires au Canada* 5, 1 (2014): n. pag.

## CHAPTER 4. SEASONALITY IN AN AGE OF ETERNAL SUMMER

1 Anne Colquhoun and Phil Lyon, "To Everything There Was a Season: Deconstructing UK Food Availability," *Food Service Technology* 1, 2 (2001): 93–102.

2 Hannah Wittman, Mary Beckie, and Chris Hergesheimer, "Linking Local Food Systems and the Social Economy? Future Roles for Farmers' Markets in Alberta and British Columbia," *Rural Sociology* 77, 1 (2012): 36–61.

3 Luis Guerrero et al., "Consumer-Driven Definition of Traditional Food Products and Innovation in Traditional Foods: A Qualitative Cross-Cultural Study," *Appetite* 52, 2 (2009): 345–54.

4 Jennifer Lynn Wilkins, "Seasonality, Food Origin, and Food Preference: A Comparison between Food Cooperative Members and Nonmembers," *Journal of Nutrition Education* 28, 6 (1996): 329–37.

5 Jennifer L. Wilkins, Elizabeth Bowdish, and Jeffery Sobal, "University Student Perceptions of Seasonal and Local Foods," *Journal of Nutrition Education* 32, 5 (2000): 261–68.

6 Jennifer L. Wilkins, "Consumer Perceptions of Seasonal and Local Foods: A Study in a U.S. Community," *Ecology of Food and Nutrition* 41, 5 (2002): 415–39.

7 See http://www.marchemaisonneuve.com/en/products/.

8 Gwendolyn Blue, "If It Ain't Alberta, It Ain't Beef," *Food, Culture, and Society* 11, 1 (2008): 69–85.

9 Henry Wetherbee Henshaw, "Indian Origin of Maple Sugar," *American Anthropologist* 3, 4 (1890): 341–52.

10 Judith Comfort, "Some Good!," in *Northern Bounty: A Celebration of Canadian Cuisine*, ed. Jo Marie Powers and Anita Stewart (Toronto: Random House, 1995), 195–202.

11  Dorothy Duncan, *Nothing More Comforting: Canada's Heritage Food* (Toronto: Dundurn Press, 2003).

12  Andrew Smith and Shelley Boyd, "Talking Turkey: Thanksgiving in Canada and the United States," in *What's to Eat? Entrées in Canadian Food History*, ed. Nathalie Cooke (Montreal: McGill-Queen's University Press, 2009), 116–44.

13  Lenore Newman, "Neige et Citrouille: Marché Atwater and Seasonality," *Cuizine: The Journal of Canadian Food Cultures/Revue des cultures culinaires au Canada* 3, 2 (2012): n. pag.

14  Lidia Marte, "Foodmaps: Tracing Boundaries of 'Home' through Food Relations," *Food and Foodways* 15, 3–4 (2007): 261–89.

15  See Newman, "Neige et Citrouille."

16  Ferguson, *Accounting for Taste*.

17  Hersch Jacobs, "Structural Elements in Canadian Cuisine," *Cuizine: The Journal of Canadian Food Culture/Revue des cultures culinaires au Canada* 2, 1 (2009): n. pag.

18  Lefebvre, *Rhythmanalysis*.

19  Mike Crang, "Rhythms of the City: Temporalised Space and Motion," in *TimeSpace: Geographies of Temporality*, ed. Jon May and Nigel Thrift (London: Routledge, 2001), 187–207.

20  Monica Degen, "Consuming Urban Rhythms: Let's Ravalejar," in *Geographies of Rhythm: Nature, Place, Mobilities, and Bodies*, ed. Tim Edensor (Burlington: Ashgate, 2010), 21–31.

21  Tim Ingold, "The Temporality of the Landscape," *World Archaeology* 25, 2 (1993): 152–74.

22  Agnes E. Van den Berg, Terry Hartig, and Henk Staats, "Preference for Nature in Urbanized Societies: Stress, Restoration, and the Pursuit of Sustainability," *Journal of Social Issues* 63, 1 (2007): 79–96.

23  Edith Adams [pen name for those in the Home Economics Department], *Edith Adams' Thirteenth Prize Cookbook* (Vancouver: Sun Printing, 1950), 25.

## CHAPTER 5. THE CANADIAN CREOLE

1  Lily Cho, *Eating Chinese: Culture on the Menu in Small Town Canada* (Toronto: University of Toronto Press, 2010), 78.

2  John Jung, *Sweet and Sour: Life in Chinese Family Restaurants* (Cypress, CA: Yin and Yang Press, 2010), 63.

3  Jennifer 8 Lee, *The Fortune Cookie Chronicles: Adventures in the World of Chinese Food* (New York: Twelve, 2008), 8.

4  David Y. H. Wu and Sidney C. H. Cheung, *Globalization of Chinese Food* (London: Routledge, 2012).

5  Lee, *The Fortune Cookie Chronicles*, 22.

6  Wu and Cheung, *Globalization of Chinese Food*.

7  Cho, *Eating Chinese*, 8.

8   Jean Duruz, "A Nice Baked Dinner...or Two Roast Ducks from Chinatown? Identity Grazing," *Continuum: Journal of Media and Cultural Studies* 14, 3 (2000): 299.

9   Wei Li, *Ethnoburb: The New Ethnic Community in Urban America* (Honolulu: University of Hawai'i Press, 2009).

10  Arlene Chan, "From Chinatown to Ethnoburb: The Chinese in Toronto," 2012, https://open.library.ubc.ca/cIRcle/collections/43391/items/1.0103074.

11  Lisa M. Heldke, *Exotic Appetites: Ruminations of a Food Adventurer* (New York: Routledge, 2003), xix.

12  Arjun Appadurai, "How to Make a National Cuisine: Cookbooks in Contemporary India," *Comparative Studies in Society and History* 30, 1 (1988): 3–24.

13  Nicholas Silich, "Authentic Food: A Philosophical Approach," in *Authenticity in the Kitchen: Proceedings of the Oxford Symposium on Food and Cookery 2005*, ed. Richard Hosking (Devon: Prospect Books, 2006), 401–02.

14  Heldke, *Exotic Appetites*, 27.

15  Richard Handler, "Authenticity," *Anthropology Today* 2, 1 (1986): 2–4.

16  Marvin Harris, *The Rise of Anthropological Theory: A History of Theories of Culture* (Lanham, MD: AltaMira Press, 2001).

17  George W. Stocking, Jr., "Franz Boas and the Culture Concept in Historical Perspective," *American Anthropologist* 68, 4 (1966): 867–82.

18  Will Kymlicka, *Multicultural Citizenship: A Liberal Theory of Minority Rights* (Cambridge, UK: Cambridge University Press, 1995).

19  Michael Dewing and Marc Leman, *Canadian Multiculturalism* (Ottawa: Library of Parliament, Parliamentary Research Branch, 2006).

20  Ibid.

21  Joyce Goldstein and Dore Brown, *Inside the California Food Revolution: Thirty Years that Changed Our Culinary Consciousness* (Berkeley: University of California Press, 2013), 31.

22  David Bell, "Fragments for a New Urban Culinary Geography," *Journal for the Study of Food and Society* 6, 1 (2002): 10–21.

23  LeeRay Costa and Kathryn Besio, "Eating Hawai'i: Local Foods and Place-Making in Hawai'i Regional Cuisine," *Social and Cultural Geography* 12, 8 (2011): 839–54.

24  Richard N. S. Robinson, "Plain Fare to Fusion: Ethnic Impacts on the Process of Maturity in Brisbane's Restaurant Sector," *Journal of Hospitality and Tourism Management* 14, 1 (2007): 70–84.

25  Eugene N. Anderson, "Malaysian Foodways: Confluence and Separation," *Ecology of Food and Nutrition* 46, 3–4 (2007): 205–19.

26  Jacobs, "Structural Elements in Canadian Cuisine."

27  Joanne Hlina, "Delicious Diversity," *BC Studies: The British Columbian Quarterly* 132 (2001): 81–84.

28  Rumiko Tachibana, "'Processing' Sushi/Cooked Japan: Why Sushi Became Canadian" (MA thesis, University of Victoria, 2008), 29.

29  Sheldon Pollock, "The Cosmopolitan Vernacular," *Journal of Asian Studies* 57, 1 (1998): 6–37.

245

30  Bell, "Fragments for a New Urban Culinary Geography," 17.

31  Kymlicka, *Multicultural Citizenship*, 22.

32  Carolyn Morris, "The Politics of Palatability on the Absence of Māori Restaurants," *Food, Culture, and Society* 13, 1 (2010): 5–28.

## CHAPTER 6. INGREDIENTS: AS CANADIAN AS MAPLE SYRUP

1  Duncan, *Canadians at Table*, 116.

2  Pierre Berton and Janet Berton, *Pierre and Janet Berton's Canadian Food Guide* (Toronto: McClelland and Stewart, 1974).

3  James Murphy and Stephen Smith, "Chefs and Suppliers: An Exploratory Look at Supply Chain Issues in an Upscale Restaurant Alliance," *International Journal of Hospitality Management* 28, 2 (2009): 212–20.

4  Amy B. Trubek, *The Taste of Place: A Cultural Journey into Terroir* (Berkeley: University of California Press 2008), 133.

5  Hashimoto and Telfer, "Selling Canadian Culinary Tourism," 42, complain about the ubiquitous nature of the maple, but research seems to bear out the impression that, as a nation, we love our national tree.

6  Carol I. Mason, "A Sweet Small Something: Maple Sugaring in the New World," in *The Invented Indian: Cultural Fictions and Government Policies*, ed. James A. Clifton (New Brunswick, NJ: Transaction Publishers, 1990), 91–106.

7  James Lawrence and Rux Martin, *Sweet Maple: Life, Lore, and Recipes from the Sugarbush* (Montpelier: Vermont Life, 1993).

8  Alexander F. Chamberlain, "The Maple amongst the Algonkian Tribes," *American Anthropologist* 4, 1 (1891): 39–44.

9  Alan R. Pierce, "Maple Syrup (*Acer Saccharum*)," in *Tapping the Green Market: Certification and Management of Non-Timber Forest Products*, ed. Patricia Shanley et al. (London: Earthscan Publications, 2002), 162–71.

10  Ken Albala, *Pancake: A Global History* (London: Reaktion Books, 2013).

11  Holly Everett, "A Welcoming Wilderness: The Role of Wild Berries in the Construction of Newfoundland and Labrador as a Tourist Destination," *Ethnologies* 29, 1–2 (2007): 60.

12  Ibid., 59.

13  Cited in Janet Clarkson, *Pie: A Global History* (London: Reaktion Books, 2009).

14  Ibid.

15  Ibid., 78.

16  Ibid., 95.

17  Anita Stewart, *The Flavours of Canada: A Celebration of the Finest Regional Foods* (Vancouver: Raincoast Books 2000), 51.

18  D. Bruce Johnsen, "Salmon, Science, and Reciprocity on the Northwest Coast" (article 43), *Ecology and Society* 14, 2 (2009): n. pag.

19  See Susan Lecompte Stacey, *Salmonopolis: The Steveston Story* (Madeira Park, BC: Harbour Publishing, 1994); and Mitsuo Yesaki, Harold Steves, and Kathy Steves, *Steveston Cannery Row: An Illustrated History* (Richmond, BC: Peninsula Publishing, 2005).

20  Yesaki, Steves, and Steves, *Steveston Cannery Row*, 81.

21  Heather Menzies, *By the Labour of Their Hands: The Story of Ontario Cheddar Cheese* (Kingston: Quarry Press, 1994).

22  Sasha Chapman, "Manufacturing Taste: The (Un)natural History of Kraft Dinner," *Walrus*, September 2012, 28+.

23  Fritz Blank, "Tafelspitz: More than a Recipe," in *Authenticity in the Kitchen: Proceedings of the Oxford Symposium on Food and Cookery 2005*, ed. Richard Hosking (Devon: Prospect Books, 2006), 65.

24  Appadurai, "How to Make a National Cuisine."

25  Cusack, "'Equatorial Guinea's National Cuisine Is Simple and Tasty.'"

26  Charles-Alexandre Théorêt, *Maudite poutine! Histoire approximative d'un fameux mets* (Montréal: Éditions Heliotrope, 2007), 9.

27  Paul R. Mullins, *Glazed America: A History of the Doughnut* (Gainesville: University Press of Florida, 2008).

28  Elaine Power and Mustafa Koc, "A Double-Double and a Maple-Glazed Doughnut," *Food, Culture, and Society* 11, 3 (2008): 263–67.

29  Steve Penfold, *The Donut: A Canadian History* (Toronto: University of Toronto Press, 2008).

30  Ibid., 74.

31  Douglas Brownlie, Paul Hewer, and Suzanne Horne, "Culinary Tourism: An Exploratory Reading of Contemporary Representations of Cooking," *Consumption Markets and Culture* 8, 1 (2005): 7–26.

32  Georges Auguste Escoffier, *Le guide culinaire* (1903; reprinted, Paris: Flammarion, 1993).

33  Elizabeth Driver, *Culinary Landmarks: A Bibliography of Canadian Cookbooks, 1825–1949* (Toronto: University of Toronto Press, 2008).

34  Catharine Parr Traill, *The Female Emigrants Guide, and Hints on Canadian Housekeeping* (Toronto: Maclear, 1854).

35  Helen Gougeon, *Helen Gougeon's Good Food Book* (1958; reprinted as *Helen Gougeon's Original Canadian Cookbook*, Don Mills, ON: Collins Publishers, 1975).

36  Canadian Home Economics Association, *The Laura Secord Cookbook* (Toronto: McClelland and Stewart, 1966).

37  Pierre Berton and Janet Berton, *The Centennial Food Guide: A Century of Good Eating* (Toronto: McClelland and Stewart, 1966).

38  Rhona Richman-Kenneally, "The Cuisine of the Tundra: Towards a Canadian Food Culture at Expo 67," *Food, Culture, and Society* 11, 3 (2008): 287–314.

39  Stewart, *The Flavours of Canada*, 9, 11.

40  Anita Stewart, *Anita Stewart's Canada: The Food, the Recipes, the Stories* (Toronto: HarperCollins, 2008).

41  Stewart, *The Flavours of Canada*, 17.

42  Franz Boas and George Hunt, *Ethnology of the Kwakiutl: Based on Data Collected by George Hunt* (Washington, DC: US Government Printing Office, 1921).

43   Nathalie Cooke, ed., *What's to Eat? Entrées in Canadian Food History* (Montreal: McGill-Queen's University Press, 2009).

## CHAPTER 7. QUEBEC AND ONTARIO

1    Jacobs, "Structural Elements in Canadian Cuisine."
2    David Bell and Gill Valentine, *Consuming Geographies: We Are Where We Eat* (London: Routledge, 1997).
3    Martin Jones and Gordon MacLeod, "Regional Spaces, Spaces of Regionalism: Territory, Insurgent Politics, and the English Question," *Transactions of the Institute of British Geographers* 29, 4 (2004): 433–52.
4    Hashimoto and Telfer, "Selling Canadian Culinary Tourism."
5    Cook and Crang, "The World on a Plate."
6    Trubek, *The Taste of Place.*
7    Evan D. G. Fraser and Andrew Rimas , *Empires of Food: Feast, Famine, and the Rise and Fall of Civilizations* (New York: Simon and Schuster, 2010), 239.
8    Julian Armstrong, *A Taste of Quebec* (Hoboken, NJ: Wiley, 2003).
9    Victoria Dickenson, "Cartier, Champlain, and the Fruits of the New World: Botanical Exchange in the 16th and 17th Centuries," *Scientia Canadensis: Canadian Journal of the History of Science, Technology, and Medicine/Revue canadienne d'histoire des sciences, des techniques, et de la médecine* 31, 1–2 (2008): 27–47.
10   Driver, *Culinary Landmarks.*
11   Stephen Gazillo, "The Evolution of Restaurants and Bars in Vieux-Québec since 1900," *Cahiers de géographie du Québec* 25, 64 (1981): 101–18.
12   Hugh MacLennan, *Two Solitudes* (1945; reprinted, Toronto: McClelland and Stewart, 2003).
13   Richard Handler, *Nationalism and the Politics of Culture in Quebec* (Madison: University of Wisconsin Press, 1988).
14   Hélène-Andrée Bizier, *Cuisine traditionnelle des régions du Québec* (Montreal: Éditions de l'Homme, 1996).
15   Laurier Turgeon and Madeleine Pastinelli, "'Eat the World': Postcolonial Encounters in Quebec City's Ethnic Restaurants," *Journal of American Folklore* 115, 456 (2002): 247–68.
16   Edward Behr, "La cuisine québécoise," *Journal of Gastronomy* 5, 4 (1990): 1–18.
17   Hashimoto and Telfer, "Selling Canadian Culinary Tourism."
18   Armstrong, *A Taste of Quebec.*
19   Catherine Turgeon-Gouin, "The Myth of Québec Traditional Cuisine at Au Pied de Cochon," *Cuizine: The Journal of Canadian Food Cultures/Revue des cultures culinaires au Canada* 3, 2 (2012): n. pag.
20   Martin Picard, *Au Pied de Cochon Sugar Shack: Maple Syrup* (Montreal: Restaurant Au Pied de Cochon, 2012).
21   David McMillan, Frederic Morin, and Meredith Erickson, *The Art of Living According to Joe Beef: A Cookbook of Sorts* (Berkeley: Potter/TenSpeed/Harmony, 2011).

22  Armstrong, *A Taste of Quebec*, 63.

23  Mordecai Richler, *The Apprenticeship of Duddy Kravitz* (New York: Simon and Schuster, 1999).

24  Jean-Pierre Lemasson, "The Long History of the *Tourtière* of Quebec's Lac-St. Jean," in *What's to Eat? Entrées in Canadian Food History*, ed. Nathalie Cooke (Montreal: McGill-Queen's University Press, 2009), 99–115.

25  Stewart, *The Flavours of Canada*, 128–65.

26  Driver, *Culinary Landmarks*, 274.

27  Carol Anderson and Katharine Mallinson, *Lunch with Lady Eaton: Inside the Dining Rooms of a Nation* (Toronto: ECW Press, 2004).

28  David J. Telfer, "Tastes of Niagara: Building Strategic Alliances between Tourism and Agriculture," *International Journal of Hospitality and Tourism Administration* 1, 1 (2000): 71–88.

29  Don Cyr and Martin Kusy, "Canadian Ice Wine Production: A Case for the Use of Weather Derivatives," *Journal of Wine Economics* 2, 2 (2007): 145–67.

30  C. Michael Hall et al., *Food Tourism around the World* (London: Routledge, 2004).

31  Bruce Erickson, *Canoe Nation: Nature, Race, and the Making of a Canadian Icon* (Vancouver: UBC Press, 2013).

32  Roy I. Wolfe, "Wasaga Beach: The Divorce from the Geographic Environment," *Canadian Geographer/ Géographe canadien* 1, 2 (1952): 57–66.

33  Stephen Svenson, "The Cottage and the City: An Interpretation of the Canadian Second Home Experience," in *Tourism, Mobility, and Second Homes: Between Elite Landscape and Common Ground*, ed. C. Michael Hall and Dieter K. Müller (Bristol: Channel View Publications, 2004), 55–74.

34  Pauline Morel, "Eating Out: The Influence of the Outdoors on Canadian Domestic Foodways," paper presented at Domestic Foodscapes: Towards Mindful Eating, Montreal, 2008.

249

## CHAPTER 8. ALBERTA AND BRITISH COLUMBIA

1  Henry C. Klassen, *A Business History of Alberta* (Calgary: University of Calgary Press, 1999).

2  J. M. S. Careless, *Frontier and Metropolis: Regions, Cities, and Identities in Canada before 1914* (Toronto: University of Toronto Press, 1991).

3  Blue, "If It Ain't Alberta, It Ain't Beef," 70.

4  James Unterschultz, Kwamena K. Quagrainie, and Michel Vincent, "Evaluating Quebec's Preference for Alberta Beef versus US Beef," *Agribusiness* 13, 5 (1997): 457–68.

5  Gail Norton and Karen Ralph, *Calgary Cooks: Recipes from the City's Top Chefs* (Vancouver: Figure 1 Publishing, 2014).

6  Henry Finck, *The Pacific Coast Scenic Tour: From Southern California to Alaska, the Canadian Pacific Railway, Yellowstone Park, and the Grand Cañon* (New York: C. Scribner's Sons, 1891).

7  D. Bruce Johnsen, "A Culturally Correct Proposal to Privatize the British Columbia Salmon Fishery," George Mason Law and Economics Research Paper 04-49 (2004), 100.

8  Goldstein and Brown, *Inside the California Food Revolution*.

9  Gary Nabhan, *Coming Home to Eat: The Pleasures and Politics of Local Foods* (New York: W. W. Norton and Company, 2009).

10  Alisa Smith and Jamie MacKinnon, *The 100-Mile Diet: A Year of Local Eating* (Toronto: Vintage, 2009).

11  Katherine Burnett, "Commodifying Poverty: Gentrification and Consumption in Vancouver's Downtown Eastside," *Urban Geography* 35, 2 (2014): 157–76.

12  David Bell, "Variations on the Rural Idyll," in *The Sage Handbook of Rural Studies*, ed. Paul Cloke, Terry Marsden, and Patrick H. Mooney (London: Sage Publications, 2006), 149–60.

13  Johnston and Baumann, *Foodies*.

14  Hashimoto and Telfer, "Selling Canadian Culinary Tourism."

15  Lenore Lauri Newman, "Notes from the Nanaimo Bar Trail," *Canadian Food Studies/ La revue canadienne des études sur l'alimentation* 1, 1 (2014): 10–19.

16  Sherrie A. Inness, *Dinner Roles: American Women and Culinary Culture* (Iowa City: University of Iowa Press, 2001), 57.

17  Diane Tye, *Baking as Biography: A Life Story in Recipes* (Montreal: McGill-Queen's University Press, 2010), 88.

## CHAPTER 9. THE EAST COAST, THE PRAIRIES, AND THE NORTH

1  Duruz, "A Nice Baked Dinner," 299.

2  Driver, *Culinary Landmarks*.

3  John T. Omohundro, *Rough Food: The Seasons of Subsistence in Northern Newfoundland* (St. John's: Institute of Social and Economic Research, Memorial University of Newfoundland, 1994).

4  Ibid.

5  Pamela J. Gray, "Traditional Newfoundland Foodways: Origin, Adaptation, and Change" (MA thesis, Memorial University of Newfoundland, 1977).

6  Everett, "Vernacular Health Moralities and Culinary Tourism in Newfoundland and Labrador."

7  Ibid.

8  Tye, *Baking as Biography*.

9  John Selwood, "The Lure of Food: Food as an Attraction in Destination Marketing in Manitoba, Canada," in *Food Tourism around the World: Management of Development and Markets*, ed. C. Michael Hall et al. (London: Routledge, 2003), 178–91.

10  Zona Spray Starks, "Arctic Foodways and Contemporary Cuisine," *Gastronomica: The Journal of Food and Culture* 7, 1 (2007): 41–49.

11  Lisa Markowitz, "Highland Haute Cuisine: The Transformation of Alpaca Meat," in *Reimagining Marginalized Foods: Global Processes, Local Places*, ed. Elizabeth Finnis (Tucson: University of Arizona Press, 2012), 34–48.

12    Edmund Searles, "Food and the Making of Modern Inuit Identities," *Food and Foodways* 10, 1–2 (2002): 55–78.

13    Martin Hand and Elizabeth Shove, "Condensing Practices: Ways of Living with a Freezer," *Journal of Consumer Culture* 7, 1 (2007): 79–104.

## CHAPTER 10. FOOD AND PUBLIC LIFE

1     Linda Biesenthal, *To Market, to Market: The Public Market Tradition in Canada* (Toronto: PMA Books, 1980), 6.

2     Helen Tangires, *Public Markets and Civic Culture in Nineteenth-Century America* (New York: W. W. Norton and Company, 2008), 36.

3     Alfonso Morales, "Marketplaces: Prospects for Social, Economic, and Political Development," *Journal of Planning Literature* 26, 1 (2011): 6.

4     Brian Stewart, "Closing of Atwater Market Confirmed," Montreal *Gazette*, September 24, 1968.

5     Sarah Musgrave, "Taste of Place, Place of Taste: Mapping Alimentary Authenticity through Marché Jean-Talon" (MA thesis, Concordia University, 2009).

6     Newman, "Neige et Citrouille."

7     Karen Johnson, *Granville Island* (Vancouver: Dreamica, 2010).

8     Ibid.

9     Michael McCullough, *Granville Island: An Urban Oasis* (Vancouver: Granville Island, 1998).

10    David Ley, *The New Middle Class and the Remaking of the Central City* (Oxford: Oxford University Press, 1996).

11    Jane Pyle, "Farmers' Markets in the United States: Functional Anachronisms," *Geographical Review* (1971): 167–97.

12    G. P. Archer et al., "Latent Consumers' Attitude to Farmers' Markets in North West England," *British Food Journal* 105, 8 (2003): 487–97.

13    Wittman, Beckie, and Hergesheimer, "Linking Local Food Systems and the Social Economy?"

14    Natalie Gibb and Hannah Wittman, "Parallel Alternatives: Chinese-Canadian Farmers and the Metro Vancouver Local Food Movement," *Local Environment* 18, 1 (2013): 1–19.

15    Newman and Burnett, "Street Food and Vibrant Urban Spaces."

16    Katherine Burnett and Lenore Newman, "Urban Policy Regimes and the Political Economy of Street Food in Canada and the United States," in *Street Food: Culture, Economy, Health, and Governance*, ed. Ryzia De Cássia Vieira Cardoso, Michèle Companion, and Stefano Roberto Marras (New York: Routledge, 2014), 46–60.

17    Ibid.

18    Alison Blay-Palmer et al., "Constructing Resilient, Transformative Communities through Sustainable 'Food Hubs,'" *Local Environment* 18, 5 (2013): 521–28.

## CHAPTER 11. BETWEEN PLACES

1   Tim Edensor, "Commuter: Mobility, Rhythm, and Commuting," in *Geographies of Mobilities: Practices, Spaces, Subjects*, ed. Tim Cresswell and Peter Merriman (Farnham: Ashgate, 2011), 197.

2   Marc Augé, *Non-Places: Introduction to an Anthropology of Supermodernity*, trans. John Howe (London: Verso, 1995).

3   Ibid., 65.

4   Daniel Boorstin, *The Image: Or, What Happened to the American Dream* (New York: Atheneum Press, 1962), 117.

5   Edward Relph, *Place and Placelessness* (London: Pion, 1976).

6   Tim Cresswell, "Towards a Politics of Mobility," *Environment and Planning D: Society and Space* 28, 1 (2010): 17–31.

7   Jon May and Nigel Thrift, eds., *TimeSpace: Geographies of Temporality* (London: Routledge, 2001).

8   John A. Jakle and Keith A. Sculle, *Fast Food: Roadside Restaurants in the Automobile Age* (Baltimore: Johns Hopkins University Press, 2002), 7.

9   Neil Wrigley and Michelle Lowe, *Retailing, Consumption, and Capital: Towards the New Retail Geography* (Harlow: Longman, 1996), 27.

10  Mike Featherstone, "Automobilities: An Introduction," *Theory, Culture, and Society* 21, 4–5 (2004): 13.

11  Darrell A. Norris, "Interstate Highway Exit Morphology: Non-Metropolitan Exit Commerce on I-75," *Professional Geographer* 39, 1 (1987): 23–32.

12  Jakle and Sculle, *Fast Food*.

13  Penfold, *The Donut*, 4.

14  Jakle and Sculle, *Fast Food*.

15  Phillip Vannini, *Ferry Tales: Mobility, Place, and Time on Canada's West Coast* (Abingdon: Taylor and Francis, 2012).

16  Cresswell, "Towards a Politics of Mobility," 17.

17  Justine Lloyd, "Airport Technology, Travel, and Consumption," *Space and Culture* 6, 2 (2003): 93–109.

18  Gillian Fuller and Ross Harley, *Aviopolis: A Book about Airports* (London: Blackdog Publications, 2004).

## CHAPTER 12. COMING HOME TO AN UNCERTAIN FUTURE

1   Brown, "Letter to Anne Brown," September 13, 1864.

2   *Halifax Morning Chronicle*, September 13, 1864.

3   *British Colonist*, September 15, 1864.

4   Robertson Davies, "The Charlottetown Banquet," in *High Spirits*, by Davies (1982; reprinted, Toronto: McClelland and Stewart, 2015).

5   Charles Perry, "The Oldest Mediterranean Noodle: A Cautionary Tale," *Petits propos culinaires* 9 (1981): 42.

6    Ibid., 44.

7    Jennifer Kidon et al., "Economic Impact of the 1998 Ice Storm on the Eastern Ontario
     Maple Syrup Industry," *Forestry Chronicle* 77, 4 (2001): 667–75.

8    Cyr and Kusy, "Canadian Ice Wine Production."

9    M. H. H. Price et al., "Ghost Runs: Management and Status Assessment of Pacific
     Salmon (Oncorhynchus Spp.) Returning to British Columbia's Central and North
     Coasts," *Canadian Journal of Fisheries and Aquatic Sciences* 65, 12 (2008): 2712–18.

10   There is a good breakdown and discussion of this in Charles A. Francis et al.,
     "Farmland Conversion to Non-Agricultural Uses in the US and Canada: Current
     Impacts and Concerns for the Future," *International Journal of Agricultural
     Sustainability* 10, 1 (2012): 8–24.

11   Statistics Canada, "Canada's Rural Population Declining since 1851," in *Canadian
     Demography at a Glance*, Catalogue 98-003-X (Ottawa: Statistics Canada, 2014).

12   Jacob Richler, "Ramps: Hands off Those Wild Leeks," *Maclean's* 127, 19–20 (2014): 74.

13   Wes Flack, "American Microbreweries and Neolocalism: 'Ale-ing' for a Sense of Place,"
     *Journal of Cultural Geography* 16, 2 (1997): 37–53.

# REFERENCES

Adams, Edith [pen name for those in the Home Economics Department]. *Edith Adams'*
*Thirteenth Prize Cookbook*. Vancouver: Sun Printing, 1950.

Albala, Ken. *Pancake: A Global History*. London: Reaktion Books, 2013.

———. "Wild Food: The Call of the Domestic." In *Wild Foods: Proceedings of the Oxford*
*Symposium on Food and Cookery 2004*, edited by Richard Hosking, 9–19. Devon:
Prospect Books, 2006.

Anderson, Benedict. *Imagined Communities: Reflections on the Origin and Spread of*
*Nationalism*. London: Verso, 2006.

Anderson, Carol, and Katharine Mallinson. *Lunch with Lady Eaton: Inside the Dining*
*Rooms of a Nation*. Toronto: ECW Press, 2004.

Anderson, Eugene N. "Malaysian Foodways: Confluence and Separation." *Ecology of Food*
*and Nutrition* 46, 3–4 (2007): 205–19.

Appadurai, Arjun. "How to Make a National Cuisine: Cookbooks in Contemporary India."
*Comparative Studies in Society and History* 30, 1 (1988): 3–24.

Archer, G. P., Judit García Sánchez, Gianpaolo Vignali, and Aurélie Chaillot. "Latent
Consumers' Attitude to Farmers' Markets in North West England." *British Food Journal*
105, 8 (2003): 487–97.

Aristotle. *Complete Works of Aristotle, the Revised Oxford Translation*. Edited by Jonathan
Barnes. Vol. 1. Princeton: Princeton University Press, 2014.

Armstrong, Julian. *A Taste of Quebec*. Hoboken, NJ: Wiley, 2003.

Augé, Marc. *Non-Places: Introduction to an Anthropology of Supermodernity*. Translated by
John Howe. London: Verso, 1995.

Barr, Ann, and Paul Levy. *The Official Foodie Handbook*. New York: Doubleday, 1985.

Barthes, Roland. "Toward a Psychosociology of Contemporary Food Consumption." In
*Food and Culture: A Reader*, edited by Carole Counihan and Penny Van Esterik, 23–30.
New York: Routledge, 2013.

Bavington, Dean. *Managed Annihilation: An Unnatural History of the Newfoundland Cod*
*Collapse*. Vancouver: UBC Press, 2011.

Behr, Edward. "La cuisine québécoise." *Journal of Gastronomy* 5, 4 (1990): 1–18.

Belasco, Warren. *Meals to Come: A History of the Future of Food.* Berkeley: University of California Press, 2006.

Bell, David. "Fragments for a New Urban Culinary Geography." *Journal for the Study of Food and Society* 6, 1 (2002): 10–21.

——. "Variations on the Rural Idyll." In *The Sage Handbook of Rural Studies*, edited by Paul Cloke, Terry Marsden, and Patrick H. Mooney, 149–60. London: Sage Publications, 2006.

Bell, David, and Gill Valentine. *Consuming Geographies: We Are Where We Eat.* London: Routledge, 1997.

Berton, Pierre, and Janet Berton. *The Centennial Food Guide: A Century of Good Eating.* Toronto: McClelland and Stewart, 1966.

——. *Pierre and Janet Berton's Canadian Food Guide.* Toronto: McClelland and Stewart, 1974.

Biesenthal, Linda. *To Market, to Market: The Public Market Tradition in Canada.* Toronto: PMA Books, 1980.

Bizier, Hélène-Andrée. *Cuisine traditionnelle des régions du Québec.* Montréal: Éditions de l'Homme, 1996.

Blank, Fritz. "Tafelspitz: More than a Recipe." In *Authenticity in the Kitchen: Proceedings of the Oxford Symposium on Food and Cookery 2005*, edited by Richard Hosking, 65–73. Devon: Prospect Books, 2006.

Blay-Palmer, Alison, Karen Landman, Irena Knezevic, and Ryan Hayhurst. "Constructing Resilient, Transformative Communities through Sustainable 'Food Hubs.'" *Local Environment* 18, 5 (2013): 521–28.

Blue, Gwendolyn. "If It Ain't Alberta, It Ain't Beef." *Food, Culture, and Society* 11, 1 (2008): 69–85.

Boas, Franz, and George Hunt. *Ethnology of the Kwakiutl: Based on Data Collected by George Hunt.* Washington, DC: US Government Printing Office, 1921.

Boorstin, Daniel. *The Image: Or, What Happened to the American Dream.* Middlesex: Penguin, 1962.

Bourdieu, Pierre. *Distinction: A Social Critique of the Judgement of Taste.* Translated by Richard Nice. Cambridge, MA: Harvard University Press, 1984.

Brillat-Savarin, Jean Anthelme. *The Physiology of Taste: Or, Meditations on Transcendental Gastronomy.* Translated by M. F. K. Fisher. Mineola: Dover Publications, 2011.

Brody, Hugh. *The Other Side of Eden: Hunters, Farmers, and the Shaping of the World.* London: Macmillan, 2002.

Brown, George. "Letter to Anne Brown." September 13, 1864. Library and Archives Canada, George Brown Papers, MG 24, B40, Vols. 5–8.

Brownlie, Douglas, Paul Hewer, and Suzanne Horne. "Culinary Tourism: An Exploratory Reading of Contemporary Representations of Cooking." *Consumption Markets and Culture* 8, 1 (2005): 7–26.

Bruce, Harry. "Confederation." In *Canada 1812–1871: The Formative Years.* Edited by James Knight. Toronto: Imperial Oil, 1967.

Burnett, Katherine. "Commodifying Poverty: Gentrification and Consumption in Vancouver's Downtown Eastside." *Urban Geography* 35, 2 (2014): 157–76.

Burnett, Katherine, and Lenore Newman. "Urban Policy Regimes and the Political Economy of Street Food in Canada and the United States." In *Street Food: Culture, Economy, Health, and Governance*, edited by Ryzia De Cássia Vieira Cardoso, Michèle Companion, and Stefano Roberto Marras, 46–60. New York: Routledge, 2014.

Campbell, Susan. "The Hunting and Gathering of Wild Foods: What's the Point? An Historical Survey." In *Wild Foods: Proceedings of the Oxford Symposium on Food and Cookery 2004*, edited by Richard Hosking, 68–78. Devon: Prospect Books, 2006.

Canadian Home Economics Association. *The Laura Secord Cookbook*. Toronto: McClelland and Stewart, 1966.

Careless, J. M. S. *Frontier and Metropolis: Regions, Cities, and Identities in Canada before 1914*. Toronto: University of Toronto Press, 1991.

——. *Statesman of Confederation, 1860–1880*. Vol. 2 of *Brown of the Globe*. Toronto: Macmillan, 1963.

Chamberlain, Alexander F. "The Maple amongst the Algonkian Tribes." *American Anthropologist* 4, 1 (1891): 39–44.

Chan, Arlene. "From Chinatown to Ethnoburb: The Chinese in Toronto." 2012. https://open.library.ubc.ca/cIRcle/collections/43391/items/1.0103074.

Chapman, Sasha. "Manufacturing Taste: The (Un)natural History of Kraft Dinner." *Walrus*, September 2012, 28+.

Cho, Lily. *Eating Chinese: Culture on the Menu in Small Town Canada*. Toronto: University of Toronto Press, 2010.

Clarkson, Janet. *Pie: A Global History*. London: Reaktion Books, 2009.

Coles, Benjamin F. "Making the Market Place: A Topography of Borough Market, London." *Cultural Geographies* 21, 3 (2014): 515–23.

Colpitts, George. "Provisioning the HBC: Market Economies in the British Buffalo Commons in the Early Nineteenth Century." *Western Historical Quarterly* 43, 2 (2012): 179–203.

Colquhoun, Anne, and Phil Lyon. "To Everything There Was a Season: Deconstructing UK Food Availability." *Food Service Technology* 1, 2 (2001): 93–102.

Comfort, Judith. "Some Good!" In *Northern Bounty: A Celebration of Canadian Cuisine*, edited by Jo Marie Powers and Anita Stewart, 195–202. Toronto: Random House, 1995.

Cook, Ian, and Philip Crang. "The World on a Plate: Culinary Culture, Displacement, and Geographical Knowledges." *Journal of Material Culture* 1, 2 (1996): 131–53.

Cooke, Nathalie, ed. *What's to Eat? Entrées in Canadian Food History*. Montreal: McGill-Queen's University Press, 2009.

Costa, LeeRay, and Kathryn Besio. "Eating Hawai'i: Local Foods and Place-Making in Hawai'i Regional Cuisine." *Social and Cultural Geography* 12, 8 (2011): 839–54.

Crang, Mike. "Rhythms of the City: Temporalised Space and Motion." In *TimeSpace: Geographies of Temporality*, edited by Jon May and Nigel Thrift, 187–207. London: Routledge, 2001.

257

Creighton, Luella. *The Elegant Canadians*. Toronto: McClelland and Stewart, 1967.

Cresswell, Tim. "Towards a Politics of Mobility." *Environment and Planning D: Society and Space* 28, 1 (2010): 17–31.

Cronon, William. "The Trouble with Wilderness: Or, Getting Back to the Wrong Nature." *Environmental History* 1, 1 (1996): 7–28.

Cusack, Igor. "'Equatorial Guinea's National Cuisine Is Simple and Tasty': Cuisine and the Making of National Culture." *Arizona Journal of Hispanic Cultural Studies* 8 (2004): 131–48.

Cyr, Don, and Martin Kusy. "Canadian Ice Wine Production: A Case for the Use of Weather Derivatives." *Journal of Wine Economics* 2, 2 (2007): 145–67.

Daschuk, James. *Clearing the Plains: Disease, Politics of Starvation, and the Loss of Aboriginal Life*. Regina: University of Regina Press, 2013.

Davies, Robertson. "The Charlottetown Banquet." In *High Spirits*, by Davies. 1982; reprinted, Toronto: McClelland and Stewart, 2015.

Davison, Janet. "Food Eats Up Less of Our Spending, but Costs Us More." October 7, 2011. http://www.cbc.ca/news/canada/food-eats-up-less-of-our-spending-but-costs-us-more-1.1054574.

de Schutter, Olivier. "Report of the Special Rapporteur on the Right to Food: Mission to Canada." Presented to the UN Human Rights Council (GE.12-18956), 2014.

Degen, Monica. "Consuming Urban Rhythms: Let's Ravalejar." In *Geographies of Rhythm: Nature, Place, Mobilities, and Bodies*, edited by Tim Edensor, 21–31. Burlington: Ashgate, 2010.

Dewing, Michael, and Marc Leman. *Canadian Multiculturalism*. Ottawa: Library of Parliament, Parliamentary Research Branch, 2006.

Dickenson, Victoria. "Cartier, Champlain, and the Fruits of the New World: Botanical Exchange in the 16th and 17th Centuries." *Scientia Canadensis: Canadian Journal of the History of Science, Technology, and Medicine/Revue canadienne d'histoire des sciences, des techniques, et de la médecine* 31, 1–2 (2008): 27–47.

Driver, Elizabeth. *Culinary Landmarks: A Bibliography of Canadian Cookbooks, 1825–1949*. Toronto: University of Toronto Press, 2008.

Duncan, Dorothy. *Canadians at Table: Food, Fellowship, and Folklore: A Culinary History of Canada*. Toronto: Dundurn Press, 2006.

———. *Nothing More Comforting: Canada's Heritage Food*. Toronto: Dundurn Press, 2003.

Duruz, Jean. "A Nice Baked Dinner…or Two Roast Ducks from Chinatown? Identity Grazing." *Continuum: Journal of Media and Cultural Studies* 14, 3 (2000): 289–301.

Edensor, Tim. "Commuter: Mobility, Rhythm, and Commuting." In *Geographies of Mobilities: Practices, Spaces, Subjects*, edited by Tim Cresswell and Peter Merriman, 189–204. Farnham: Ashgate, 2011.

Erickson, Bruce. *Canoe Nation: Nature, Race, and the Making of a Canadian Icon*. Vancouver: UBC Press, 2013.

Escoffier, Georges Auguste. *Le guide culinaire*. 1903; reprinted, Paris: Flammarion, 1993.

Everett, Holly. "Vernacular Health Moralities and Culinary Tourism in Newfoundland and Labrador." *Journal of American Folklore* 122, 1 (2009): 28–52.

———. "A Welcoming Wilderness: The Role of Wild Berries in the Construction of Newfoundland and Labrador as a Tourist Destination." *Ethnologies* 29, 1–2 (2007): 49–80.

Featherstone, Mike. "Automobilities: An Introduction." *Theory, Culture, and Society* 21, 4–5 (2004): 1–24.

Ferguson, Priscilla Parkhurst. *Accounting for Taste: The Triumph of French Cuisine.* Chicago: University of Chicago Press, 2006.

Finck, Henry. *The Pacific Coast Scenic Tour: From Southern California to Alaska, the Canadian Pacific Railway, Yellowstone Park, and the Grand Cañon.* New York: C. Scribner's Sons, 1891.

Finnis, Elizabeth, ed. *Reimagining Marginalized Foods: Global Processes, Local Places.* Tucson: University of Arizona Press, 2012.

Fischler, Claude. "Commensality, Society, and Culture." *Social Science Information* 50, 3–4 (2011): 528–48.

Flack, Wes. "American Microbreweries and Neolocalism: 'Ale-ing' for a Sense of Place." *Journal of Cultural Geography* 16, 2 (1997): 37–53.

Francis, Charles A., et al. "Farmland Conversion to Non-Agricultural Uses in the U.S. and Canada: Current Impacts and Concerns for the Future." *International Journal of Agricultural Sustainability* 10, 1 (2012): 8–24.

Fraser, Evan D. G., and Andrew Rimas. *Empires of Food: Feast, Famine, and the Rise and Fall of Civilizations.* New York: Simon and Schuster, 2010.

Fuller, Gillian, and Ross Harley. *Aviopolis: A Book about Airports.* London: Black Dog Publications, 2004.

Gazillo, Stephen. "The Evolution of Restaurants and Bars in Vieux-Québec since 1900." *Cahiers de géographie du Québec* 25, 64 (1981): 101–18.

Geertz, Clifford. *The Interpretation of Cultures.* London: Fontana Press, 1993.

Gibb, Natalie, and Hannah Wittman. "Parallel Alternatives: Chinese-Canadian Farmers and the Metro Vancouver Local Food Movement." *Local Environment* 18, 1 (2013): 1–19.

Gibbons, Euell. *Stalking the Wild Asparagus.* New York: David McKay, 1962.

Gitelson, Joshua. "Populox: The Suburban Cuisine of the 1950s." *Journal of American Culture* 15, 3 (1992): 73–78.

Goldstein, Joyce, and Dore Brown. *Inside the California Food Revolution: Thirty Years that Changed Our Culinary Consciousness.* Berkeley: University of California Press, 2013.

Gougeon, Helen. *Helen Gougeon's Good Food Book.* 1958; reprinted as *Helen Gougeon's Original Canadian Cookbook,* Don Mills, ON: Collins Publishers, 1975.

Gray, Pamela J. "Traditional Newfoundland Foodways: Origin, Adaptation, and Change." MA thesis, Memorial University of Newfoundland, 1977.

Guerrero, Luis, et al. "Consumer-Driven Definition of Traditional Food Products and Innovation in Traditional Foods: A Qualitative Cross-Cultural Study." *Appetite* 52, 2 (2009): 345–54.

Hall, C. Michael, Liz Sharples, Richard Mitchell, Niki Macionis, and Brock Cambourne, eds. *Food Tourism around the World.* London: Routledge, 2004.

259

Hand, Martin, and Elizabeth Shove. "Condensing Practices: Ways of Living with a Freezer." *Journal of Consumer Culture* 7, 1 (2007): 79–104.

Handler, Richard. "Authenticity." *Anthropology Today* 2, 1 (1986): 2–4.

——. *Nationalism and the Politics of Culture in Quebec.* Madison: University of Wisconsin Press, 1988.

Harris, Marvin. *The Rise of Anthropological Theory: A History of Theories of Culture.* Lanham, MD: AltaMira Press, 2001.

Hashimoto, Atsuko, and David J. Telfer. "Selling Canadian Culinary Tourism: Branding the Global and Regional Product." *Tourism Geographies* 8, 1 (2006): 31–55.

Heldke, Lisa M. *Exotic Appetites: Ruminations of a Food Adventurer.* New York: Routledge, 2003.

Henshaw, Henry Wetherbee. "Indian Origin of Maple Sugar." *American Anthropologist* 3, 4 (1890): 341–52.

Hlina, Joanne. "Delicious Diversity." *BC Studies: The British Columbian Quarterly* 132 (2001): 81–84.

Hluchly, Patricia. "Taste of the True North." *Maclean's* 116, 26–27 (2003): 67–72.

Holloway, Lewis, and Moya Kneafsey. "Reading the Space of the Farmers' Market: A Preliminary Investigation from the UK." *Sociologica Ruralis* 40, 3 (2000): 285–99.

Hosking, Richard, ed. *Authenticity in the Kitchen: Proceedings of the Oxford Symposium on Food and Cookery 2005.* Devon: Prospect Books, 2006.

——, ed. *Wild Food: Proceedings of the Oxford Symposium of Food and Cookery 2004.* Devon: Prospect Books, 2006.

Huskins, Bonnie. "From Haute Cuisine to Ox Roasts: Public Feasting and the Negotiation of Class in Mid-19th-Century Saint John and Halifax." *Labour/Le travail* 37 (1996): 9–36.

Ingold, Tim. "The Temporality of the Landscape." *World Archaeology* 25, 2 (1993): 152–74.

Inness, Sherrie A. *Dinner Roles: American Women and Culinary Culture.* Iowa City: University of Iowa Press, 2001.

Jacobs, Hersch. "Structural Elements in Canadian Cuisine." *Cuizine: The Journal of Canadian Food Culture/Revue des cultures culinaires au Canada* 2, 1 (2009): n. pag.

Jakle, John A., and Keith A. Sculle. *Fast Food: Roadside Restaurants in the Automobile Age.* Baltimore: Johns Hopkins University Press, 2002.

Johnsen, D. Bruce. "A Culturally Correct Proposal to Privatize the British Columbia Salmon Fishery." George Mason Law and Economics Research Paper 04-49. 2004.

——. "Salmon, Science, and Reciprocity on the Northwest Coast" (article 43). *Ecology and Society* 14, 2 (2009): n. pag.

Johnson, Karen. *Granville Island.* Vancouver: Dreamica, 2010.

Johnston, Josée, and Shyon Baumann. *Foodies: Democracy and Distinction in the Gourmet Foodscape.* New York: Routledge, 2010.

Jones, Martin, and Gordon MacLeod. "Regional Spaces, Spaces of Regionalism: Territory, Insurgent Politics, and the English Question." *Transactions of the Institute of British Geographers* 29, 4 (2004): 433–52.

Jowett, Benjamin, trans. *Dialogues of Plato: Translated into English, with Analyses and Introduction.* Vol. 4. Cambridge, MA: Harvard University Press, 2010.

Jung, John. *Sweet and Sour: Life in Chinese Family Restaurants.* Cypress, CA: Yin and Yang Press, 2010.

Kidon, Jennifer, Glenn Fox, Dan McKenney, and Kimberly Rollins. "Economic Impact of the 1998 Ice Storm on the Eastern Ontario Maple Syrup Industry." *Forestry Chronicle* 77, 4 (2001): 667–75.

Klassen, Henry C. *A Business History of Alberta.* Calgary: University of Calgary Press, 1999.

Kramer, Steven. "Tracking the Wild in 'Wild' Foods." In *Wild Food: Proceedings of the Oxford Symposium of Food and Cookery 2004,* edited by Richard Hosking, 184–92. Devon: Prospect Books, 2006.

Kurlansky, Mark. *Cod: A Biography of the Fish that Changed the World.* New York: Random House, 2011.

Kymlicka, Will. *Multicultural Citizenship: A Liberal Theory of Minority Rights.* Cambridge, UK: Cambridge University Press, 1995.

Lawrence, James, and Rux Martin. *Sweet Maple: Life, Lore, and Recipes from the Sugarbush.* Montpelier: Vermont Life, 1993.

Lee, Jennifer 8. *The Fortune Cookie Chronicles: Adventures in the World of Chinese Food.* New York: Twelve, 2008.

Lefebvre, Henri. *Rhythmanalysis: Space, Time, and Everyday Life.* Trans. Stuart Elden and Gerald Moore. New York: Continuum, 2004.

Lemasson, Jean-Pierre. "The Long History of the *Tourtière* of Quebec's Lac-St. Jean." In *What's to Eat? Entrées in Canadian Food History,* edited by Nathalie Cooke, 99–115. Montreal: McGill-Queen's University Press, 2009.

Ley, David. *The New Middle Class and the Remaking of the Central City.* Oxford: Oxford University Press, 1996.

Li, Wei. *Ethnoburb: The New Ethnic Community in Urban America.* Honolulu: University of Hawai'i Press, 2009.

Lloyd, Justine. "Airport Technology, Travel, and Consumption." *Space and Culture* 6, 2 (2003): 93–109.

Lowitt, Kristen. "Fish and Fisheries in the Evolution of Newfoundland Foodways." In *World Small-Scale Fisheries: Contemporary Visions,* edited by Ratana Chuenpagdee, 117–32. Delft: Eburon, 2011.

Lupton, Deborah. *Food, the Body, and the Self.* London: Sage, 1996.

MacLennan, Hugh. *Two Solitudes.* 1945; reprinted, Toronto: McClelland and Stewart, 2003.

Markowitz, Lisa. "Highland Haute Cuisine: The Transformation of Alpaca Meat." In *Reimagining Marginalized Foods: Global Processes, Local Places,* edited by Elizabeth Finnis, 34–48. Tucson: University of Arizona Press, 2012.

Marte, Lidia. "Foodmaps: Tracing Boundaries of 'Home' through Food Relations." *Food and Foodways* 15, 3–4 (2007): 261–89.

Mason, Carol I. "A Sweet Small Something: Maple Sugaring in the New World." In *The Invented Indian: Cultural Fictions and Government Policies*, edited by James A. Clifton, 91–106. New Brunswick, NJ: Transaction Publishers, 1990.

May, Jon, and Nigel Thrift, eds. *TimeSpace: Geographies of Temporality*. London: Routledge, 2001.

McCullough, Michael. *Granville Island: An Urban Oasis*. Vancouver: Granville Island, 1998.

McMillan, David, Frederic Morin, and Meredith Erickson. *The Art of Living According to Joe Beef: A Cookbook of Sorts*. Berkeley: Potter/TenSpeed/Harmony, 2011.

Menzies, Heather. *By the Labour of Their Hands: The Story of Ontario Cheddar Cheese*. Kingston: Quarry Press, 1994.

Miller, Jeff, and Jonathan Deutsch. *Food Studies: An Introduction to Research Methods*. London: Berg Publishing, 2009.

Mitchell, Katharyne. "Educating the National Citizen in Neoliberal Times: From the Multicultural Self to the Strategic Cosmopolitan." *Transactions of the Institute of British Geographers* 28, 4 (2003): 387–403.

Morales, Alfonso. "Marketplaces: Prospects for Social, Economic, and Political Development." *Journal of Planning Literature* 26, 1 (2011): 3–17.

Morel, Pauline. "Eating Out: The Influence of the Outdoors on Canadian Domestic Foodways." Paper presented at Domestic Foodscapes: Towards Mindful Eating, Montreal, 2008.

Morris, Carolyn. "The Politics of Palatability on the Absence of Māori Restaurants." *Food, Culture, and Society* 13, 1 (2010): 5–28.

Mullins, Paul R. *Glazed America: A History of the Doughnut*. Gainesville: University Press of Florida, 2008.

Murphy, James, and Stephen Smith. "Chefs and Suppliers: An Exploratory Look at Supply Chain Issues in an Upscale Restaurant Alliance." *International Journal of Hospitality Management* 28, 2 (2009): 212–20.

Musgrave, Sarah. "Taste of Place, Place of Taste: Mapping Alimentary Authenticity through Marché Jean-Talon." MA thesis, Concordia University, 2009.

Nabhan, Gary. *Coming Home to Eat: The Pleasures and Politics of Local Foods*. New York: W. W. Norton, 2009.

Newman, Lenore. "Blackberries: Canadian Cuisine and Marginal Foods." *Cuizine: The Journal of Canadian Food Cultures/Revue des cultures culinaires au Canada* 5, 1 (2014): n. pag.

——. "Neige et Citrouille: Marché Atwater and Seasonality." *Cuizine: The Journal of Canadian Food Cultures/Revue des cultures culinaires au Canada* 3, 2 (2012): n. pag.

——. "Notes from the Nanaimo Bar Trail." *Canadian Food Studies/La revue canadienne des études sur l'alimentation* 1, 1 (2014): 10–19.

Newman, Lenore Lauri, and Katherine Burnett. "Street Food and Vibrant Urban Spaces: Lessons from Portland, Oregon." *Local Environment* 18, 2 (2013): 233–48.

Norris, Darrell A. "Interstate Highway Exit Morphology: Non-Metropolitan Exit Commerce on I-75." *Professional Geographer* 39, 1 (1987): 23–32.

Norton, Gail, and Karen Ralph. *Calgary Cooks: Recipes from the City's Top Chefs.* Vancouver: Figure 1 Publishing, 2014.

Omohundro, John T. *Rough Food: The Seasons of Subsistence in Northern Newfoundland.* St. John's: Institute of Social and Economic Research, Memorial University of Newfoundland, 1994.

Penfold, Steve. *The Donut: A Canadian History.* Toronto: University of Toronto Press, 2008.

Perry, Charles. "The Oldest Mediterranean Noodle: A Cautionary Tale." *Petits propos culinaires* 9 (1981): 42–45.

Picard, Martin. *Au Pied de Cochon Sugar Shack: Maple Syrup.* Montreal: Restaurant Au Pied de Cochon, 2012.

Pierce, Alan R. "Maple Syrup (*Acer Saccharum*)." In *Tapping the Green Market: Certification and Management of Non-Timber Forest Products,* edited by Patricia Shanley, Alan R. Pierce, Sarah A. Laird, and Abraham Guillén, 162–71. London: Earthscan Publications, 2002.

Pimentel, David, et al. "Biofuel Impacts on World Food Supply: Use of Fossil Fuel, Land, and Water Resources." *Energies* 1, 2 (2008): 41–78.

Pollock, Sheldon. "The Cosmopolitan Vernacular." *Journal of Asian Studies* 57, 1 (1998): 6–37.

Power, Elaine, and Mustafa Koc. "A Double-Double and a Maple-Glazed Doughnut." *Food, Culture, and Society* 11, 3 (2008): 263–67.

Powers, Jo Marie, and Anita Stewart, eds. *Northern Bounty: A Celebration of Canadian Cuisine.* Toronto: Random House, 1995.

Price, M. H. H., C. T. Darimont, N. F. Temple, and S. M. MacDuffee. "Ghost Runs: Management and Status Assessment of Pacific Salmon (*Oncorhynchus Spp.*) Returning to British Columbia's Central and North Coasts." *Canadian Journal of Fisheries and Aquatic Sciences* 65, 12 (2008): 2712–18.

Pyle, Jane. "Farmers' Markets in the United States: Functional Anachronisms." *Geographical Review* (1971): 167–97.

Rath, Eric C. "Banquets against Boredom: Towards Understanding (Samurai) Cuisine in Early Modern Japan." *Early Modern Japan: An Interdisciplinary Journal* 16 (2008): 43–55.

Relph, Edward. *Place and Placelessness.* London: Pion, 1976.

Richler, Jacob. "Ramps: Hands off Those Wild Leeks." *Maclean's* 127, 19–20 (2014): 74.

Richler, Mordecai. *The Apprenticeship of Duddy Kravitz.* 1959; reprinted, New York: Simon and Schuster, 1999.

Richman-Kenneally, Rhona. "The Cuisine of the Tundra: Towards a Canadian Food Culture at Expo 67." *Food, Culture, and Society* 11, 3 (2008): 287–314.

Robbins, Maria Polushkin. *The Cook's Quotation Book: A Literary Feast.* New York: Viking Press, 1984.

Robinson, Richard N. S. "Plain Fare to Fusion: Ethnic Impacts on the Process of Maturity in Brisbane's Restaurant Sector." *Journal of Hospitality and Tourism Management* 14, 1 (2007): 70–84.

Roy, Suman, and Brooke Ali. *From Pemmican to Poutine: A Journey through Canada's Culinary History*. Toronto: Key Publishing House, 2010.

Sandlos, John. *Hunters at the Margin: Native People and Wildlife Conservation in the Northwest Territories*. Vancouver: UBC Press, 2011.

Searles, Edmund. "Food and the Making of Modern Inuit Identities." *Food and Foodways* 10, 1–2 (2002): 55–78.

Selwood, John. "The Lure of Food: Food as an Attraction in Destination Marketing in Manitoba, Canada." In *Food Tourism around the World: Management of Development and Markets*, edited by C. Michael Hall, Liz Sharples, Richard Mitchell, Niki Macionis, and Brock Cambourne, 178–91. London: Routledge, 2003.

Silich, Nicholas. "Authentic Food: A Philosophical Approach." In *Authenticity in the Kitchen: Proceedings of the Oxford Symposium on Food and Cookery 2005*, edited by Richard Hosking, 401–02. Devon: Prospect Books, 2006.

Smith, Andrew, and Shelley Boyd. "Talking Turkey: Thanksgiving in Canada and the United States." In *What's to Eat? Entrées in Canadian Food History*, edited by Nathalie Cooke, 116–44. Montreal: McGill-Queen's University Press, 2009.

Smith, Alisa, and Jamie MacKinnon. *The 100-Mile Diet: A Year of Local Eating*. Toronto: Vintage, 2009.

Soja, Edward W. *Seeking Spatial Justice*. Minneapolis: University of Minnesota Press, 2010.

Spang, Rebecca L. *The Invention of the Restaurant: Paris and Modern Gastronomic Culture*. Cambridge, MA: Harvard University Press, 2001.

Stacey, Susan Lecompte. *Salmonopolis: The Steveston Story*. Madeira Park, BC: Harbour Publishing, 1994.

Starks, Zona Spray. "Arctic Foodways and Contemporary Cuisine." *Gastronomica: The Journal of Food and Culture* 7, 1 (2007): 41–49.

Statistics Canada. "Canada's Rural Population Declining since 1851." In *Canadian Demography at a Glance*. Catalogue 98-003-X. Ottawa: Statistics Canada, 2014.

Steel, Carolyn. *Hungry City: How Food Shapes Our Lives*. London: Vintage Books, 2009.

Steeves, Taylor A. "Wild Rice—Indian Food and a Modern Delicacy." *Economic Botany* 6, 2 (1952): 107–42.

Stewart, Anita. *Anita Stewart's Canada: The Food, the Recipes, the Stories*. Toronto: HarperCollins, 2008.

——. *The Flavours of Canada: A Celebration of the Finest Regional Foods*. Vancouver: Raincoast Books, 2000.

Stewart, Brian. "Closing of Atwater Market Confirmed." Montreal *Gazette*, September 24, 1968.

Stocking, George W. Jr. "Franz Boas and the Culture Concept in Historical Perspective." *American Anthropologist* 68, 4 (1966): 867–82.

Svenson, Stephen. "The Cottage and the City: An Interpretation of the Canadian Second Home Experience." In *Tourism, Mobility, and Second Homes: Between Elite Landscape and Common Ground*, edited by C. Michael Hall and Dieter K. Müller, 55–74. Bristol: Channel View Publications, 2004.

Tachibana, Rumiko. "'Processing' Sushi/Cooked Japan: Why Sushi Became Canadian." MA thesis, University of Victoria, 2008.

Tangires, Helen. *Public Markets and Civic Culture in Nineteenth-Century America*. New York: W. W. Norton, 2008.

Telfer, David J. "Tastes of Niagara: Building Strategic Alliances between Tourism and Agriculture." *International Journal of Hospitality and Tourism Administration* 1, 1 (2000): 71–88.

Théorêt, Charles-Alexandre. *Maudite poutine! Histoire approximative d'un fameux mets*. Montréal: Éditions Heliotrope, 2007.

Traill, Catharine Parr. *The Female Emigrants Guide, and Hints on Canadian Housekeeping*. Toronto: Maclear, 1854.

Trubek, Amy B. *The Taste of Place: A Cultural Journey into Terroir*. Berkeley: University of California Press, 2008.

Turgeon, Laurier, and Madeleine Pastinelli. "'Eat the World': Postcolonial Encounters in Quebec City's Ethnic Restaurants." *Journal of American Folklore* 115, 456 (2002): 247–68.

Turgeon-Gouin, Catherine. "The Myth of Québec Traditional Cuisine at Au Pied de Cochon." *Cuizine: The Journal of Canadian Food Cultures/Revue des cultures culinaires au Canada* 3, 2 (2012): n. pag.

Tye, Diane. *Baking as Biography: A Life Story in Recipes*. Montreal: McGill-Queen's University Press, 2010.

Unterschultz, James, Kwamena K. Quagrainie, and Michel Vincent. "Evaluating Quebec's Preference for Alberta Beef versus U.S. Beef." *Agribusiness* 13, 5 (1997): 457–68.

Van den Berg, Agnes E., Terry Hartig, and Henk Staats. "Preference for Nature in Urbanized Societies: Stress, Restoration, and the Pursuit of Sustainability." *Journal of Social Issues* 63, 1 (2007): 79–96.

Van den Berghe, Pierre L. "Ethnic Cuisine: Culture in Nature." *Ethnic and Racial Studies* 7, 3 (1984): 387–97.

Vannini, Phillip. *Ferry Tales: Mobility, Place, and Time on Canada's West Coast*. Abingdon: Taylor and Francis, 2012.

Vennum, Thomas Jr. *Wild Rice and the Ojibway People*. St. Paul: Minnesota State Historical Society Press, 1988.

Watson, Julie V. *Ardgowan: A Journal of House and Garden in Victorian Prince Edward Island*. Charlottetown: Seacroft Books, 2000.

Webb, Margaret. *Apples to Oysters: A Food Lover's Tour of Canadian Farms*. Toronto: Viking Canada, 2008.

Whatmore, Sarah. *Hybrid Geographies: Natures, Cultures, Spaces*. London: Sage, 2002.

White, Richard. "From Wilderness to Hybrid Landscapes: The Cultural Turn in Environmental History." *Historian* 66, 3 (2004): 557–64.

Whyte, William H. *The Social Life of Small Urban Spaces*. Washington, DC: Conservation Foundation, 1980.

Wilk, Richard. "Loving People, Hating What They Eat." In *Reimagining Marginalized*

265

*Foods: Global Processes, Local Places,* edited by Elizabeth Finnis, 15–33. Tucson: University of Arizona Press, 2012.

Wilkins, Jennifer L. "Consumer Perceptions of Seasonal and Local Foods: A Study in a U.S. Community." *Ecology of Food and Nutrition* 41, 5 (2002): 415–39.

——. "Seasonality, Food Origin, and Food Preference: A Comparison between Food Cooperative Members and Nonmembers." *Journal of Nutrition Education* 28, 6 (1996): 329–37.

Wilkins, Jennifer L., Elizabeth Bowdish, and Jeffery Sobal. "University Student Perceptions of Seasonal and Local Foods." *Journal of Nutrition Education* 32, 5 (2000): 261–68.

Williams, Judith. *Clam Gardens: Aboriginal Mariculture on Canada's West Coast.* Vancouver: Transmontanus, 2006.

Wittman, Hannah, Mary Beckie, and Chris Hergesheimer. "Linking Local Food Systems and the Social Economy? Future Roles for Farmers' Markets in Alberta and British Columbia." *Rural Sociology* 77, 1 (2012): 36–61.

Wolfe, Roy I. "Wasaga Beach: The Divorce from the Geographic Environment." *Canadian Geographer/Le géographe canadien* 1, 2 (1952): 57–66.

Wrigley, Neil, and Michelle Lowe. *Retailing, Consumption, and Capital: Towards the New Retail Geography.* Harlow: Longman, 1996.

Wu, David Y. H., and Sidney C. H. Cheung. *Globalization of Chinese Food.* London: Routledge, 2012.

Yesaki, Mitsuo, Harold Steves, and Kathy Steves. *Steveston Cannery Row: An Illustrated History.* Richmond, BC: Peninsula Publishing, 2005.

Zukin, Sharon. *Naked City: The Death and Life of Authentic Urban Places.* Oxford: Oxford University Press, 2009.

# INDEX

# ABOUT THE AUTHOR

 Lenore Newman holds the Canada Research Chair in Food Security and Environment at the University of the Fraser Valley, where she is an Associate Professor of Geography. Lenore is a member of the College of New Scholars, Artists and Scientists of the Royal Society of Canada. She researches regional cuisine, agricultural land use, and urban food systems. Her love affair with food began on her family's fishing boats, where she gained an early introduction into the world of direct marketing of local products, and she is a strong advocate for fresh, local food. Lenore lives in Vancouver with her partner, Katherine, and spends her spare time tending her family's orchard.